CU00642192

THE FAMOUS DRUIDS

1. The Chief Druid: *see p.* 101.

THE FAMOUS DRUIDS

A survey of three centuries
of English literature on the Druids

BY

A. L. OWEN

CLARENDON PRESS · OXFORD

Oxford University Press, Great Clarendon Street, Oxford OX2 6DP

Oxford New York

Athens Auckland Bangkok Bogota Bombay
Buenos Aires Calcutta Cape Town Dar es Salaam
Delhi Florence Hong Kong Istanbul Karachi
Kuala Lumpur Madras Madrid Melbourne
Mexico City Nairobi Paris Singapore
Taipei Tokyo Toronto Warsaw
and associated companies in
Berlin Ibadan

Oxford is a trade mark of Oxford University Press

Published in the United States by
Oxford University Press Inc., New York

First published by Oxford University Press 1962
Special edition for Sandpiper Books Ltd., 1997

British Library Cataloguing in Publication Data
Data available

ISBN 0-19-811602-0

3 5 7 9 10 8 6 4 2

Printed in Great Britain by
Bookcraft Ltd
Midsomer Norton, Somerset

TO
MY MOTHER

FOREWORD

The author warmly thanks Professor David Nichol Smith and Professor Idris Foster for the many kindnesses they have shown him.

CONTENTS

LIST OF PLATES

NOTE ON ABBREVIATIONS

References to the Druids in classical and patristic literature (with the abbreviations used here in parentheses), are found in:

(Am.M.) Ammianus Marcellinus, *The History* xv, 9, 4; xv, 9, 8.

(Aur.) Aurelius Victor, *On the Caesars*, IV, 2.

(Aus.) Ausonius, *The Professors of Bordeaux*, IV, x.

(Caes.) Caesar, *The Gallic War*, VI, 13; VI, 14; VI, 16; VI, 18; VI, 21.

(Cic.) Cicero, *On Divination*, I, xli; Clement of Alexandria, *Miscellanies*, I, 15; St. Cyril of Alexandria, *Against Julianus*, IV, 133; Dio Chrysostom, *Orations*, XLIX.

(Dio.L.) Diogenes Laertius, *Lives of Eminent Philosophers*, I, 1; I, 6.

(Dio.S.) Diodorus Siculus, *The Library of History*, V, 28, 6; V, 31, 2–5; Hippolytus, *The Refutation of All Heresies*, I, ii; I, xxv; 'Lampridius', *Alexander Severus*, LIX, 5.

(Luc.) Lucan, *The Civil War*, I, 447 ff.; Origen, *Against Celsus*, I, 16.

(P.Mela) Pomponius Mela, *De Situ Orbis*, III, 2; 18–19.

(Pl.) Pliny the Elder, *Natural History*, XVI, 249; XXIV, 103; XXIV, 104; XXIX, 52; XXX, 13.

(Str.) Strabo, *The Geography*, IV, 4, 4; IV, 4, 5.

(Su.) Suetonius Tranquillus, *Claudius*, 25.

(Tac.) Tacitus, *Annals*, XIV, 30, *Histories*, IV, 54; Valerius Maximus, II, vi, 10; 'Vopiscus', *Numerianus*, XIV, *Aurelianus*, XLIII, 4, 5.

Translations, unless otherwise acknowledged, are taken from the Loeb Classics and from T. D. Kendrick, *The Druids*, 1928, chapter III.

In the footnotes, the place of publication of works referred to is, unless otherwise stated, London.

Jer. refers to *Jerusalem*, and K., followed by a number, to pages in *Blake's Poetry and Prose*, ed. G. Keynes, 1946, an edition which has been superseded but which may be convenient for most readers to consult.

Contractions in quotations from printed texts have been expanded.

INTRODUCTION

'THE famous Druids', as they are described here, are not the Druids of classical antiquity. 'Our *Druids*', '*the famous and mysterious* Druidae', 'the ancient *Druids*, so renowned in Story'[1] are literary figures. It is hard to see what else they could be, for those who attempted to rediscover the Druids of history had set themselves an impossible task. Not only is little known about the Druids as they really were, but when Elias Ashmole calls them the '*mysterious* Druidae' he rightly suggests that this little fits insecurely into familiar frames of reference. Yet while the Druids as they are described by the scholar of the Renaissance, the virtuosi and the clerical antiquary have little contact with historical reality, they are not the products of the imagination alone. Their creation owes much to widely held assumptions that coloured the thought of the sixteenth to the nineteenth centuries, and these have given the Druid as he was then seen some characteristics which he originally lacked and which he has since shed. The most far-fetched of the eighteenth-century conjectures on Druidism, too much at variance with each other to evoke any single contemporary image of a Druid, still belong firmly to their own day, to a time which may be lightly stencilled 'the Age of Reason', even if they hint at attitudes of mind which reeled on their Georgian pedestals.

English literature on the Druids stems from a few passages in classical and patristic literature which, brief as they are, have possibly never yielded two identical

---

[1] 'Lycidas', l. 54; W. Camden, *Britannia*, ed. E. Gibson, 1695, col. xviii; Elias Ashmole, *Theatrum Chemicum Britannicum*, 1652, vol. i, sig. A2 v; Sir William Temple, *Works*, 1720, vol. ii, p. 531.

interpretations. They have also provided a starting-point
for dissertations in which the name alone of the Druid
may recall what Caesar and Pliny have said of him. The
flash of insight that blinded, the enterprise that hurried
the seeker away from his goal, and the conscription of
evidence have given much writing on the Druids a character of its own, and in this literature, as it reads today, the
shadow claims as much attention as the substance. It
needs some commentary, but if this comes too officiously
between the reader and the original texts, the short an-
thology which opens this book leaves it to him to form his
own impressions.

The remarks of Greek and Roman historians and geo-
graphers on the Druids, though they are the earliest and
most intelligible of the primary sources, are not the only
authorities to consult. It should, however, be added here
that neither the archaeologist nor the student of Celtic
religion have contributed anything substantial to our
knowledge of the subject. 'Archaeologically,' as Professor
Stuart Piggott says of the Druids, 'they are almost in-
tangible.'[1] Sotion, writing in 200 B.C., says that 'among
the Celts and Gauls there are people called the Druids or
Holy Ones';[2] at this time, the culture of La Tène had
spread to both sides of the Channel. Here the Druids have
their earliest known setting, but there is nothing to show
that they inspired or owed anything to this culture, and
it seems that what is missing is a firm link between the
Druids and some established fact which can then serve
as a stepping-stone to what is already known about the
Celtic past. As it is, any conclusions on the Druids and
Druidism which may be drawn from a survey of Gaul at
this date, for example, must be founded on conjecture.

Stonehenge will be frequently mentioned in this book,

[1] Stuart Piggott, *British Prehistory*, 1949, p. 193.
[2] Diogenes Laertius, *Lives of Eminent Philosophers*, tr. R. D. Hicks
(Loeb), I, I.

and what has been written about it as a temple of the Druids may be compared with the findings of modern archaeology. It is a composite monument: the bank, ditch, and Aubrey Holes were constructed—to give provisional and very approximate dates—between 1900 and 1700 B.C., and a timber structure and certain stones were also erected at this time; between 1700 and 1600 B.C. its bluestones were brought there from Prescelly, and its sarsen stones were brought there from the neighbourhood of Marlborough in about 1500 B.C. The structure was subsequently remodelled at different dates.[1] The site, then, was held in great veneration at least fifteen hundred years before Sotion mentioned the Druids, and since he lacks any proof of a corresponding antiquity for Druidism —to say nothing further of his reasoning—the archaeologist necessarily rejects any theory of a Druid origin for Stonehenge.

Material for the study of Celtic religion is relatively abundant, but the problems which arise out of its interpretation only incidentally hamper efforts to reconstruct from it anything which can properly be called Druidism. From the remarks of Caesar and others it is known that the Druids did 'not wish the rule to become common property'. What is recorded of their ethical and doctrinal teaching is a self-evidently incomplete and external version of Druidism. If the Druids' 'rule' was ever communicated to any outside their own 'consortia', no record of this survives, and so serious a gap must give this branch of Celtic studies a permanent background of enigma.

It is possible to learn more about the Druids from early Irish literature, for the 'druïd'—the nominative plural of 'druí'—are the Irish equivalents of the Gallic 'druidae' of Caesar's description. Later forms and meanings of the word are 'draí' and 'draoi', magician, wizard and diviner. It was also used to describe the counterparts of the Druids

---

[1] R. J. C. Atkinson, *Stonehenge*, 1960, pp. 68–101.

among other races: the Magi were called 'na dráide
Indecdai', a phrase which recalls that in four classical and
patristic texts the Druids are spoken of as though they
were the peers of the Brahmins and the Magi.[1] The
soothsayers of the second rank or order of the Druid
hierarchy are called Vates by Strabo; this word and the
Irish 'fáith', seers and prophets, are cognate.[2] But while
classical and Irish literature corroborate each other at
points, they also have very different things to say about
the Druids. In the brief remarks that follow, no attempt
is made to give any kind of outline which in effect sums
up what has been recorded of the Druids of Ireland, but
it is noticeable that while Greek and Roman references to
the Druids dwell heavily on the human sacrifice, the
Irish texts have next to nothing to say about it. They have,
on the other hand, far more to say about the Druids' use
of magic. The Druids raised storms, laid curses on places,
killed by the use of spells, declared auspicious occasions,
and created magic obstacles. Their persons were sacro-
sanct, and they were therefore employed as ambassadors.
They were physicians, and they investigated crimes. They
opposed the Christian missions, but there were Druids
at the courts of Christian princes. Christian priests inherited their property and took over some of their functions.[3]

The circumstances in which the materials for a history
of early Ireland were recorded left the evidence of
monastic editing on what was said about the men who had
once resisted the coming of Christianity, and in one text
it is said that they will be among the damned on Dooms-
day.[4] Yet evidence of strong spiritual associations that

[1] *Contributions to a Dictionary of the Irish Language*, 'dodénta-dúus',
ed. M. E. Byrne and M. Joynt, Dublin, 1960, col. 409.
[2] Ibid., 'F-fochraic', 1950, p. 33.
[3] Charles Plummer, *Vitae Sanctorum Hiberniae*, Oxford, 1910, vol. i,
pp. clix ff.
[4] *Dictionary of Irish*, 'dodénta-dúus', loc. cit.

were attached to their memory still survives, for in early
Christian Ireland the words saint and Druid were once
interchangeable.[1] In lines attributed to St. Columba, the
name of the Druids is exalted by the very comparison
which extinguishes it:

> I adore not the voice of the birds,
> Nor the *sreod*, nor a destiny in the earthly world,
> Nor a son, nor chance, nor woman,
> My Druid is Christ, the son of God.[2]

[1] C. Plummer, op. cit., p. clxvii.
[2] J. O'Donovan, 'An ancient Poem attributed to St. Columkille',
Miscellany of the Irish Archaeological Society, Dublin, vol. i, 1846, pp.
5–6, 12–13.

THE DRUIDS, BY SEVERAL HANDS

Holinshed's Druids

IT is not to be doubted, but at the first and so long as the posteritie of Japhet onlye, reigned in this Islande, that the true knowledge and forme of religion brought in by *Samothes*, was exercised among the Britains. . . . What other learning *Magus* the sonne of *Samothes* taught after his fathers death when he also came to the kingdome, beside thys which concerned the true honoring of God, I can not easily saye, but that it shoulde bee naturall Philosophie, and Astrology (whereby his disciples, gathered a kinde of foreknowledge of things to come) the verye use of the worde *Magus*, among the Persians doth yeeld no incertaine testimony.

In lyke maner, it shoulde seeme that *Sarron* sonne unto the sayde *Magus*, diligentlye followed the steppes of hys father, & thereto opened Schooles of learning in sundrie places, both among the Celtes and Britaines, whereby such as were his Auditors, grewe to be called *Sarronides*, notwithstanding, that aswell the *Sarronides* as the *Magi* (otherwise called *Magusei*) & Druiydes, were generally called Samothei, or Semnothei, of *Samothies* stil among the Græcians, as *Aristotle* in his *de magia*, doth confesse, and calling them Galles, hee addeth thereunto that they first brought the knowledge of Letters, and good learning unto the Greekes.

Druiyus the sonne of Sarron (as a scholler of his fathers owne teaching) seemed to be exquisite in all things, that pertayned unto the deuine or humaine knowledge: and therfore I may safely pronounce, that he excelled not onely in the skill of Philosophie: and the Quadriualles,

but also in the true Theologie, wherby the right seruice
of God was kept & preserved in puritie. He wrote more-
over sundry precepts, and rules of religious doctrine,
which among the Celtes were reserved very religiously,
and had in great estimation among such as sought unto
them . . .

After the death of Druiyus, Bardus his sonne, and king
of the Celtes succeeded not onely over the sayde kingdome, but also in his fathers vertues, whereby it is very
likely, that the winding and wrapping up of the sayde
Religion, after the afore remembered sorte into Verse,
for he was an excellent Poet. . . . But as to procede, as
the chiefe estimation of the Druiydes remained in the
ende among the Britons only, for their knowledge in
religion, so dyd the same of the *Bardes* for their excellent
skill in musicke, and Heroicall kind of song, which at the
first contayned only the high misteries of their religion.
There was little difference betweene them and the
Druiydes, till they so far degenerated from their first institution, that they became to be minstrels at feastes,
droncken meetings, and abhominable sacrifices of Idols.

The First Volume of the Chronicles of England, 1577,
ff. 7 ff.

'The same spirit has a body again elsewhere'

Ye sacred Bards, that to your Harps melodious strings
Sung th'ancient Heröes deeds (the monument of
    Kings) . . .
If, as those *Druides* taught, which kept the British rites,
And dwelt in darksome Groues, there counsailing with
    sprites
(But their opinion faild, by error led awry,
As since cleere truth hath shew'd to their posterity)
When these our soules by death our bodies doe forsake,
They instantlie againe doe other bodies take;

I could haue wished your spirits redoubled in my breast,
To giue my verse applause, to time's eternall rest.

Michael Drayton, *Poly-Olbion*, 1612, p. 2.

John Selden annotates Michael Drayton's Poly-Olbion

The fearles British Priests *vnder an aged* Oake

He means the *Druids*; because they are indeed, as he
cals them, *British* Priests, & that this Island was of old
their Mother: whence, as from a Seminary, *Gaule* was
furnisht with their learning. . . . The name of *Druids*
hath beene drawne from δρύς . i. *an Oake*, because of their
continuall vsing that Tree as superstitiously hallowed.
. . . To compare the *British* word Derw of the same
signification, and, the Originall here sought for, will
seeme surely found. But one, that deriues all from *Dutch*,
and prodigiously supposes that the first tongue spoken,
makes them so stiled from Trow wis .i. *truely wise*, so
expressing their nature in their name. Nor is this without
good reason of coniecture (if the ground were true)
seeing that their like in proportion among the *Iewes* and
Gentiles were call'd (vntill *Pythagoras* his time) *Wise-men*,
and afterwards by him turned into the name of philosophers .i. *Louers of wisedome*; and perhaps the old *Dutch*
was, as some learned thinke, communicated to *Gaule*, and
from hence hither; the coniecture being somewhat aided
in that attribute which they haue in *Pomponius*, calling
them *Masters of wisedome*. A late great Scholler draws it
from Trutin, in an old *Dutch* copy of the Gospel, signi-
fying, as he saies, *God*; wch might be given them by
Hyperboly of superstitious reuerence: nay, we see that it
is iustifiable by holy Writ, so to call great Magistrates
and Iudges. . . . But that word *Trutin* or *Truchtin* in
the old Angellical salutation, *Zacharies* Song . . . is
alwayes *Lord*. . . . These are the etymologies which
sauour of any iudgement. . . . For their PROFESSION,

it was both of learning Profane and Holy (I speake in all, applying my words to their times:) . . . In a multitude of verses they deliuered what they taught, not suffering it to be committed to writing, so imitating both *Cabalists*, *Pythagoreans*, and ancient Christians.

Poly-Olbion, 1612, p. 151.

The origin of Druidism

Farther, thou mayest demand whence this *Oke Religion* (of the *Druides*) sprang? namely from the *Okes* of *Mamre*: under which, in times past, those holy men (in whose hands the administration of *Divine* Service and Worship was) lived most devoutly: the shadow of which *Okes* afforded an *house* to *Abraham*, and a *Temple* to *God*. This I sucked from the *Dugs* of *Truth*, namely from the sacred *Scriptures*. *Abraham dwelt* . . . *in*, or (as the *Arabick* has it) *among the Okes of Mamre*. . . . Under which *Oke* he fixed his *Tabernacle*, erected an Altar, and offered to the Lord Calves, Goats, Rams, and other Sacrifices of like kind; and performed all *Sacerdotal Offices*. Yea under this tree he entertained *God himself*, together with *Angels*. He here had *conference* with *God*, and entred into *covenant* with him, and was blessed of him. These are indeed admirable *præconia* of *Okes*. Lo the *Oke priests*! Lo the *Patriarchs* of the *Druides*! For from these sprang the *Sect* of the *Druides*, which reached up at least, as high as *Abraham*'s time (for they report that the *Druides Colleges* flourished in the time of *Hermio*, who was King of the *Germans*, immediately after the death of *Abraham*). For because this holy man and Priest, *Abraham* lived under *Okes*, and enjoyed God for his companion, performing worship to him, our Divines (the *Druides*) from this so famous example, chose Goves of *Okes* for their *Religious* Services, &c.

Theophilus Gale, *The Court of the Gentiles*, Part II, Oxford, 1671, p. 82.

The diffusion of Druidism

When I had thus far satisfied myself, I began to take the RISE of the BRITISH DRUIDS into Consideration; and after collating all the Circumstances touching KING BLADUD, the reputed FOUNDER of the Hot Waters, and the City of BATH, as well as of the antient UNIVERSITY of STANFORD, with what is recorded of ABARIS, the *Hyperborean Priest* of the SUN, I could not avoid concluding that they were one and the same Man: Neither could I avoid concluding, that the *Britons* and the *Hyperboreans* were one and the same people. . . .

By the circumstances that led me to these Conclusions it appeared, even beyond probability, that BLADUD assumed the gift of Prophecy, and became a great Philosopher while he was a Youth. . . . And that he became the favourite Disciple, the Colleague, and in many things, the Master of the *Samian* Philosopher; since the antient Writers that speak of these celebrated Men, unanimously agree that they reciprocally communicated their Knowledge to each other.

It also appeared that after BLADUD had made himself famous all over *Greece* for his ORACLES, he was there dignified with the Title of ABARIS; and then built TEMPLES in that Country. . . . And it likewise appeared that our *British* Philosopher, after having been Initiated into the *Samothratian Mysteries*, and continuing abroad for eleven Years, returned to his native Land about the Year PYTHAGORAS died at *Crotona*; succeeded his Father soon after in the *British* Throne; and FOUNDED that ORDER of PRIESTHOOD, which, in the antient times of Paganism, was of such high Renown as to make *Cicero* himself, on one hand, declare the DRUIDS, or PRIESTS admitted into it, to have been the very INVENTORS of MYTHOLOGY; and *Pliny*, on the other, to suppose them to have been the MASTERS of the *Persian* MAGI.

And when the PRIESTHOOD was FOUNDED, BLADUD, as ARCH-DRUID, appeared to have seated himself near the Hot Springs of BATH; and to have placed his *Grecian* Refugees at STANTONDREW, as the Heads of so many Orders of Priests to act under him, and instruct the *Britons* in the Liberal Sciences; making them a stupendous Model of the Planetary World for that purpose, with Blocks of Marble dugg out of OKEY-HOLE to enlarge that dreadful DEN, and make the Initiating CAVE really great and tremendous to all that should enter it.

FROM this Institution the *British* Fable of SAM-OTHES, and the four next Kings in a continued Succession from Father to Son seems to have it's Rise: For SAMOTHES was a Title given to BLADUD from his Initiation into *Samothratian Mysteries*; and the Names of *Magus, Sarron, Druis*, and *Bardus*, by which the four other Kings were distinguished, express the very functions assigned to each Order of Priests among the DRUIDS; who were so denominated from their esteeming Trees, and particularly Oaks, as Symbols of the Deity. From the same Institution the Fable of *Apollo*'s ARROW, concealed by him in the *Hyperborean Island*, seems likewise to have it's Rise; and ABARIS'S carrying, or being carried by it through all parts of the World, without eating, seems to imply that DRUIDISM immediately spread itself from BRITAIN Eastward to the utmost Corners of the Earth, instead of coming from the Extremity of the Eastern World to us. The INDIAN HYLOBII seem therefore to have had their Rise from the BRITISH DRUIDS; and the Learning of the latter seems to have soon reached *China* itself, CONFUCIUS rising up in that Country, and appearing as a great Philosopher at the Head of four Orders of Priests in about thirty Years after the death of PYTHAGORAS.

John Wood, *Choir Gaure*, Oxford, 1747, pp. 9–12.

The Sacrifices of the Druids

Although some useful truths charm'd in the song
Of Druid wisdom, and with awe their groves
Beheld the natural light through thickest shades
Oft' shew her radiant presence, yet the pomp
Of bloody Altars, knives and death prepar'd
For human victims, where by force compell'd
They shed their blood bewailing, made their groves
The bloody shambles of misguided zeal,
And the vile Priests the butch'ring tools of Heav'n.

James Foot, *Penseroso*, 1771, p. 164.

The studies of the Druids

AMONG the *arcana* of nature which our Druids were
acquainted with, there are many presumptive, if not
positive, proofs for placing the art of gunpowder, or
artificial thunder and lightning; though like all other
mysteries, they kept the invention of it a secret. Some
learned men allow, that the priests of Delphos were in
possession of this art. . . . Why may we not suppose,
that those great searchers into nature, the Druids, might
also light upon the secret? The impressions of which
thunder and lightning are so apt to make upon the mind,
would certainly induce the Druids to try, if possible,
to counterfeit the awful phenomena; as the invention of
anything like them would be a most useful engine to
keep the wondring world in awe of them. And if we con-
sider the deep and long researches of those colleges of
philosophers, their being possessed of the experiments of
a series of ages before, and an extensive communication
with other countries, we can hardly suppose the mystery
of the nitreous grain could escape them.

John Smith, *Galic Antiquities*, Edinburgh, 1780, p. 73.

The secrets of the Druids

Many particulars of this allegory may be interpreted
from what has gone on before in this essay; and it may
be admitted as additional evidence, of two curious facts:
namely, that the superstitious rites of Druidism were
avowedly practiced, in certain corners of Britain, as late
as the close of the sixth century; and that the Bards of
that age, used all the means in their power, to conceal
their secrets from the knowledge of the populace, to
prevent them from the persecution of Christian princes
and ministers, and at the same time, to transmit them safe
and unblemished, to future ages.

In support of this assertion, I shall produce abstracts
from the several stanzas of the *Avallenau,* translated as
literally as the darkness of the subject, and the faults of
the copies, will permit: and to these, I shall add a few
occasional remarks:

'To no one has been exhibited, at one hour of dawn,
what was shewn to Merddin, before he became aged;
namely, seven score and seven delicious apple trees, of
equal age, height, length, and size, which sprang from the
bosom of *Mercy.* One bending veil covers them over.
They are guarded by one maid, with crisped locks: her
name is *Olwedd,* of the luminous teeth.'

Edward Davies, *The Mythology and Rites of the British
Druids,* 1809, pp. 481–2.

The dress of the Druids

The figures in this plate are an Awenydd or Bardic
disciple, and a candidate for that initiatory order. The
former having been admitted wears a variegated dress of
the Bardic colours, blue, green, and white; while the
candidate retains his original habit. . . . In the right
hand of the disciple is a cup, which it is conjectured contained some of the sacred juice, the *Gwin a bragawd,*

'wine and bragget', or perhaps only the mead drunk at great festivals; and in his left hand a bird, the symbol of an aspirant, for such Taliesin mystically says he was, when speaking of his initiation. Mr. Davies, however, conceives that the bird was the Dryw, a name implying both a wren and a Druid; and if such be correct the bird here represented cannot be this symbol for it is a nearer resemblance to a dove. The dove was the bird of good omen, as the raven was that of bad, among the nations of antiquity, the former having returned to Noah with the olive sprig of peace, when the latter wholly deserted him. The other youth has under his arm a pig, and in the hands of the other a box, perhaps to contain its food. The pig was also a symbol of Druidism. The Druids are frequently termed Swine, the Lunar-arkite goddess is as often alluded to under the character of a mystical sow; and the bard Myrddin commences his address to a disciple with the words *Oian porchellan*, 'listen, little pig'.

S. R. Meyrick and C. H. Smith, *The Costume of the Original Inhabitants of the British Isles*, 1821, p. 25.

I

DISCIPLINA IN BRITANNIA REPERTA . . . EXISTIMATUR

ENGLISH literature on the Druids is mainly based on descriptions of the Druids of Gaul. The Druids of Britain are mentioned by name only in the works of Caesar and Tacitus, though when the elder Pliny speaks of the extent to which magic was practised in Britain, his comments are very probably aimed at her Druids. Yet nearly everything that was said about them in classical antiquity has been appropriated by writers in this country, for Caesar records that it was believed that Druidism had originated in Britain, adding, as though to clinch the matter: 'Today those who would study the subject more accurately journey there, as a rule, to learn it.'[1] The English antiquary therefore thought that he might legitimately apply to this island's first philosophers and poets what Strabo, for example, has to say of the Druids of Gaul, and thus English literature on the Druids is ultimately derived from the five words that head this chapter.

Caesar's is the most authoritative description of the Druids. Towards the end of *The Gallic War* he breaks off his narrative in order to describe the Gauls themselves, and the earlier part of his history, with its details of battles and negotiations, is thus related to the general situation in Gaul as he had first found it. The portrait of Caesar as the deliverer of the Gauls from their own anarchy is then complete.

[1] Caes., VI, 13.

It is at this point that he first mentions the Druids.
The supreme caste of the Gallic social hierarchy, the
Druids, he writes, held annual assemblies in the geo-
graphical centre of Gaul, and public and private disputes
were then brought to them for arbitration. They taught a
doctrine which, as Caesar remarks, they held 'to be the
greatest incentive to valour'. On the face of it, the Druids
might have been expected to inspire and lead the Gallic
opposition to the Roman invasions.

Yet it is not recorded that these leaders who fired the
Gauls with a martial spirit did anything to resist the
invaders. Caesar's account of the Druids thus seems to be
inconsistent with everything that he had already written
about his campaigns. Such apparent contradictions in the
original texts raise problems that are sometimes of the
reader's making, and when he depends on extraneous
assumptions in order to solve them, interpretation is
allowed a latitude which helps to give English literature
on the Druids its characteristic variety.

Here it is evident that the Druids were not in any way
involved in Caesar's war, but if they are thought of as
militant patriots, it is not at all clear why they should
have disassociated themselves from their own people at
so critical a time. Caesar himself saw nothing anomalous
in their behaviour, and he accounts quite simply, if incidentally, for their absence from the battlefields: 'The
Druids', he says, 'usually hold aloof from war.' Nevertheless, he leaves room for further questions, though these
on the whole seem to arise from the assumption that the
Druids can be comfortably fitted into familiar social
patterns, that they can be thought of as statesmen,
power-seekers, administrators, and patriots—and in this
context, it has also been hinted that they were traitors.
Yet Caesar's account of the Druids is incompatible with
his account of the campaigns only when they are seen as
militant patriots or the like. Without going outside

Caesar's text, it can also be inferred that the Druids did not exercise direct control over Gaul, but made themselves accessible to the Gauls as a court of appeal. Theirs was a moral authority, and when they intervened in the affairs of others, this was when normal administration by others had broken down. It is consistent with Caesar's description of the Druids that they had much in common with the highest of the castes of the Hindus, with the Brahmins with whose name their own is coupled in classical and patristic literature. If this analogy holds, then the relationship of the Druids to the rest of the Gauls is intelligible, and both what Caesar says and what he does not say of the Druids are consistent with the general state of affairs which he describes. His total picture of Gaul is that of a country which has lost its head; and thus *The Gallic War*, which was written in defence of his policy, both shows Caesar bringing the Pax Romana to a divided and turbulent people and briefly describes the caste whose guidance the 'equites', the *de facto* rulers of Gaul, no longer heeded.

The three castes of Gaul, as Caesar names them, were the druidae, the equites, and the plebs.[1] The Druids, Vates, and Bards were members of the same caste;[2] all were called Druids, but the Vates and Bards were subordinate to the Druids proper, to these 'men of greater talent'.[3] The Bards celebrated 'the brave deeds of their famous men in epic verse' sung to the lyre.[4] The Vates practised soothsaying and studied natural philosophy.[5] The Druids 'were concerned with divine worship, the due performance of sacrifices, public and private, and the interpretation of ritual questions'.[6] The supreme authority was vested in the chief Druid; his successor was appointed

---

[1] Caes., loc. cit.
[2] Str., Am.M.: the Vates are here called 'euhages'.
[3] Am.M.   [4] Am.M., Str., Dio.S., Luc.
[5] Str., Am.M.   [6] Caes., loc. cit.

either because of his acknowledged eminence, or by voting, or even by force of arms when the succession was contested.[1]

The Druids tried both 'public and private matters', meeting annually at the centre of Gaul in a 'consecrated spot' within the tribal boundaries of the Carnutes for that purpose. Murderers were sentenced to be sacrificed; dissidents from the Druids' verdicts in civil cases suffered the same penalties as medieval excommunication and outlawry.[2]

The Druids were excused from military service and the payment of war taxes.[3] So great was their prestige that when intertribal disputes came to a head, they would intervene, and simply by showing themselves, prevent a battle even when the armies were face to face.[4] At the same time, as Caesar notices, they taught the doctrine of the immortality of the soul, holding this 'to be the greatest incentive to valour'.[5]

Theologians, philosophers, and teachers, they recruited their 'consortia'[6] from the young men who wished to join them in order, as Caesar says, to share their privileges and avoid military conscription. When Druidism was proscribed and such privileges became meaningless, the Druids still continued to attract recruits.[7] These, as part of their training, had to learn by heart a large body of verses, a task which sometimes took twenty years. Pomponius Mela supplements Caesar's remarks on this 'course of instruction', adding that the pupils of the Druids were the nobles of Gaul, and that they met in secret in caves and secluded dales. The Druids had 'many discussions as touching the stars and their movements, the size of the universe and of the earth, the order of nature, the strength and powers of the immortal gods',

---

[1] Caes., loc. cit. [2] ibid. [3] Caes., VI, 14.
[4] Dio.S., Str. [5] Caes., loc. cit., P.Mela.
[6] Am.M. [7] P.Mela.

and they studied moral philosophy.[1] Though they made use of Greek letters 'in their public and private accounts', they committed none of their doctrine to writing. Caesar suggests that the reason for this was that 'they do not wish the rule to become common property', and that 'the assistance of writing tends to relax the diligence of the student'.[2] Details of their actual teaching are very scarce; they thought that 'men's souls and also the universe, are indestructible, although both fire and water will at some time or other prevail over them'.[3] Sotion records what seems to be a general summary of their teaching: 'They uttered their philosophy in riddles, bidding men to reverence the gods, to abstain from wrongdoing, and to practise courage'.[4] The Gauls affirmed that they were descended from Dis, giving as their authority a Druidic tradition. Hence they regarded the twenty-four-hour day as starting in the evening.[5] They followed a lunar calendar, and observed 'saeculae' of thirty years.[6]

The cardinal doctrine which they sought to teach was that souls did not die, but after death passed 'from one to another';[7] but there are so many different interpretations of the fate of the soul that it appears that the exact Druidic teaching on the subject was not precisely known. Diodorus Siculus thought the doctrine was Pythagorean. Pomponius Mela said they thought that life continued in the infernal regions; Lucan explicitly denied this theory, saying that the spirit has a body 'in a different scene' and that 'death is but a point in the midst of continuous life'. The Gauls, in consequence, would lend each other sums to be repaid after death, or throw themselves on the pyres of their relatives in order to share the new life with them.[8]

Diogenes Lartius's mention of their 'riddles', Caesar's remark that 'they do not wish the rule to become common

---

[1] Caes., VI, 14; Str.   [2] Caes., loc. cit.   [3] Caes., loc. cit.; Str.
[4] Dio.L., I, 6.   [5] Caes., VI, 18.   [6] Pl., XVI, 249.
[7] Caes., VI, 14.   [8] Val. Max.

property', Ammianus Marcellinus's allusion to their 'searching into secret and sublime things', Pomponius Mela's statement that their instruction was given during secret meetings in caves 'or secluded dales', Lucan's sneer 'to you alone it is given to know the truth about the gods', and some allusions to the similarity between the esoteric teaching of Pythagoras and the Druids make it fairly clear that knowledge of their doctrine and methods of instruction was confined to the Druids alone. Even within the caste, there was a sharp distinction between the studies of the Druids and the Vates, for the latter were not directly concerned with the main doctrinal studies of the Druids proper: their own studies were confined to soothsaying and natural philosophy.

These men, however, who were 'experienced in the nature of the divine',[1] and the mediators between men and the gods, whose abodes were in 'the innermost groves of far-off forests',[2] and who, 'held in exceptional honour' as 'the most just of men',[3] were venerated as judges, priests, and teachers by the communities among whom they lived, were also notorious in the Graeco-Roman world for their human sacrifices. It may be noted in passing that more details were known about these rites than about any other aspect of Druidism.

Caesar noted that the practice was so widespread that a human sacrifice could be made as a thanks offering for deliverance from sickness or danger in battle. Only the Druids could officiate as ministers. They sometimes used 'figures of immense size . . . of twigs', which, filled with living men and animals, were then set on fire. Thieves, robbers, and murderers made sacrifices 'more pleasing to the immortal gods'; 'when the supply of such fails they resort to the execution even of the innocent'.[4]

Diodorus Siculus states that their victims were stabbed and that the convulsions of the dying were studied for the

[1] Str. [2] Luc. [3] Str. [4] Caes., VI, 16; Str.

11. The Human Sacrifice: *see pp.* 20, 158.

purpose of divination. The entrails were also examined. The presence of a Druid was essential for the performance of a sacrifice, for it was 'through their agency that the blessings of the gods should properly be sought'. Strabo adds that when the supply of victims was plentiful, it was thought that there would be a big yield from the land. They also shot their victims with arrows, or impaled them in temples. Caesar notes that for the Gauls exclusion from participation in the sacrifice was the greatest disaster that could happen to them.[1]

The Druids were also notorious for their practice of magic, and for their superstitions. As an example of the latter, Pliny describes their veneration of the serpent's egg: this had to be caught in a cloak when the mating snakes flung it into the air, and the possessor had to make off on horseback until he was safely over a stream. This talisman ensured 'success in lawsuits and a favourable reception with princes'; a knight of the Vocontii who carried one was put to death by the Emperor Claudius for this reason alone. Pliny's description of such an 'egg' is sufficiently precise to make it clear that whatever this object was, it was not a snake's egg. He also affirms that Druids were cannibals.[2]

The texts in which the Druids are mentioned cover the period 200 B.C. to A.D. 400, though early students of Druidism had some excuse for believing that they went back to 500 B.C., for Diogenes Laertius cites Aristotle's *Magic*, now known to be apocryphal. Sotion, in a fragment quoted by Diogenes Laertius in the first half of the third century A.D. first speaks of the Druids, together with the Magi of Persia and the Brahmins of India, as the originators of the study of philosophy. Caesar, covering the period 58–52 B.C., describes the Druids as the priests, judges, and teachers of the Gauls, and as ministers at human sacrifices.

[1] VI, 13. [2] XXXIX, 52; XXX, 13.

Cicero, writing in 46 B.C., states that Caesar's Aeduan friend Divitiacus, who is mentioned in *The Gallic War*, was a Druid. Divitiacus studied natural philosophy and soothsaying, and he was therefore a member of the order of the Vates. Diodorus Siculus (*c.* 8 B.C.) was the first to say that the Druids' doctrine was Pythagorean; after expressing astonishment at their human sacrifice, he pays tribute to the Druids as spiritual leaders and peacemakers. Strabo, who lived until A.D. 21, writes of the Druids with evident respect as 'the most just of men', but he puts the period when disputes were brought to them for settlement 'in former times'. He also notices that the Romans had 'put a stop to' human sacrifice and 'divinations that are opposed to our usages'.

Ammianus Marcellinus (b. A.D. 330), the last of the great Roman historians, drew upon the now lost history of Gaul by Timagenes—who lived under Augustus—for his eulogy of the Druids. According to the Druids, he says, part of the population of Gaul was indigenous, but the rest came from islands and lands beyond the Rhine, driven from their homes by the inroads of the sea and frequent invasions. The Druids, he adds, 'being loftier than the rest in intellect, and bound together in fraternal organizations, as the authority of Pythagoras prescribed, were elevated by their investigation of obscure and profound subjects, and scorning human affairs pronounced the soul immortal'.

The Emperor Augustus merely forbade Roman citizens to participate in the rites of the Druids. Under Tiberius (A.D. 14–37) the Druids were themselves persecuted; under Claudius (A.D. 41–54) Druidism was 'very thoroughly suppressed'.[1] Valerius Maximus, in about A.D. 31, says that the Gauls still believed in the immortality of the soul, and he shows surprise that these trousered barbarians should profess what he calls the beliefs of

[1] Su.

Pythagoras. Pomponius Mela, writing immediately before the Claudian persecution, states that a symbolical drawing of blood had been substituted for the original sacrifice. The Druids, he says, kept their doctrines secret, but he adds that their teaching on the immortality of the soul was permitted to be taught publicly, since it encouraged bravery in war.

Lucan, writing in A.D. 62, does not speak of the Druids as contemporaries: in *The Civil War* he apostrophizes the Druids of the past, and he sneers at their monopoly of 'the truth about the gods'. But he exempts from his censure

> You Poets, Bards, that of those valiant souls,
> Dying in warres, do Caroll their renowne,
> Know how t'eternize to perpetuall worlds
> Their endlesse praise: Many sweet songs you sing.[1]

In the preceding lines he describes a famous grove near Marseilles, the haunt of awesome powers;[2] he mentions the gods Teutates, Esus, and Taranis,[3] but he does not say that these gods were worshipped by the Druids, nor that this was a grove of the Druids.

Tacitus describes the massacre by Suetonius Paulinus of the Druids on Mona in A.D. 60. The Roman soldiers were confronted by armed warriors, women bearing brands, and Druids 'lifting up their hands to heaven and pouring forth dreadful imprecations'. Mutually encouraging each other not to quail before these 'frenzied women', the Romans advanced and 'smote down all resistance, and wrapped the foe in the flame of his own brands'. They then destroyed the groves of the Druids.[4] Tacitus does not make it clear why Suetonius led an expedition to

---

[1] Pedro Mexia, *Ten Following Bookes to the former Treasurie*, 1619, p. 39.
[2] *Civil War*, III, 399 ff.
[3] ibid., I, 445–6.
[4] Annals, XIV, 30.

Mona. By speaking of the Druids' 'inhuman superstitions', he implies that Suetonius had been moved by moral indignation, but in Rome his action was attributed to jealousy at another general's successes.[1] Though the country was unsettled, Suetonius went off to Mona and left the seat of his administration unguarded; the Iceni then rose in 'Boadicea's' rebellion. In Rome, the situation which Suetonius as an eyewitness could not see was obvious to Seneca, among others,[2] but the wider context of Tacitus' description throws no further light on the reasons which prompted an ambitious general and incompetent administrator to invade this remote island. Perhaps as a result of the massacre there was no centre of Druidism left in Britain: the Druids are not mentioned in *Agricola*. But they reappear in Tacitus's *Histories*, and he dismisses with scorn the interpretation by the Druids of the significance of a fire in the Capitol in A.D. 70. It portended, they said, 'the passage of the sovereignty of the world to the peoples beyond the Alps'. Since Druidism had been proscribed in Gaul, it is difficult to see who these Druids were: possibly they were the Vates, who may have been tolerated, and they were of course entitled to be called Druids.

In his *Natural History* (A.D. 77) the elder Pliny says that the Druids 'held nothing more sacred than the mistletoe' and the oak, 'and they never perform any of their rites except in the presence of a branch of it'. 'They choose groves formed of oaks for the sake of the tree alone.' They specially venerated the mistletoe that grew on an oak, regarding it as a particular sign of the divine favour. When one was found, on the sixth day of the moon preparations were made for the sacrifice of two white bulls which were for the first time tethered by the

[1] Annals, XIV, 29.
[2] R. G. Collingwood and J. N. L. Myres, *Roman Britain*, Oxford, 1937, p. 99.

horns, and for a banquet under the trees; a priest clad in white then cut down the mistletoe with a golden sickle. It was received in a white cloth when it fell. A panacea, it imparted fecundity to barren animals, and it was an antidote to poison.[1] Pliny also describes the ritual gathering of two herbs, 'selago' and 'samolus'.[2] He describes the snake's egg, and he comments with asperity on the magic which the Gallic Druids used to practise, and which was still being practised in Britain: 'it almost seems as though it was she who had imparted the cult to the Persians'. For him, Druidism was a 'monstrous cult', and his hostility to the Druids led him to throw in the charge of cannibalism as a parting shot.[3]

Dio Chrysostom, who died in A.D. 112, compares the Druids to the Brahmins and Magi, and says of the Celtic kings that though they 'fared sumptuously in their palaces', they were 'mere ministers of the Druids' will'.[4] His remarks are obviously anachronistic. In A.D. 120 Suetonius Tranquillus wrote briefly and sharply of their barbarous and inhuman religion. In about A.D. 200, St. Clement of Alexandria stated that philosophy had been studied by the Druids before the Greeks; on the authority of Alexander Polyhistor, he says that Pythagoras was a 'hearer' of the Galatae and Brahmins, and thus, by implication, of the Druids. In the third century, Hippolytus, who was hostile to them, stated that they had used Pythagorean methods of reckoning in their prophecies, and he mentions them in the prolegomena to his *Refutation of All Heresies* as though they were the equals of Pythagoras, Socrates, Plato, and Aristotle.

Lampridius and Vopiscus, in about A.D. 300, speak of the 'dryades' who entered the lives of Alexander Severus (A.D. 235), Diocletian (before A.D. 285), and Aurelianus (A.D. 270) as soothsayers, and sixty years later Aurelius Victor briefly alluded to the superstitions of the Druids.

[1] XVI, 249.   [2] XXIV, 103.   [3] XXX, 13.   [4] *Orations*, XLIX.

The last mention of the Druids in the literature of classical antiquity comes at the end of the fourth century, and for the first time a glimpse of the Druids is caught through the eyes of a Gaul. In two poems from *The Professors of Bordeaux* which commemorate Attius Patera and Phoebicius, Ausonius makes a point of alluding to their descent from the Druids of Bayeux and Brittany. Three and a half centuries had passed since their religion was 'very thoroughly suppressed', but the men who had once been 'held in exceptional honour' were not forgotten, and among their own people, pride was still taken in a pedigree which went back to the Druids.

II

THE LEARNED THOUGHTFUL DRUIDS

THE English poets have some odd things to say of
the Druids. Drayton's are drawn through the air
by dragons; Milton calls on Parliament to follow
the example of the Druids; Pope's Druids may be taken
for Scythian heroes; Marvell and Wordsworth picture
themselves as Druids, Collins calls Thomson a Druid,
and Blake calls Adam a Druid. The first allusion to the
Druids in English poetry is particularly mystifying, and
Alexander Barclay's lines on his 'Druydans' thus establish a precedent. In his case, they must have puzzled not
only his readers but the author himself.

Very early in the sixteenth century Barclay published
The Shyp of folys of the worlde: on board are the seven
deadly sins and various misdemeanours and nuisances,
and here the Druids appear as a simile for intoxicated
dancers

> Rennynge about in this theyr furyous vyce
> Like as it were in Bacchus sacrifice
>
> Or as the Druydans rennyth in vayne about
> In theyr mad fests vpon the hylle of yde
> Makynge theyr sacrafyce with furour noyse and shout
> Whan theyr madnes settyth theyr wyt asyde.[1]

These Druids are quite unrecognizable. The Druids had
nothing to do with Mount Ida, and their deportment when
gathering mistletoe or pacifying belligerent tribes seems
to have been, if anything, assured and sedate. The possibility that the 'Druydans' are not Druids at all must be

---

[1] *The Shyp of folys of the worlde*, 1509, f. cxxii v.

ruled out: Barclay's marginal gloss explains that they come from Caesar's *Gallic War*.

The Latin text which Barclay translates does not at once make it clear why the Druids are thought of as dancers on Ida. The original *Ship of Fools*, Sebastian Brant's *Das Narren schyeff*, 1498, contains no mention of Druids, but Jacob Locher published a very free Latin translation of Brant, and the verse which Barclay even more freely translates contains both the words 'druidae' and 'galli', and it also has a reference to the priests of Cybele.[1] Locher must have had the frenzied corybants in mind, for this gives point to the simile. The Galli were in fact the priests of Attis, whose worship was often confused with that of Cybele; and since 'galli' was used both for Cybele's priests and as an adjective meaning Gallic, Locher evidently thought that these Galli were the same Gallic priests, the Druids, about whom he had read in Caesar. (This word had given rise to comment in classical antiquity, and Ovid and St. Jerome both offer explanations of the apparent connexion between Gaul and the Galli.)[2] The perplexed Barclay did not mention Cybele in his own translation, and he thus gives his reader no clue whatsoever to Locher's intended meaning. Henry Watson's prose version of the *Ship of Fools*, which was also published in 1509, is equally garbled,[3] and it would seem that at this date no one in England was particularly interested in the Druids.

It was, then, with Hector Boece's *Scotorum Historiae a prima gentis origine*, which was published in Paris in 1526 and translated by John Bellenden in 1536, that the reputation of the Druids as persons 'of definite account and dignity' was revived in this island. In his introductory

[1] *Stultifera navis*, Basle, 1497, f. LXIX v.
[2] *Fasti*, iv, 361; *Sancti Eusebii Hieronymi . . . Operum Tomus Sextus*, Verona, 1736, col. 41 B.
[3] *The Grete Shyppe of Fooles of this Worlde*, 1517, sig. O iii v.

'Discription of Albion', Boece looks over the scene of his history and remarks:

in thay dayis wer the preistis of Britane, namit Driades, richt expert baith in naturall and morall philosophie.

The principall sect of thir preistis wes in the Ile of Man, quhilk wes in that time the spectacle and fontane of all honest eruditioun and letteris; and, fra thir preistis wer anis profest in Catholik faith, thay perseverit with gret constance in it, bot ony spot of herise.[1]

Both Anglesey and Man were once called Mona; such was Boece's esteem for these early moral philosophers that presumably he removed them to the more northern island in order to bring them nearer to Scotland. From Tacitus' description, however, it is evident that a narrow strait rather than a sea gave the Druids their last line of defence. But what emerges from Boece's history is that he strove to give his narrative a continuity which would show that Scotland had a long tradition of piety and learning, and if parts of his history are, as John Selden says, 'infinit Fables',[2] this does not affect the truth which Boece was embellishing. Yet while the Druids, as he saw them, fit easily into Scotland's past as he saw it, they were not entirely the Druids of Caesar, the Druids of Dio Chrysostom. In his account of '*King Fynnane and his Lawis; and of the College of Clerkis in the Ile of Man*', Boece says that he 'wes the first king that institute Prelatis and Clerkis to be in this realme', adding:

Thir preistis war namit Druides; and wes institute in this Ile, be advise of the king and his nobillis, to make sacrifice in honour of thair Goddis, and to instruk the sonnis of nobill men in virtew and science, siclik as thay war lernit at Athenes.[3]

This last phrase is evocative. What Boece valued in the Druids was their apparent kinship with the scholars of

[1] *Hystory and Croniklis of Scotland*, Edinburgh, 1821, p. xxv.
[2] Michael Drayton, *Poly-Olbion*, 1612, p. 151.
[3] Bellenden, op. cit., p. 54.

the Renaissance, and for the rest of the sixteenth century
it was as 'wise Clerkis' that they were mainly held in
regard by the learned.

He adds a picturesque detail to his description of the
Druids which is reminiscent of the fire ceremonies of the
Celts. Among the Druids, he says, there was 'a bischop
and maister . . . before quhom wes borne ane gleib of fire,
in signe of his honour and divinite'.[1] It is not altogether
certain that Boece's testimony can here be relied on, for
this is also a description of the *daduchos* of the Hierophantes, the head of the Eleusinian cult; elsewhere, Boece
says that Diana was worshipped in Scotland,[2] and it seems
that he was quite ready to draw on the classics in order to
supplement his material. Of special interest, since later it
was widely thought that the Druids had built them, is his
mention of stone circles; he says that King Maynus ordered

certane grete stanys in diverse partis of euery regioun, quhare was
maist convenient, suld be invirone and in cirkill, and ye gretest
stane suld be errectit towart ye south, to be vsit for ane altare.
Apoun ye samyn to immortall goddis suld hoistis be offerit and
sacrifice be brynt.[3]

He adds that even in his own day 'are sene thir roundis of
stanys and ar callit the ald temple of goddis be ye vulgare
pepill'. He maintains that the rites celebrated there were
like those described in 'the ald bukis of Egipcianis',
and it would seem from this remark that he did not have
the Druids in mind here. William Stewart, who wrote a
metrical version of the *Historiae*, renders this passage:

> Ane tempill als of greit authoritie,
> Quhairin their godis placit wer full hie,
> This king gart make for habitatioun
> Of Drewides witht greit possessioun.[4]

[1] loc. cit.   [2] op. cit., p. 56.
[3] *The Mar Lodge Translation*, ed. G.Watson, Edinburgh, 1946, pp. 83, 84.
[4] *The Buik of the Croniclis of Scotland*, tr. William Stewart (1535),
ed. W. B. Turnbull, *Rolls Series*, VI, vol. i, p. 99.

His loose paraphrase thus fortuitously links the Druids with 'roundis of stanys' a century and a half before more cogent reasons were advanced for believing that these were the remains of temples of the Druids.

It is most unlikely that Boece's interest in the Druids was originally inspired by Scottish folklore. What he says of them is plainly derived from Caesar, from a literary source, and what he selected from Caesar produced a picture of an early humanist which much resembles the Druid who was currently admired in France. Though early sixteenth-century French literature on the Druids made little stir in England—for its fervently patriotic nature created an effective copyright—Boece must certainly have been acquainted with it, if only at second hand, for he had lived for some years in Paris, and in France at that time interest in the Druids was not at all confined to literary circles. The citizens of Dreux were then proud to call themselves 'les Druydes'.[1] In many parts of France the customary New Year's Day greeting was 'Aguillanneuf', then widely regarded as *an ancient tearme of reioycing, deriued from the Druides*.[2] They had caught popular fancy even before Chaucer's day, when it was recorded that a temple of the Druids once stood on Montmartre.[3] In the crypt of the cathedral at Chartres there is a grotto which, according to medieval tradition at latest, was thought of as a cave of the Druids. Specially remarkable was the story about them which had attached itself to a much venerated statue of the Virgin in the crypt, and Boece may well have heard of it, for in his time the legend was well known. The *Virgo Paritura*, as it was called, showed the Virgin seated with closed eyes and

---

[1] *Recuiel de poésies françoises de 15e et 16e siècles*, ed. A. de Montaiglon, Paris, 1858, tom viii, p. 234.

[2] R. Cotgrave, *A Dictionarie of the French and English Tongues*, 1611, 'Au-guy-l'an-neuf'.

[3] R. de Presles [b. 1314], *Monseigneur saint Augustin dela cité de Dieu*, Abbeville, 1486, sig. si v.

holding the infant Saviour in her lap, and the interpretation of its symbolism was made particularly striking by
the theory that it had been carved by the Druids in anticipation of the Nativity.[1] Thirteenth-century verses on the
cathedral do not mention this legend, but a Latin poem
of the early fifteenth century contains a reference to the
crypt and the Druids, and the poem then goes on immediately to speak of the Virgin. The two subjects were
juxtaposed, and defective punctuation then led to a
misreading of the text, and in this way the legend was
started.[2] That it was not thought intrinsically implausible
testifies, if indirectly, to the regard in which the Druids
were then held. As for current French literature on the
Druids, this shows that in the early sixteenth century
they were greatly admired for their learning, and apparent parallels between Catholicism and Druidism attracted some attention.

The King's Antiquary John Leland (1506?–1552) also
studied for a time in Paris, and there he may well have
noticed the interest of the French in their scholarly
ancestors, in men who had been established in Britain as
well. It was his life's ambition to write a comprehensive
account of the literature, history, and antiquities of
Britain, and for years he travelled extensively in search
of his material. He carefully noted down everything that
he had read about Britain's earliest men of learning, and,
in fact, he had some justification for making much of
them in the context of his literary studies, for—if the
labels are not looked at too closely—the Druids and their
Bards are certainly the earliest known philosophers and
poets of this island. A small irritant may also have helped
to stimulate his sense of mission, for when Polydore
Vergil published his *Anglicae Historiae libri XXVI* in

[1] See S. Rouillard, *Parthénie*, Paris, 1609.
[2] Y. Delaporte, 'Les Druides et les traditions Chartrains', *La Voix
de Notre-Dame de Chartres*, n.p., Sept. 1936.

1534—the year in which Leland started on his travels—
the Italian described them as 'preestes, being Druides,
that is to say of hethen religion, sainge their accursed
prayers'.[1] Leland, a patriot as well as a scholar, greatly
resented this kind of remark, and his observations on the
Druids offset those of a man who had shown both a
Roman disdain for the ancient Briton and a Christian
disdain for the pagan.

Leland cherished the Druids. Caesar's account of their
'discussions' encouraged some of his readers to believe
that the Druids studied, among other things, astronomy,
mathematics, history, and jurisprudence. The Renaissance scholar might easily feel drawn to the men with
whom, it seemed, he shared so many interests. The
humanist Petrus Ramus, for example, expatiates at great
length on their learning, and lamenting over his country's
vanished glories, he exclaims that long ago Gaul, too,
had her own Euclids, Platos, and Aristotles.[2] Leland's
understandable enthusiasm was typical of his age, and it
also appears to have found some response in a few of his
eighteenth-century readers. His biographies of British
authors, with 'the firste booke begynning at the Druides',[3]
first appeared in print—though in an imperfect edition—
in 1709,[4] and even at so late a date reminiscences of
Leland's approach show themselves in Joseph Spence's
brief allusion to 'Druidical poetry' in a short essay on the
English poets, and in Thomas Warton's original intention
to introduce his *History of English Poetry* with an allusion
to the lost poems of the Druids.[5] In a remark in *The*

---

[1] *Polydore Vergil's English History*, ed. H. Ellis (Camden Soc.), 1846,
p. 18.
[2] Petrus Ramus, *Liber de Moribus veterum Gallorum*, Paris, 1559, ff.
40 ff.
[3] *The Itinerary of John Leland*, ed. L. T. Smith, 1907, p. xl.
[4] *Commentarii de Scriptoribus Britannicis*, Oxford, 1709.
[5] *Pope and his Contemporaries*, ed. J. L. Clifford and L. A. Landa,
1949, pp. 230 ff.; C. Rinaker, *Thomas Warton*, Urbana, 1916, p. 83.

Polite Correspondence, 1747, Leland's attitude to the Druids is fairly summed up:

as soon as we read any Thing of *Britain* either in our old Authors, or in the Writings of Strangers, we hear of Poets, and which is very remarkable, not of miserable wretched Rhimers, but of wise and powerful Men.[1]

But Leland's influence was felt far earlier than this. John Bale drew heavily on the other's manuscript for his own biographies of British authors, and strangely enough, he was also to share Leland's pride in the Druids. A former priest of the Catholic Church who had married a nun, Bale never found peace of mind inside or outside the Church to which he had once belonged, and his persistent and vindictive attacks on Catholic belief and practice alienated Protestants who had a distaste for his kind of polemic. He often shot at targets which did not exist, and in *The Actes of Englysh Votaries*, 1546, which is dedicated to the proposition that lewdness is the inevitable outcome of vows of chastity, he illustrates his thesis by citing the Druids as an example of clerical incontinence.[2]

The charge throws more light on Bale than on the Druids. As he saw them, they exercised too much authority in their handling of religious matters: they appointed ceremonies, educated the young and settled controversies; and he must also have noticed that they had a hierarchy headed by the chief Druid, exemption from conscription, and the power to excommunicate. Looked at in this way, the Druids seem to have provided the Catholic Church with a model, yet he was in two minds about them. On the one hand he stated that they were monotheists—even if this claim arose out of his mistranslation of a sentence in Boece's *Historiae* which says precisely the opposite.[3] On the other, his hostility is

[1] op. cit., n.p., 1747, p. 249.
[2] op. cit., 1546, ff. 10-11 v.
[3] ibid., f. 12; op. cit., f. XXII.

plain enough in his comments on 'the Druydes and their chastyte', and elsewhere in *The Actes* he shows it in less obvious a fashion. Though he borrowed from Annius of Viterbo's version of the history of postdiluvian Europe, he was reluctant to endorse it by stating that the study of philosophy had started in Britain, and of the island's earliest philosophers who were later known as Druids he says: 'Rather shulde they seme to come first hyther from Athens, a most famouse cytie of the Grekes.'[1] But the leaven of Leland's ideas was working on his imagination, and when he came to write *Scriptorum Illustrium Maioris Brytanniae Catalogus*, 1557, his reservations vanished. He wholeheartedly accepted Annius's account of the origins of Druidism, a story that he had hitherto merely toyed with, and it was with pride that Bale asserted that the studies of the Druids had flourished, particularly in Britain, long before Greece had any literature to speak of.[2]

His tribute to their pre-eminence was soon to appear restrained. In a controversy over the priority of the foundation of the universities of Oxford and Cambridge, Thomas Caius of Oxford claimed that philosophers had come to Britain with Brutus and settled at Oxford. John Caius of Cambridge replied that the Druids, who thrived from 1013 B.C. to A.D. 179, had been in Britain before the arrival of Brutus, and their establishment at Cambridge had therefore antedated that of the Oxford philosophers. In the augmented second edition of *De Antiquitate Cantabrigiensis Academiae*, posthumously published in 1574, a revised estimate of the age of Druidism then helped to place a seat of learning beside the Cam long before the name of Isis was heard on the banks of the Nile, let alone in the neighbourhood of Folly Bridge.[3]

[1] op. cit., f. 10.
[2] *Scriptorum Illustrium Maioris Brytanniae Catalogus*, Basle, 1557, p. 4.
[3] *De Antiquitate Cantabrigiensis Acadamiae*, 1568, p. 18; 1574, p. 15.

The first severe blow to the Druids' reputation came in 1577, when the historian Raphael Holinshed attacked them for perverting the doctrine of the immortality of the soul. Holinshed saw history as a succession of events linked together by cause and effect, a story to be told by a man with the Ancient Mariner's ability to hold the listener. He very ingeniously rearranged his data in order to keep his narrative moving, and it so happens that out of the spurious he produced, as far as the Druids are concerned, the entirely bogus. His rather magisterial comments on men who never existed and events that never took place give his history an altogether disconcerting appearance of reality. But the King Druiyus and his Druids of the *Chronicles* are not Holinshed's invention. It was in 1498 that, as Selden puts it,

THERE came forth, and in Buskins too (I mean with Pomp and State) some parcels of years ago, and is still handled about everywhere, an Author, called *Berosus* a *Chaldee* Priest (take heed how you suffer yourself to believe him to be the same that *Flavius Josephus* so often quotes up and down for a witness) with a commentary of Viterbiensis.[1]

The Berosus whom Josephus quotes was a Chaldean historian who in 250 B.C. wrote a history covering a period of 36,000 years; of this history only some fragments have been preserved. The object of Selden's scorn was the fifteenth-century Italian historian Annius of Viterbo, who wrote a long commentary on a text purporting to come from the hand of Berosus. Assuming for the sake of argument that its editor had forged this text—for the original and the commentary fit each other so well as to suggest some connivance—Annius divided the Chaldean annals into sections which were each headed by the name of an Assyrian king. Following the name of each king

---

[1] John Selden, *The Reverse . . . of the English Janus*, tr. R. Westcot (Adam Littleton), 1683, p. 1.

were some brief remarks on his contemporaries in other lands. In the section devoted to Jupiter Belus, for example, there is a significant mention of one Comerus, and incidentally of Tyras the founder of Tyre.[1]

The ostensible intention of the forger, then, was to provide a record of the Assyrian dynasties. It was, however, not this part of the text that caught the Western reader's eye, but the asides of Berosus, for he supplied a complete list of Gaul's earliest rulers from its first settlement down to Paris, the founder of Paris. In this way, Annius filled a great gap in the postdiluvian history of Europe.

According to Annius, after the Flood the posterity of Noah at once went their several ways: Ganges settled in east Asia, and Samotes the son of Japhet founded Celtic colonies in Western Europe. He was followed by Magus, who was in turn succeeded by Sarron, Dryius, Bardus, Longo, Bardus Junior, Celte, and so on.[2] The commentary enlarged on these names, and it is clear that Annius had based the names of the earliest monarchs of Gaul and Britain on Greek and Latin texts in which the Druids are mentioned. Samotes he derived from Diogenes Laertius's 'semnotheoi', Magus was taken from Pliny, Dryius came from Caesar's druidae, and Sarron from a scribal error for 'drovidas' in Poggio Bracciolini's Latin translation from the Greek of Diodorus Siculus which had been published twenty-six years before.[3] By the time he came to Bardus the reader had every reason to be suspicious.

Nevertheless, Annius found an audience which was probably willing to be deceived. He had not only painstakingly produced a commentary in which the best

[1] J. Annius Viterbiensis, *Commentaria super opera diversorum auctorum de antiquitatibus loquentium*, Rome, 1498, sig. R iii.

[2] ibid., sig. R ff.

[3] *Diodori . . . a Poggio in Latinum traducti*, Bologna, 1472, f. 80: 'quos uocant sarronidas'. The accepted transliteration is 'drovidas'.

authorities were called on to bear witness to the authenticity of his annals, but he had above all appealed to national pride. As far as the Druids were concerned, the most telling passage in his book gave special prominence to remarks by Diogenes Laertius on the barbarian origin of philosophy. As king succeeded king, Annius went on, these philosophers changed their names. Under Sarron they were called Zarronidas, and under Dryius, Dryiudes.[1] It was thus more explicitly demonstrated how the philosophers of Gaul had long antedated those of Greece.

Holinshed mixed the inventions of Annius with the fictions of Geoffrey of Monmouth, and thus produced his own version of early British history. While the immediate posterity of Japhet reigned here, he writes, the true knowledge taught by Samothes was uncontaminated. The posterity of Cham, however, were in the meantime developing their magic arts. Sarron opened schools; Dryius excelled in philosophy and theology, and his followers the Druids were called Samothei or Semnothei. Druiyus taught that the soul is immortal, and he wrote precepts and rules of doctrine.

Religion subsequently decayed: it had grown corrupt when it was said that the soul went from one body to another. Yet the Druids were powerful, and many flocked to them 'to learne their trades'. They taught orally to hide from outsiders the contemptible quality of their instruction, but they committed their laws and histories to writing: this island was literate from the first.

Then Albion the grandson of Cham introduced idolatry, superstition, and sorcery. This situation permitted Holinshed to digress and attack Catholicism. When a prince died, he says, some 'forme of starres' was dedicated to him: this was 'their translation in heauen'. The prince then 'was properlye sayde to haue place amonge the goddes. A toye much lyke to the Catalogue of Romish

[1] op. cit., sig. S vi, sig. T v.

saintes, (although the one was written in the celestiall orbes, the other in sheepe skinnes, and verye brickle paper).' The 'Druiysh' and 'Bardike' ceremonies grew more elaborate; Samothes was given divine honours and called Dis; and they built huge temples for the twenty-five Flamines, the equivalents of Bishops, who subjected the rest to their 'jurisdiction in cases of religion, and super-sticious ceremonies'.[1] Thus, by ingeniously adapting Annius and Geoffrey of Monmouth, Holinshed produced a picture of the Druids which gave his country a high reputation for learning, and at the same time left much for the Christian missionaries to reform.

Annius's reputation declined quickly, and Camden excluded him from the pages of *Britannia*. Yet Camden was eclectic. He thoroughly explored the classics for everything which had the least bearing on British history, and he was particularly interested in the Druids. Though the standard sources offered much scope for speculation, he read them in a very different temper from that of a 'Dr. Druid the Antiquarian'[2] of the eighteenth century. He expanded his material, however, by reading into the classics references to the Druids which were not explicitly there. Sometimes uncritical, he at least based his remarks on established authorities. There was a strong demand for his work, and edition after edition of *Britannia* quickly followed each other. If any man made the Druids famous, it was Camden.

They were 'our Druids' from the first edition of 1586, and this phrase was never changed.[3] The nuances of this proprietory attitude differed: in the second edition of 1587 he claimed, on the basis of a passage in Origen, that the Druids had prepared the Britons for the Faith, but by the fourth edition of 1594 their religion had become 'a

[1] *The First Volume of the Chronicles of England*, 1577, ff. 7 ff.
[2] A character in Richard Cumberland's *Fashionable Lover*, 1772.
[3] op. cit., p. 14.

dismal and confused heap of superstition'.[1] Yet the
interest which Camden had showed as a man was sustained even when he had become an institution: so trivial
a thing as the finding of an alleged 'Druid amulet' was
thought sufficiently important to record in Gibson's
second edition of *Britannia*, 1722.[2]

From the first, then, Camden shows how he had been
extending the scope of his researches. He records the
names of Celtic gods; he thought that the Bardocucullus
was a reference to the cloak of the Bards, and he suggests
that 'Drẏ', from Aelfricus, might mean Druid.[3] Going
far outside the standard classical texts on the Druids, he
mentions Solinus Polyhistor, (who merely repeats that
men were sacrificed in Gaul); he also refers his readers
to a fourth-century play and to the works of Lactantius
and Eusebius for more information about Druidism.[4] His
allusion to the play, (which he calls the *Psuedo-Plauti
Aulularia*), the only surviving comedy of the Late
Empire, is misleading; here, however, Camden was
himself misled. He had read this play in an edition
edited by Peter Daniel under the title of *Querolus*.[5] In
the course of the play the hero asks his Lar Familiaris
to help him become a powerful man: he wishes to beat
foreigners and despoil his neighbours. The Lar replies
that Querolus sought brigandage, not power, and he
suggests that Querolus should live on the banks of the
Loire, the home of men who follow 'natural right'.
Capital sentences there were performed on the trunk of
an oak; peasants were advocates, private persons judges,
and there everything was permitted. Querolus rejects this
advice: he does not care for this 'sylvan law'. Daniel in
his notes took this scene to refer to the Druids, but the

---

[1] op. cit., 1587, p. 33; 1594, p. 33; 1594, p. 32, 1695, col. xxxv.
[2] ibid., ed. E. Gibson, 1722, p. 585.
[3] ibid., 1586, pp. 14, 16 (from Martial, xiv, 28); p. 11 (from a manuscript: the meaning is 'mage').   [4] ibid., 1607, p. 11.
[5] Paris, 1564.

allusion was in fact to the Bagaudae, who from their head-
quarters at the mouth of the Loire ravaged Gaul during
the fourth century. The Druids had disappeared long
before this date.[1]

Lactantius and Eusebius do not mention the Druids.
The former states that Esus and Teutates were placated
by human sacrifice,[2] a remark which reinforces Lucan's
brief allusion to Taranis, Esus, and Teutates, whom a
scholium of 1486 identifies as the Jupiter, Mars, and
Mercury of the Gauls.[3] But a wider reading in Lactantius
shows that Camden had a by no means negligible influence on the students he guided to the *Divine Institutes*.
'While Saturnus reigned . . . God was manifestly worshipped':[4] such a phrase lent powerful support to the
later antiquaries' conviction that in the earliest age there
was one universal religion. Eusebius states that the Celts
offered human sacrifices to Kronos,[5] and the picture he
paints of corrupt paganism could be taken to show how
swiftly the first religion of men had declined. With hints
from the early Fathers to support them, later antiquaries
could place their Druids in a far wider context, and claim
that the Druids had kept the first religion in its purest
form. These brief notices in Camden, then, suggest that
patristic literature had more influence on students of
Druidism than might be apparent from too narrow a
reference to his sources.

Camden's curiosity was inherited by his editor, Edmund Gibson, who translated and republished *Britannia*
with copious notes in 1695. The older antiquary remarked
that at '*Cerig-y-Drudion*, id est, *Lapides Druydarum*' in

[1] L. Havet, *Le Querolus*, Paris, 1880, pp. 1, 217 ff.
[2] *Opera*, ed. X. Betuleius Augustanus, Basle, 1563, p. 72. Camden
may have consulted this edition: on this page there are notes on the
Druids.
[3] *Pharsalia*, ed. Vincentius Omnibonus, Venice, 1486, sig. b vij.
[4] *Divine Institutes*, v, 5; *Works*, tr. W. Fletcher, Edinburgh, 1871,
p. 302.
[5] *The Preparation for the Gospel*, IV, xvi.

North Wales there was a monument with a then un-
deciphered inscription which he tentatively attributed to
the Druids.[1] Between 1594 and 1695, however, it was
discovered that it had been erected '*to the memory of the
excellent Prince, Lhewelin*'.[2] Gibson says of '*Kerrig y
Drùdion*' that it was 'highly probable, tho' not unquestion-
able' that it was 'so denominated from the *Druids*'.[3] But
he could not trace these 'Druid-stones'. The first intimation that Stonehenge may have been a temple of the
Druids was then in print: Gibson alludes to Aubrey's
theory that circular monuments were temples of the
Druids—if only as a supposition[4]—and he had also learned
that in Scotland these circles were called 'Chapels and
Temples', and in local tradition they were regarded as
'places of worship in the time of Heathenism' which had
belonged to the 'Drounich'.[5] Cerrig y Drudion had no
stone circles, but in this locality there were two '*Kistieu
maen* or *Stone-chests*': '*two solitary prisons that are
generally supposed to have been used in the time of the
Druids*'.[6] Gibson suggests that these may have been the
stones commemorated in 'Kerrig y Drùdion'.

He was always prepared to print his correspondents'
ready remarks on the Druids. Mr. Walker's article on
early British coins gives them a mention.[7] Another correspondent discovered, and mistranslated as '*Druids-Town*,' a
'village' in Anglesey which he called '*Tre'r Druw*.' (It
was in fact a farm-house.) The sufficiently correct translation of '*Tre'r Beirdh*' as '*Bards Town*' strengthened the
district's apparent association with the Druids, and
'*Maen y Druw*' was thought to have commemorated a
vanished sepulchral monument.[8] '*Kèrig y Brỳngwyn*', it
was conjectured, might have been 'a burial place of some
of the most eminent Druids'.[9] As though to compensate

[1] op. cit., 1594, p. 519
[2] *Britannia*, 1695, col. 685.   [3] ibid., col. 681.
[4] ibid., col. 618.   [5] ibid., col. 637.   [6] ibid., col. 681.
[7] ibid., col. xciv.   [8] ibid., col. 675.   [9] ibid., col. 676.

for these 'reveries', as the Reverend Edward Ledwick called such speculations,[1] the etymology of Stanton Drew in Somerset was shown to have nothing to do with the Druids. (The marginal note refers to John Aubrey, but the mistaken etymology originated with the philologist Samuel Bochart in 1646.)[2] These contributions to the 1695 edition of *Britannia*, which was republished with minor additions in 1722, greatly stimulated interest in the Druids, and when Gibson said of a rocking stone in Pembrokeshire 'I suspect it rather an effect of human industry, than chance' in a context where the Druids are thought of as builders of cromlechs,[3] his casual remark finally suggested the Druid rocking stone of William Mason's *Caractacus* and William Blake's 'Stone of Trial'.

Camden had ranged so far in searching for the Druids that mention might be made here of two texts which he did not see, or chose to disregard. An early scholium on Lucan calls them 'Driadae gens Germaniae', adding that they used to divine with acorns and that they had altars of turf.[4] In the *editio princeps* (1521) of Seneca's satirical *Death of Claudius* the spirit of Augustus addresses a senate of gods in support of Claudius's supplication for elevation to divine rank. Augustus declares that princes became gods when they displayed piety and justice, but the reasons he puts forward for raising Claudius, that pious and just man, to divine rank do little to help the candidate; among them is mention of his extirpating the perfidious tribe of the Druids.[5] The passage does not occur in any known manuscript of Seneca; it appears for the first time only in the earliest printed edition, and possibly it was interpolated by a sixteenth-century scholar

[1] J. B. Nichols, *Illustrations of Literary History*, 1848, vol. vii, p. 512.
[2] op. cit., col. 81; S. Bochart, *Geographia Sacra*, Caen, 1646, Part II, p. 755.
[3] op. cit., col. 638.
[4] *Scholia in Lucani Bellum Civile*, ed. H. Usener, Leipzig, 1869, p. 451.
[5] *Ludus L. Annei Senecae, De Morte Claudij Caesaris*, Basle, 1521, p. 14.

who took the opportunity of contributing some further satire to the 'pumkinification'—as a much later editor translates Seneca's word for the 'deification' of Claudius[1] —of a man who had persecuted the learned Druids.

Towards the end of the sixteenth century growing interest in the subject led to some indiscriminate gleaning in the classics for more information about the Druids. They had nothing more to yield, and 'W.B.', the English translator of Ortelius's *Theatrum Orbis Terrarum*, 1606, had no authority for saying that at the Druids' musters, late-comers were put to death, that the skulls of enemies were gilded and converted into cups, and that they slaughtered the older men. W. B. was strongly of the opinion that the ancestors of the English, as well as those of the Welsh and the French, had Druids of their own: Britain, he argues, was formerly colonized from the Low Countries, and therefore, he claims, 'Druthin', the German for 'deus', established a German etymology for the word Druid.[2]

W.B.'s miscellany, with its items collected at random and with few scruples about their authenticity, reads rather like gossip about the Druids. He remarks, for example, that the 'Drudenfuss'—a magic pentagram which he describes as 'that same kind of night-bug, commonly called the Philosophicall shoe'—was still being used as a charm. The notion that it was a Druid symbol probably dates from the turn of the fifteenth century, when the poet Conrad Celtes speculated on the meaning of a pentagram which he had seen on an early Frankish coin: since in Germany this figure was then known as the 'druiden fues', as he spells it, he thought it had a Druid origin.[3] Subsequently, the seventeenth-century antiquary

[1] *The Satire of Seneca on the Apotheosis of Claudius*, ed. A. P. Ball, New York, 1902, pp. 50, 56.

[2] Abraham Ortelius, *Theatrum Orbis Terrarum*, tr. W.B., 1606, leaves 1–4 between ff. xij and xiij.

[3] 'Norinberga', *Conradis Celtis . . . quatuor libri*, Nuremberg, 1502, sig. m viii v.

Elias Schedius thought that the word referred to an actual shoe,[1] and Petrus Lescaloperius in turn suggested that from this Gallic footwear came the word 'galoshes';[2] little was heard of it in England, where opinion was probably summed up by William Borlase's reflection that as a shoe it had 'a singular shape'.[3]

W.B. also took part in a little international bickering, if it can be called such, over the origins of Druidism. Caesar's remarks on this subject were not well received in France, where they were challenged with some acerbity; the English continued to quote him with an urbane indifference to Gallic discomposure. Noël Taillepied, for example, claims that Caesar was speaking of Brittany, where the learned retired in order to enjoy its quiet, and where the young went to learn their ABC. France owed nothing to England, and even Alcuin's part in the foundation of the University of Paris provoked the comment: 'quant à dire parmy les rues, science à vendre'.[4] De Chasseneux interrupts his long *Catalogus Gloriae Mundi* in order to refute Caesar with a quotation from Juvenal: 'Gallica causidicos docuit facunda Britannos'— 'Eloquent Gaul has trained the pleaders of Britain'.[5] Juvenal's, however, was a reference to the Gallic schools of rhetoric which flourished long after the days of the Druids. (Nevertheless, in French literature, an occasional glimpse is thereafter caught of the newly discovered Druid order of Causidiques.) In England, little attention was paid to these barbed remarks, but they stung W.B. into translating Juvenal's line as: 'The prating Frenchmen first did teach, The Englishman to plead at barre.'

By the time that the Druids were being taken up by the

---

[1] *De Diis Germanis*, Halle, 1728, p. 411.
[2] 'Theologia Veterum Gallorum', in Cicero, *De Natura Deorum*, Paris, 1660, p. 726.
[3] *Observations on the Antiquities of Cornwall*, 1754, p. 120.
[4] *Histoire de l'Estat et Republique des Druides*, Paris, 1585, ff. 83 ff.
[5] op. cit., Lyons, 1546, sig. Viij; juvenal, *Satires*, xv, 1.111.

poets, of whom Drayton was the first to write about them at all frequently, the classical descriptions offered rather hackneyed material to work on. But Drayton handled his new literary image with ease and conviction; starting with pure invention, he rapidly discovered and developed some of the potentialities of his sources, and he found novel ways of working within their limitations. His Druids first appear in the second edition of *Englands Heroicall Epistles*, 1598. In '*Elinor Cobham* to Duke *Humfrey*' the banished duchess writes of her place of exile:

> They say the *Druides*, once liud in this Ile,
> This fatall *Man*, the place of my exile,
> Whose powerful charmes, such dreadful wonders wrought,
> Which in the gothish Island tongue were taught:
> O that their spels to me they had resign'd,
> Wherewith they raised, and calm'd, both sea and wind,
> And made the moone, pause in her palid spheare,
> Whilst her grym Dragons, drue them through the ayre;
> Their hellish power, to kill the plowmans steed,
> Or to forespeake the flocks as they did feed,
> To nurse a damned spirit, with humaine bloud,
> To carry them through earth, ayre, fire and floud.[1]

Ultimately derived from Pliny's remarks on their use of magic, these Druids are otherwise entirely fanciful. They live on Man, to which Elinor Cobham, on her conviction for witchcraft, had been banished; in this context, they lend a little local colour to the abode of an alleged sorceress who had been exiled to a place where Thomas Nashe had placed his Druids and their familiars.[2]

A roundabout series of events may have helped Drayton to revise his ideas on the Druids. In 1567, the cartographer Abraham Ortelius was interested in the discovery off the Dutch coast of a stronghold called the 'Huys te Britten',

---

[1] op. cit., p. 43.
[2] Thomas Nashe, *The Terrors of the Night*, 1594, sig. B4.

and he asked the antiquary Humphrey Llwyd if he could throw any light on it. As a result of their exchange of letters, Llwyd sent him a description of Anglesey, 'De Mona Druidum Insula', and in 1570 Ortelius printed this brief survey of the home of the Druids as an appendix to his *Theatrum Orbis Terrarum*.[1] Though Llwyd died when Drayton was only five, Drayton spoke of him as though he had personally known 'his loued (the learned) Humphrey Floyd';[2] he appears to have read 'De Mona' and realized that he had made a mistake by putting his Druids on Man. Thereafter he kept more closely to historical fact.

By more frequently writing of the Bards than of 'the Druydes imbrew'd with Gore',[3] Drayton seems to have shared, if only by chance, the general preference of the Welsh for their Bards. From his 'friends the Camberbritans' (to quote from the proper title of his 'Ballad of Agincourt')[4] he had a first-hand knowledge of Welsh music, and he heard for himself the Welsh poetry which enabled him to speak with conviction of the 'true Poëtick rage' and 'genuin vaine' of the Bard.[5] It is very likely that he discussed the Druids with them: though for the most part his allusions to the Druids in *Poly-Olbion*, 1612, his topographical poem on British rivers, are based on the classics, his lines on the River Parret in Somerset mention a curious prophecy which quite possibly he might have heard about from a Welsh antiquary. They run:

For, from the *Druides* time, there was a prophecie
That there should come a day (which now was near at hand
By all fore running signes) that on the Easterne Strand
If *Parret* stood not fast vpon the English side,
They all should be supprest.[6]

[1] T. M. Chotzen, 'Some sidelights on Cambro-Dutch relations', *Transactions of Cymmrodorion*, 1938, pp. 129 ff.
[2] *Poly-Olbion*, sig. A v.
[3] *Poemes*, 1606, sig. B.   [4] ibid., sig. C 5 v.
[5] *Poly-Olbion*, p. 93   [6] op. cit., p. 47. (Song III).

Giraldus Cambrensis in his *Itinerary through Wales* says of the River Dee:

The inhabitants of these parts assert that the waters of this river change their fords every month, and, as it inclines more towards England or Wales, they can, with certainty, prognosticate which nation will be successful or unfortunate during the year.[1]

Drayton tells this story of the Dee—which he therefore calls 'ominous'—in his XIth Song, but why he repeats it of the Parret—which also changes its course—is not all clear. What is remarkable about this prophecy dating back to the Druids is that it is set, not in the time of the Romans, but in the period of the struggles between the Welsh and English—a theme that runs through much of *Poly-Olbion*. This is far too late to be properly called 'the *Druides* time', but in the then unpublished tenth century Welsh poem 'Armes Prydein' in the *Book of Taliesin* there is a mention of 'derwyddon' (which W. F. Skene translates as Druids,[2] though the meaning is more correctly 'vaticinators') who prophesy of a forthcoming battle with the English on the banks of a River 'Perydon'. According to the eighteenth century Welsh scholar Lewis Morris a former name for the Dee was 'Peryddon', a word which was also spelled 'Periton';[3] perhaps both Dee and Parret once had a similar name. Precisely what Drayton was told is obscure—and 'Armes Prydein' was likely to have had in his day a very limited circulation— but from this background of early Welsh poetry, history and river lore it would appear that he based his 'prophecie' on the remarks of a Welsh antiquary who somehow linked the *Itinerary*, 'Armes Prydein', and the Parret through the word 'Peryddon'.

Drayton's verses on the Druids are not very striking,

[1] op. cit., tr. R. Colt Hoare, 1808, p. 131.
[2] *Four Ancient Books of Wales*, Edinburgh, 1868, vol. i, p. 438. (His translations are unreliable.)
[3] 'Celtic Remains', *Archaeologia Cambrensis*, [1877], n.p., n.d., pp. 148, 355.

yet one faint reminiscence of his Druids survives in later poetry. He would add small touches of his own to what he had read about them, and when he placed his Druids in 'darksome' groves, so unforced is this adjective that it reads as though one of their historians had used the word. A consequence of this almost imperceptible improvement on his original is that in minor poetry of the eighteenth century—when a new edition of his works was published —his Druids are sometimes seen indistinctly, in deep shadow, and Wordsworth in particular very noticeably associates the Druids with darkness. The militantly patriotic Druids of later poetry also seem to have risen out of Drayton's interpretation of their place in British history. If his lines on the Druids stay at an unexciting level, he sustains interest in them by the quiet exercise of his powers of imagination, of a skill which might pass notice if he had no imitators.

Poly-Olbion is a poet's version of *Britannia*, and its alexandrines mingle topography, history and legend as Drayton follows the rivers of Britain along their courses. Unlike Camden, he made much of Geoffrey's *Historia*, and he united the appropriately winding directions of his poem in the theme of Trojan Brutus, whose issue had at last regained their rightful heritage and were ruling once more. The poem was entertainingly 'illustrated' by John Selden, who as an annotator had a difficult task. A cautious historian who had read widely in his search for firmly established legal precedents, Selden was critical of his authorities, and in particular he disbelieved in the authenticity of by far the greater part of the *Historia*. Drayton's frequent references to the Trojan ancestry of the Britons put Selden at some disadvantage; nevertheless, he good-naturedly humoured the poet and in his commentary faithfully echoed him, though at the same time he made it clear that he did so only as 'an Advocat for the Muse'.[1]

[1] *The Works of Michael Drayton*, vol. iv, *Poly-Olbion*, ed. J. W. Hebel, Oxford, 1933, p. viii.*

When Drayton, then, comparing the Britons with the Romans, affirmed that learning had been 'long with us, ere 'twas with them in use',[1] (since the Bards, as he points out, were of Trojan origin and *ipso facto* older than the Romans), Selden must have felt that the other was taking the implications of the *Historia* to extreme lengths. But he was never at a loss as an advocate, and he loyally supported Drayton by observing that 'the *Druids*, being in profession very proportionat in many things to *Cabalistique* and *Pythagorean* doctrine, may well be suppos'd much ancienter then any that had note of learning among the *Romans*'.[2]

Here he advances a suggestion as though he were unwilling to let a case go by default. But his imagination was not only stimulated by Drayton's brave flights of fancy: in explaining to the poet's readers exactly who the Druids were, Selden gives his own theories plenty of latitude. Digressing at some length on the religion of the Druids, he says that though the vulgar Gauls were polytheists, he thought that the Druids themselves were monotheists, for, taking his cue from Pliny's description of the mistletoe as a panacea, Selden claims that their invocation was to 'one *All-healing* or *All-saving* Power'. This deity, he argues, was Apollo, who was also called Medicus, the god whom the Druids worshipped under the name of Belin, and he adds that Apollo's memory was still preserved in Britain in an inscription in Cumberland. Nor was it surprising, he goes on to say, that such a monument should be found so far to the North, 'seeing that . . . *Abaris* (about the beginning of the *Olympiads*) an *Hyperborean* is recorded for *Apollo*'s Priest among the utmost *Scythians*, being farther from *Hellenisme* then our *British*'.[3] As it will be seen, this particular argument was not adopted by the learned—Selden starts few hares[4]—

---

[1] *The Works of Michael Drayton*, vol. iv, p. 207.   [2] ibid., p. 214.
[3] ibid., pp. 193–5.
[4] Eighteenth century pictures of the Druid, 'cloakt and hooded', with

for the Druids were later to be thought of as monotheists for quite different reasons, but his obvious approval of these early scholars and theologians must have been remarked by those of his readers who noticed that they had impressed a man who was hard to please, and it is very likely that Milton's attitude to the Druids was in the first place influenced by his study of Selden's 'Illustrations'.

Selden especially enjoyed a chance to scrutinize what others had said of the Druids, a chance to compare, castigate and emend, and this habit of his gives part of the commentary a rather wayward appearance. A few of the topics he discusses come from remoter branches of studies of the Druids, for though Caesar explicitly states that the Germans 'have no Druids',[1] some Continental scholars insisted that the Germans once had Druids of their own, and Selden here recalls among other things their ingenious refutations of Caesar. (To a certain extent they were encouraged to think this: the Druids themselves remembered in their traditions a time when Celtic tribes lived beyond the Rhine.) The first of their colleges in Germany had been founded by Druius Germanorum Pontifex in *Anno Mundi* 2900; later they became the wandering scholars, and they also practised their magic arts on Venusberg.[2] Or they lived in the Hercynian forest, where 'sub quercubus de natura rerum, & Deorum' they philosophized.[3] The Druidesses of ancient Germany were still remembered in the Christian name 'Gerdrudis'.[4] As Selden's 'Illustrations' show, on the Continent interest had for many years past been sustained in these noteworthy men, and in calling them

a bag, book, staff and a long beard are probably derived from Selden's descriptions of statues seen by Conrad Celtes: op. cit., p. 197, and see below, p. 101.

[1] VI, 21.
[2] H. Pantaleon, *Prosopographiae Heroum atque Illustrium Vivorum totius Germaniae*, Basle, 1565, pp. 40 ff.
[3] J. Aventinus, *Annalium Boiorum*, [1517], Leipzig, 1710, p. 96.
[4] W. Lazius, *De gentium aliquot migrationibus*, Frankfort, 1600, p. 130.

'famous', John Milton was echoing a phrase used over a hundred years earlier in an edition of Caesar published in Venice.[1]

Milton first speaks of the Druids in 'Lycidas', but here he places a small crux before the reader. In his manuscript the lines run:

> where were yee nymphs when ye remorselesse deepe
> clos'd ore the head of yor *youn* [*del.*] lov'd Lycidas
> For neither were yee playing on the steepe
> where yor old bards the famous Drüids lie
> nor on the shaggie top of Mona high.[2]

As an occasional poem, 'Lycidas' contains specific allusions to the circumstances in which Edward King was drowned. Its references to the calm air and the level brine recall details of the disaster, for when the ship in which King was sailing went down the sea was perfectly still. Milton at this point describes the coast in the general vicinity of the wreck: King was sailing from Chester to Dublin, and this sea-route skirts the northern side of Anglesey.

The outstanding features of this coast are mentioned as though they invite instant recognition: a steep which holds a burial-ground of Druids, and the wooded and mountainous island of Mona. But the nymphs could not possibly have played here. To anyone who knows North Wales, the steep at once suggests Penmaenmawr, but there was in Milton's day no printed or local tradition about a graveyard which connects the Druids with this great cliff;[3] and as for the second place which Milton speaks of, Anglesey was very lightly wooded in his time,

---

[1] *Caij Julii Caesaris: Inuictissimi imperatoris commentaria*, (ed. Lucas Panaetius), Venice, 1511, f. 29 v.

[2] *Facsimile of the Manuscripts of Milton's Minor Poems*, ed. W. A. Wright, Cambridge, 1899, pl. 29.

[3] A stone circle in the parish of Dwygyfylchi in Penmaenmawr is now called 'The Druids' circle': Royal Commission's *Inventory: Caernarvonshire*, vol. i, 1956, pp. 89, 90, Plate I. It is described in *Britannia*, 1695, cols. 673–4; no Druids are mentioned here.

and it is not mountainous. It was not Milton's intention to describe an imaginary coastline, and since he had never visited North Wales he probably based his lines on an imperfectly remembered topographical description of the district. In Camden's *Britannia* there is a short passage which brings these details from 'Lycidas' back to mind; as it is translated by Philemon Holland it runs:

this Iland, which towards the East mounteth aloft with a high promontory . . . harboured in old time so many holy men, that . . . ancient histories record that there were twenty thousand Saints buried heere. Next unto this lieth MONA.[1]

A steep, a burial ground of holy men of great antiquity, and the introductory mention of a Mona which, as Milton would have remembered from Tacitus, was once 'shaggie': the coincidence is close. Here, however, Camden describes Bardsey, which is fifty miles south of the Chester-Dublin route. Nevertheless, a glance at Camden's text explains why Milton may well have thought that Bardsey was in the immediate vicinity of Mona, and therefore quite near the scene of the wreck. Camden's remarks form part of a description not of North Wales, but of the islands of Britain, and he obviously intends to say 'After Bardsey, the next island to be met with is Mona'. But he does not make this perfectly clear, for on finishing with Bardsey he at once goes on to say 'Proxima hinc MONA'. Even Holland was misled by this sentence, and he translated it as 'Next unto this lieth MONA'. To a reader who knows nothing about North Wales and who is here following Camden alone, Camden's meaning may very easily be taken for 'Adjacent to Bardsey is Mona'.[2]

[1] *Britain*, 1610, p. 203.

[2] Mr. G. W. Whiting (in *Milton's Literary Milieu*, Chapel Hill, 1938, pp. 103–5) suggests that this passage is also based on Milton's study of Ortelius; if so, Milton must have overlooked Leland's remark, quoted in *Theatrum*, 1595, f. 13, that Mona was no longer heavily wooded. A cogent explanation of Mona 'high' will be given in the first volume, edited by A. S. P. Woodhouse, of the forthcoming Columbia Variorum Commentary on Milton's Poems.

Milton's mention of the Druids in 'Lycidas' was probably suggested by the proximity of the shipwreck to Mona
of the Druids, and in these lines—though perhaps the
symmetry is fortuitous—he links the poet, the Fellow of
Christ's College, and the promising divine with Britain's
earliest poets, learned men, and priests: some such parallel
may have been in his mind, for in the original manuscript
a deletion shows that he had at first intended to write
'young Lycidas' as an antithesis to 'yoʳ old bards'. But
when he next alluded to the Druids, no obvious literary
associations prompted the reference. He opens *Mansus*,
the best of his Latin poems and the first poem to be written after 'Lycidas', with respectful compliments to his
host in Italy, the Marquis of Villa; then, changing the
mood of the poem, he lightheartedly speaks of three
famous Hyperborean maidens, whose tombs at Delos had
been the object of pilgrimages in classical antiquity, as
though they had been British girls, and Britain becomes
by inference the land of the Hyperboreans. He adds:

We even worship Phoebus and . . . we have sent him gifts,
yellowing ears, rosy apples in baskets, crocuses breathing fragrance,
and troops of maidens chosen from the Druid race. The Druids,
an ancient people skilled in the rites of the gods, used to sing the
praise of heroes and their emulative deeds.[1]

Milton here pictures his Druids as the priests of the
most highly venerated people of classical antiquity. Free
from toil, war, and sickness, the Hyperboreans lived in an
anachronistic Golden Age of their own. They dwelt in
the most distant of lands, and it was with their remoteness
in mind that Milton asked his friend Charles Diodati in a
letter dated 1637 how long he intended to stay among the
Hyperboreans of far-off Cheshire.[2] In framing his compliments for *Mansus*, Milton, with a kind of mock-Chinese

[1] *The Latin Poems of John Milton*, tr. W. MacKellar, New Haven,
1930, p. 155.
[2] D. Masson, *Life of John Milton*, 1875, vol. i, p. 507.

politeness, speaks deprecatingly of his 'foreign Muse, but sparely nourished under the frozen Bear'.[1] Distance and the Bear are already in his mind, and by the amusing device of calling Britain the land of the Hyperboreans, he places England and Italy on the same level: the ancient Briton then addresses the classical Roman as an equal.

'Ypre,' writes Ludovicus Guiccardini, 'selon aucuns print tel nom d'vn Capitaine de l'ancienne Bretaigne, auiord'huy appellée Angleterre, nommé Hipperbore.'[2] Claudian mentions the Hyperborean seas off Scotland.[3] But it is quite possible that the idea was suggested to Milton by a fragment of Hecataeus of Abderos preserved by Diodorus Siculus. Hecataeus places the home of the Hyperboreans on an island 'off the Celtic' coast which Apollo used to visit, an island where there was a large circular temple which was decked with votive offerings. Its keepers were the Boreads, the descendants of Boreas; and here there is a link between Hecataeus and *Mansus*, for Boreas was the father of Loxo, Upis, and Hecaerge, Milton's British Hyperborean maidens.[4]

In his poetry Milton shows a partiality for the Druids that he might not have cared to defend seriously; but when he next alluded to the Druids, this was in support of some impassioned special pleading on matters of public interest. In 1643 he published *The Doctrine and Discipline of Divorce*, but he felt that his closely reasoned arguments for new legislation which would permit divorce needed reinforcing, and in the following year he published a second edition with a 'revis'd and much augmented' address to Parliament. It was obviously added to the original text only after careful thought, and Milton evidently meant what he said. Aware that he is urging

---

[1] tr. MacKellar, op. cit., p. 155.
[2] *Description de tout les Pays-Bas*, Antwerp, 1586, p. 302.
[3] *Third Consulship of Honorius*, I, 56.
[4] *Histories*, II, 47; see also P. Wesseling's edition, Amsterdam, 1745, vol. i, p. 158, and Rolls Series, vol. 26a, p. cxvi.

Parliament to pass radically new laws, he reminds its
members that Britain in the past had not been afraid of
innovation, that any enterprise they showed would thus
be based on precedent:

It would not be the first, or second time, since our ancient *Druides*,
by whom this Island was the Cathedrall of Philosophy to *France*,
left off their pagan rites, that England hath had this honour
vouchsaft from Heav'n, to give out reformation to the World.[1]

He concludes with the exhortation: 'Let not England,
forget her precedence of teaching nations how to live.'

'Cathedrall of philosophy . . . precedence of teaching
nations': more remarkable things were yet to be said of
the Druids, but not by a man of Milton's stature. He
seems to have borrowed the idea as a debating point from
Selden, who in his notes to *Poly-Olbion* remarks: 'Thus
hath our Isle beene as Mistris to Gaule twice. First in the
Druidian doctrine, next in the institution of their own
famous University of Paris.'[2] The grandiloquence of the
phrasing, however, is Milton's own, and so strong then
was his attachment to the Druids that he failed to see the
incongruity which Selden's milder language avoids.

Areopagitica appeared in the same year, and praising the
'quick, ingenious and piercing spirit' of his nation, 'acute
to invent, suttle and sinewy to discours, not beneath the
highest that human capacity can soar to', Milton adds:

Therefore the studies of learning in her deepest Sciences have bin
so ancient, and so eminent among us, that Writers of good
antiquity, and ablest judgement have bin perswaded that ev'n the
school of *Pythagoras*, and the *Persian* wisdom took beginning
from the old Philosophy of this Iland.[3]

Diodorus Siculus states that the Druids followed Pythagorean doctrine, Ammianus Marcellinus that they were
'members of the intimate fellowship of the Pythagorean

[1] op. cit., sig. A 4.   [2] op. cit., p. 96.   [3] op. cit., p. 30.

faith', Hippolytus notes that 'the Druids applied themselves very thoroughly to the Pythagorean philosophy',
and Valerius Maximus, describing the Gauls, says that
'what these trousered barbarians believe is the very faith
of Greek Pythagoras himself'. St. Clement of Alexandria
passes on the story that Pythagoras had been 'a hearer of
the Galatae';[1] Diogenes Laertius speaks of his being
initiated into the mysteries of foreign countries,[2] and
Iamblichus in his *Life of Pythagoras* states that Pythagoras was acquainted with the Celtic mysteries.[3] Milton,
however, quite lacks any authority for his remarks on the
Persian wisdom. Diogenes Laertius and Dio Chrysostom
mention the Druids as though they were the peers of the
Magi, and St. Clement of Alexandria states that both the
Druids and the Magi studied philosophy before the
Greeks, but no 'writer of good antiquity' even hints that
the Persians were the pupils of the Druids. Pliny, on the
other hand, says that it almost seems as though Persia
had learned her magic from Britain, and Milton must have
had this remark in mind; like his reading of Camden on
Bardsey, this appears to be yet another example of Milton's imperfect reading or faulty recollection of a text.

His mention of Pythagoras in this context is significant.
As a young man, Milton had thought of Pythagoras as the
philosopher who had arrived at the truth, the master of
the harmony of mathematics who could hear the harmony
of the spheres. If men's souls could become like that of
Pythagoras, the world around them would spontaneously
return to its primordial state.[4] To the younger Milton,
Pythagoras was the pattern of regenerate man, and even
if in 1644 he no longer saw him in quite this visionary
light, some afterglow still remained to shine over the
Druids as well. Three years later he finished his *History*

---

[1] *Misc.*, I, xv, 70, 1.
[2] *Lives*, viii, 2.   [3] op. cit., ch. 28.
[4] 'Prolusiones quaedam Oratoriae', *Works*, ed. F. A. Patterson, New
York, 1930–40, vol. xii, p. 157; see also his 'Sixth Latin Elegy'.

of Britain, and presumably he had studied his material for the early history of the island with Pythagoras and the Druids still in mind.[1] He thought that the Britons' abstention from eating certain fish, for example, followed Pythagorean precept, and he took it for granted that the ethics of the ancient Britons were founded on the teachings of the Druids. But the classical historians had a tendency to dwell on the shortcomings of the barbarians who came under their inspection: they saw little to admire in the ancient Britons, and Milton repeats their remarks with additional asperity. He calls them 'Progenitors not to be glori'd in', and he thoroughly approved of the Roman invasion: it 'beate us into some civilitie'. The responsibility for the deplorable moral condition of the ancient Britons was put by Milton squarely on the Druids.

With scorn he calls them 'a sort of Priests or Magicians'. He concedes that they might have studied Pythagoras, 'yet philosophers I cannot call them, men reported factious and ambitious'. His comments were harsh, and he saddled the Druids with faults that even Pliny had not found in them. Paraphrasing Tacitus on the massacre on Mona, he calls the Druids 'a barbarous and lunatic rout'.[2] The language of the translation is more savage than that of the original text, and this vehemence perhaps owes its sharpness to disappointment. Milton had associated the Druids with matters about which he felt deeply: the poets and philosophers who had given such a lustre to early Britain, the men who had given England her precedence in teaching nations how to live, the glorious Hyperboreans, the tutors of Persia and of great Pythagoras—they could not stand up to his more critical examination. Their 'Cathedrall of Philosophy' came crashing down. Milton never again spoke of them. For the author of the phrase 'the famous Druids', the Druids had become infamous.

[1] *The History of Great Britain* was not published until 1670.
[2] op. cit., pp. 2, 62, 49.

III

THE HEIRS OF THE PATRIARCHS

IN his history of the University of Oxford, which was published in 1674, Anthony Wood glances with pride at the liberal arts of the Druids.[1] There is a touch of the quaintly old-fashioned in the relish with which he sets out their imposing curriculum, for by this time the Druids were no longer being admired only for their learning. Already in 1621 William Slatyer had indicated the direction which studies of the Druids were to take, for when he says that the Druids

> taught diuine *Philosophie*,
> What *Vertue* meant, what *Pietie*[2]

he gives his paraphrase of Caesar perceptible Christian nuances.

Leland initiated the process by means of which the Druids became, as Wordsworth calls them, 'auxiliars of the Cross'.[3] Geoffrey of Monmouth, on whom Leland depended for much of his knowledge of the history of early Britain, states that Pope Eleutherius sent missionaries to King Lucius in the second century. Lucius then converted the country's twenty-eight temples into churches, and three Archbishops took the place of the former Archiflamines.[4]

Geoffrey did not say that his pagan priests were Druids. Though the Archiflamines of *Historia Regum Britanniae*

---

[1] *Historia et Antiquitates Universitatis Oxoniensis*, Oxford, 1674, p. 2.
[2] *Palae-Albion*, 1621, p. 17.
[3] *Commentarii*, Oxford, 1709, pp. 4, 7, 21; *Ecclesiastical Sonnets*, x.
[4] *Historia Regum Britanniae*, IV, xix, which is partly based on Bede, *Historia Ecclesiastica*, Bk. I, I.

may call the Druids to mind, Geoffrey was certainly not thinking of Caesar when he used these titles for his pagan dignitaries: the word is an invention of the ninth century, and the context in which it is first used is strikingly similar to Geoffrey's own story of Lucius.[1] There is nothing to suggest the Druids here. But it is entirely likely that Leland thought that Geoffrey's pagan priests were Druids simply because he could not see who else they might have been. For the same reason, Bale, William Lambard,[2] Archbishop Matthew Parker,[3] and John Pits[4] accepted and helped to popularize Leland's version of what had happened when Britain was converted, and the prevailing view was that the Druids had not greatly objected to the change. Bishop Francis Godwin, however, disapproved of anything that might lead to the notion that Druidism and Christianity had anything in common, and he declares:

these seedes of the Gospell had proued but badly (we may suppose) had not God as it were made way for their growth, by pulling up the weedes of that so long continued superstition of the Druides.

He thus saw the hand of Providence in the Roman persecution of the Druids, and in Godwin's opinion, when the Papal envoy came to Lucius, there was no smooth transition but a final break with the past: the missionary 'reformed the error of the King . . . by refining in him the olde British Philosophy & taking away the dregs of the Druids'.[5]

But the consensus of opinion was with Leland, and it only remained for others to add further details to his story in order to make it more plausible. Stow says that the second Archbishop of London built a library in Corn-

---

[1] Migne, *P.L.*, vol. 130, p. 30 b.
[2] *An Alphabetical Description of England and Wales* (1570), 1730, p. 205.
[3] *De Antiquitate Britannicae Ecclesiae*, 1605, p. 4.
[4] *Relationum Historicum*, Paris, 1619, pp. 14 ff.
[5] *A Catalogue of the Bishops of England*, 1615, pp. 19, 33.

hill and 'conuerted many of the Druides, learned men in the Pagan Law, to Christianity'.[1] John Speed points out that Claudius had persecuted both the Christians and the Druids: he infers that Claudius thought that Druidism savoured 'too much of *Christianitie*' for his taste, and since both religions were evidently alike, Speed claimed that the teaching itself of the Druids greatly facilitated the conversion of Britain.[2]

John Selden, always alert to these undercurrents of contemporary thought, acknowledges that formerly,

the natural wisdom of the Druides (who were Masters of the Consciences of the *Britons* . . . in a Devotion beyond the reach of other Nations . . .) stood in the way and rendered the people more uncapable of any new Light.[3]

But the Druids soon changed their minds, and at the time of the Christian missions they became the 'leaders of the blind people in a better way, and unto a better hope'. Richard Broughton, the Catholic historian, in spite of his many strictures on the Druids also thought that the Druids had supported the missionaries. The Druids, he says, being soothsayers, were able to anticipate and reflect upon the Nativity, and they had been alarmed by portents at the time of the Crucifixion; being learned men, and therefore keeping in constant touch with Rome, they soon understood what had happened. Further, being natural philosophers, they understood from the phenomenal disturbances at that time that the devils had been overcome. Though at first the Druids hindered the conversion of the Britons, when their chief Doctors had become 'perplexed' and their religion 'conuicted to be abominable Idolatrie, and Superstition, the Professors of it generally embraced the faith of Christ, detesting their former Infidelities'. The conversion of Cambridge, he says, a

[1] *A Survay of London*, 1603, p. 195.
[2] *The History of Great Britaine*, 1611, p. 204.
[3] N. Bacon, *An Historical and Political Discourse*, 1689, p. 3.

centre of Druid learning, materially contributed to the conversion of the entire country.[1]

In 1645 John Colgan published his *Acta Sanctorum Veteris et Maioris Scotiae* at Louvain. In this account of the lives of the early Irish saints, there is occasional mention of the ineffectual resistance of the Druids to the work of the Celtic missionaries. It was curiously neglected, and it would seem that so firm was the hold of the classics on the thought of this age that its historians and antiquaries would accept the Druids only as the Greeks and Romans had seen them.

The rapidity of their conversion, then, earned for the Druids the indulgence of most of the seventeenth-century divines who mentioned them, and an Archbishop of St. Andrews who did not mince his words about heathenish superstition also admitted that the Druids were 'men of moral conversation' and that they 'ruled their affairs very politickly'.[2] A rhetorical line in Origen's commentary on Ezekiel, repeated in edition after edition of *Britannia*, which as a standard work of reference long continued to sustain interest in the Druids, further enhanced their reputation. Camden refers to 'Origen's account of the Britains embracing the faith, and finding their way to God by the Druids who always inculcated the divine unity'.[3] This was an impressive testimonial, but Camden had understandably missed the point of a passage which yields a clearer meaning in a loose paraphrase than in a literal translation, and Bishop Stillingfleet rightly wondered

what should make two such learned Antiquaries as Mr. *Camden* and bishop *Godwin*, so far to mistake the sense of *Origen* to understand him as if he had said, *That* Britain, *by the help of the* Druids,

---

[1] *The Ecclesiastical Historie of Great Britain*, Douai, 1633, pp. 17, 240, 207.

[2] J. Spotswood, *History of the Church of Scotland*, 1655, p. 3.

[3] *Britannia*, tr. R. Gough, 1789, vol. i, p. l.

always consented in the belief of one God, whereas it is very plain,
That *Origen* speaks of it as a great alteration that was made in the
Religion of the *Britains* after the coming of *Christ*.[1]

This passage from Origen was known to Thomas
Fuller as well, and in his *Church History*, 1655, he charged
the Druids with polytheism. But he was out of touch with
opinion. Dr. Peter Heylyn, who discovered well over two
hundred debatable points in Fuller's book, attacked him
at length, and in defending the Druids, Heylyn taught
him that their alleged polytheism was a subject which
should be approached with caution. High feelings lent
sharpness to an otherwise leisurely clash: the two royal
chaplains—who were later reconciled and became good
friends—were well matched. Heylyn doggedly worried
Fuller's arguments, while Fuller, that 'flashly jeering
Author'[2] as another enemy calls him, replied with rather
more vivacity.

'And secondly our Author tells of the *Druides*', Heylyn
says,

that they were *Philosophers*, *Divines*, and *Lawyers*, to the rest of
the *Brittains*; and if Philosophers, they might by their long study
in the book of Nature, and their Industrious inquiry into naturall
Causes, attaine to the knowledge of the one and onely Super-
naturall Cause, (as others of the *Heathen Philosophers* in their
severall Countries,) from which the works of Nature had their
first Originall . . . For though they did admit a multitude of
Inferiour Gods, *Topical* in respect of Countries, and *Tutelar* in
respect of particular Persons; yet in the middle of that darknesse
they discerned one Supreme God over all the rest. . . .

Nor did those old Philosophers keep the great truth unto themselves . . . but plac'd it like a great Light on the top of a Mountain, that all the people might discern it; who thereupon lifting
their hands unto the Heavens, did frequently make their addresses
but to one God onely, saying in common SPEECH unto one

[1] E. Stillingfleet, *Originae Britannicae*, 1685, p. 57.
[2] Cornelius Burgess, *No Sin to Purchase the Lands of Bishops*, 1659,
p. 134.

another, that *God was great*, and *God was true*, and, *If God permit*.
Of which, my Author (the same Christian Advocate) seems to
make a question: *Vulgi iste naturalis sermo est, an Christiani
consitentis oratio?* that is to say, Whether these expressions savoured
not rather of the *Christian*, than the vulgar *Heathen*. And hereupon
I may conclude, in the behalf of the Druides, (or rather of those
learned Pens who affirm it of them) that being *Philosophers* in
Study, and *Divines* by *Office*, and very eminent in their times in
both capacities, they might as well instruct the People in the
knowledge of one onely God, as any other of the *Heathen Sages*,
either *Greeks* or *Romans*.

Fuller answers:

In this long *Harangue*, I know not what the *Animadvertor aimes
at*; this I know, he *hits not* me, nor alledgeth any thing in opposition to what I have written. If he desireth only to prove, that the
refined Heathens worshipped one God above all the rest, he shall
not onely have my free consent, but the adjection of this my
Symbole thereunto.

He then states that monotheism is quite incompatible
with the recognition of other gods, even if they are solely
regarded as God's 'Attributes under other Titles; *wisdom*,
of *Apollo*; *Omni-presence*, *Swiftness*, of *Mercury*'. With
a touch of triumph he produces an analogy which, he
thinks, will silence the Animadvertor:

Now for quietnesse sake, let the result of this long discourse (so
far as I can understand) be granted him, and it amounts to no
more, then to put the *Brittains* in the same form with the *Grecians*;
instructed by their *Druids* in the worship of one God, as well and
as far as the *Grecians* were in the same Lesson by their *Philosophers*.
Now what the *Grecians* held and did in this point, will appear by
the practise of the *Athenians*, whose City was the *Mistris* of
Greece, *Staple of Learning*, and *Palace* of *Philosophers*; and how
well the *Athenians* worshipped one God, we have from the infallible witness of St. *Paul, whose Spirit was stirred within him,
whilst he saw the City wholly given to idolatry*. Whence it will follow,
that the *Brittaines, form-fellowes* with the *Grecians*, were wholly
given to Idolatry: which is as much, and more then I said before.

And now the Reader may judge, what progress the *Animadvertor* hath made in confuting what I have written; yea, less then the Beast *Pigritia* in *Brasil*, which, as he telleth us elsewhere, goes not so far in *fourteen* daies, as one may throw a stone. Yea, our *Adversary* hath not gone at all, (save backward) and if he doth not mend his pace, it will be late before he commeth to his lodging.[1]

The controversy ends with Heylyn patiently repeating 'that though the *Brittains* had many *Topical* and *Tutelar* Gods', nevertheless, 'the *Druides* instructed them in the knowledge of one supream deity'; and where Fuller had compared them to the Athenians, Heylyn thought a more apt parallel was provided by 'the present *Papists*', who were certainly monotheists 'notwithstanding their superstitious worshipping of so many National, Typical, and Tutelar Saints'.[2] It is apparent from this argument that the Druids attracted much goodwill, and Heylyn's parallel was at least in keeping with current sentiment. Just at the time when Anthony Wood was speaking of the encyclopaedic learning of the Druids, yet another royal chaplain was arguing that the 'sublime and unparallel'd Metaphysicks' of the Druids 'touching God, and Soul, and Holy Discipline' proved that they were quite capable of appreciating and responding to the merits of Christianity.[3] Acclaim had thus produced a Druid who was as near to being a Christian as makes no difference; he was then to be linked even more closely to the Bible when the origins of Druidism were discovered in Genesis.

The theory that the Druids had learned their wisdom from the mouths of the Patriarchs was not entirely fanciful. It was partly inspired by the Renaissance historian's attitude to history itself; if John More does in fact speak for him, he thought that

THE WAY to knowe what times of the worlde the thinges that be

---

[1] T. Fuller, *The Appeal of Injured Innocence*, 1655, pp. 54–55.

[2] P. Heylyn, *Certamen Epistolare*, 1659, p. 343.

[3] Thomas Jones, *The Heart and its Right Sovereign*, 1678, pp. 542–3.

mentioned in prophane Histories were done, is this: namely, we must first bring them to that account which is set downe in Scriptures, from the beginning of the Worlde till the suffering of Christ, most exactly, and so labour to make the times of forreine histories to agree with that account of the holy Scripture unto the account of prophane writers.[1]

His deference to Biblical chronology led the Renaissance historian to believe that world history spanned only a few thousand years, and at one time it was not unusual for events to be dated *Anno Mundi*. In consequence, he had no idea of prehistory in the sense in which it is now understood, for recorded history started with the words 'In the beginning'. As for British history, this was divided into pre-Roman, Roman, Saxon, Norman, and modern periods, and speaking very broadly—for not everyone believed in the authenticity of Geoffrey's narrative—the period covered by the *Historia* accounted for most of the island's pre-Roman past. Since, according to Geoffrey, Brutus and his band had come from Troy—and Ammianus Marcellinus records a theory current in his day that the Gauls were of Trojan descent—the history of the Britons could be traced back to a time when their national identity had not yet emerged.

William Warner, just at the time when Camden shows that he was himself sceptical of the truth of Geoffrey's story, follows the national pedigree, by way of the mythical ancestors of the Trojans, back to Noah:

> and thus the *Brutons* bring
> Their pedigree from *Iupiter*, of Pagane Gods the King:
> And adde they may, that *Brute* his Syer of *Venus* sonne did
> springe.
> Thrise five degrees from *Noe* was *Brute*, and fower times six was he
> From *Adam*: and from *Iaphets* house doth fetch his pedigree.[2]

[1] *A Table from the Beginning of the World to this Day*, 1593, sig. A 6 v. xv, 8, 4. See also Robin Flower, *The Irish Tradition*, Oxford, 1947, pp. 4–5.
[2] *The First and Second Parts of Albion's England*, 1589, p. 55.

No one took these verses seriously, but they show how
Warner's thoughts and More's had at least the same
orientation, and Camden as well was interested in tracing
the Britons back to the Ark. Warner's mention of Japhet
is a reminder that the line from Adam to Noah belonged
to world history: European history started with Japhet.
The Celtic dynasts who vanished when Annius' version
of Berosus was discredited had left a large gap in the
immediately postdiluvian history of Europe, but it was
over the erasures in Annius' record that later antiquaries
lightly sketched the outlines of the growth of Western
civilization, and at the same time they brought the Druids
from the neighbourhood of Ararat to British soil.

By conflating data from the Bible and the classics,
some major stages of their journey could still be identified. Briefly: Stow and Selden thought that the mention
of the Isles of the Gentiles in Holy Writ gave this country
a providential rather than a fortuitous place in history.[1]
It was ultimately reached by the descendants of Gomer,
a grandson of Noah, for it was widely assumed, by Camden among others,[2] that the Biblical Gomer was identical
with the Gomar whom Josephus mentions: 'For Gomer
founded those whom the Greeks called Galati, but were
then called Gomerites', as a late nineteenth-century translation puts it.[3] St. Jerome in his commentary on Genesis
briefly echoes Josephus, and the eighth-century historian Nennius speaks of Gomer 'a quo Galli',[4] thus link-
ing Gomer and the Galatians with the Gauls. According to
St. Cyril of Alexandria there were Druids among the
Galatae,[5] and it was therefore inferred that there were

[1] *Annales*, 1631, p. 6; N. Bacon, op. cit., p. 2.
[2] op. cit., 1586, p. 8.
[3] *Jewish Antiquities*, VI, I; (Bohn) 1889, p. 86. R. L'Estrange's
translation, 1720, has Gomer in the text, Gomar in the Index.
[4] Migne, *P. L.*, vol. 23, col. 950; F. Lot, 'Nennius', *Bib. de l' École
des Hautes Études*, Paris, 1934, p. 162.
[5] *Opera*, Basle, 1546, vol. iii, col. 90 D.

Druids in Gomer's retinue. That there were Druids among the Gauls was well known, and since, according to Orosius, the transrhenian tribe of the Cimbri were Gauls, it could be taken for granted that the Cimbri had Druids.[1] Because the Cymry of Wales had a name which seemed to be markedly similar to that of the Cimbri, Humphrey Llwyd in 1572 thought that the ancient Britons were originally Cimbri:[2] the Druids were thus brought to Britain to end their postdiluvian wanderings.

Camden produced further evidence in order to strengthen the bonds between Britain and Genesis: he thought that there was a significant similarity between Gomer and 'Kumero', a Welshman.[3] His theories received the support of another contemporary historian when John Lewis asserted that the Welsh spoke 'Cymbraeg', a variant spelling which more closely associates Cymraeg with the Cimbri.[4] The eighteenth-century historian Thomas Carte thought that Homer had placed the 'Cimmeri' in the British Isles,[5] and James Macpherson also supports the Elizabethan antiquary's views on the Cimbri by stating that it was the Druids' attitude to death that had inspired the remark of Valerius Maximus: 'Cimbri in acie gaudio exultabant.'[6] Aylett Sammes not only accepts the general assumptions that enabled this route to Britain to be traced, but he also provides in *Britannia Antiqua Illustrata*, 1676, a map showing what seems to be a well trodden section of the highway from Ararat to an embarkation point on the French coast. On the other hand, he points out that the Cimbri were Teutons; and

[1] *Seven Books of History*, v, 16.
[2] *Commentarioli Brytannicae Descriptionis Fragmentum*, Cologne, 1572, f. 42.
[3] op. cit., p. 8.
[4] *The History of Great Britain*, ed. H. Thomas, 1729, p. 44 (written c. 1611).
[5] *A General History of England*, vol. i, 1748, p. 67.
[6] *Introduction to the History of Great Britain*, Edinburgh (3rd edition), 1773, p. 243; Valerius Maximus, II, vi, 11.

III. 'The Procession of the antient CIMBRI' along part of the route from Ararat to Britain: see pp. 67–69.

therefore, he insists, the English were the original inhabitants of Britain.[1]

With the publication of David Jones's translation of the Abbé Pezron's *Antiquities of Nations* in 1706, Gomer was firmly established in the public mind as the ancestor of the Celts. Pezron argued that Gomer himself had never left Asia, and that the settlement of the West was accomplished by very easy stages. The groups who detached themselves from the parent stock produced what were later kindred peoples, and therefore, with cognate languages: 'a separation of Parthians took place from the Gomarians, which accounts for the large number of *Celtick* or *Gaulick* Words in the *Persian* Language'. Having made themselves masters of lesser Asia and Greece, the Gomarians '*affected the Name of* Titans'; those who went to upper Asia and beyond the Danube became Cimbri and Cimmerians. On settling '*in the Provinces of* Europe', the Gomarians were known as Celtae, and on peopling the country between the Alps and the Pyrenees, as Gauls. In classical mythology, the Titans are the children of Heaven and Earth, and as such they were of particular interest to Pezron, who was more concerned with investigating the origins of peoples than their subsequent history. He studied the legends of Greece and Rome as though they were fanciful versions of events that had actually happened, and in the matter-of-fact manner of the euhemerist he declared that '*those of the* Titans *who were called* Uranus, Saturn *and* Jupiter, *were not Gods, as the* Greeks *and* Romans *vainly believed, but Potent Princes and Mortal Men.*'[2] Classical mythology, then, was a by-product of the history of the ancestors of the French before Gaul was discovered and settled. Pezron's thoughts on the Titans encouraged those who during the eighteenth century tentatively explored familiar

---

[1] *Britannia Antiqua Illustrata*, 1676, pp. 12 ff.

[2] op. cit., pp. 11 ff.; p. 26; pp. iv–vi.

fables for the secrets of the Druids; the comparative etymologist scanned on his map the areas over which the descendants of Gomer had deployed themselves, and if John Cleland stopped far short of Ararat, the lexicographer Rowland Jones left his guide far behind when in the course of his researches he believed that he had found the palaeographical symbol of the point at which the universe had burst into being.

Yet another kind of connexion between the Druids and the Patriarchs was discovered after Samuel Bochart published *Geographia Sacra* in 1646. He wished to show that Phoenician was the parent of the European languages, and he claimed that the Celts still preserved the original Phoenician roots in their language, and though he paid little attention to the Druids in his sacred geography, his theories lent some support to the arguments of those who contended that Druidism had originated in the Middle East. His chief English disciple was Theophilus Gale, who demonstrates in *The Court of the Gentiles* that classical literature was only an adulterated version of the teaching of the Old Testament. The Druids, according to Gale, had also absorbed their wisdom from the same source, and he points to the precise time and place at which Druidism had started. He took this information from a book which is remarkable both for its contents and the circumstances in which it was published.

The first book on the Druids to be published in England appeared in 1664, but in 1655 a short study of Druidism was published as an appendix to Edmund Dickinson's *Delphi Phoenicizantes*. Anthony Wood, however, says that 'a harmless innocent, careless and shiftless person' called Henry Jacob was the book's true author. Jacob became a Probationer-Fellow of Merton College in 1629. He was 'the prodigie of his age' for philological and Oriental learning, and in 1636 he helped Selden with his Hebrew. Being 'over-busie with critical notions' which left him 'little better than craz'd', he neglected his official duties; in 1648 he lost his Fellowship.

He left a manuscript in his chambers at Merton, where it was found by Edmund Dickinson. Wood says that Dickinson then rewrote it 'with another stile', and then learned Oriental languages in order to 'blind the world'. Jacob died in 1652, leaving Dickinson free to publish the book in 1655. Jacob's ghost then appeared to a Dr. Jacob, in a state of great distress about the fate of the manuscript.[1]

This little book is full of ingenious theories, and it reminds one how compact was the world of Biblical and classical antiquity to some seventeenth-century minds, for it was a world where Seth by crossing the Hellespont might chance upon a god, and Joseph see an Argonaut. But euhemerism killed such fancies: Dickinson thought, for example, that the statue of Hercules Ogmius which Lucian had seen on his visit to Marseilles commemorated Josuah after he had slain Og the king of Bashan.[2] Dickinson's main concern was with etymologies, and he was of the opinion that the word Druid was derived from a rare Greek word for oak. The oak religion of the Druids had come '*è quercubus Mamre*', or, as Theophilus Gale translates it:

from the *Okes* of *Mamre*: under which, in times past, those holy men (in whose hands the administration of *Divine* Service and Worship was) lived most devoutly . . . Lo the *Oke Priests*! Lo the *Patriarchs* of the *Druides*! For from these sprang the *Sect* of the Druides, which reached up at least, as high as *Abraham's* time.[3]

This apparently novel approach to the subject of the Druids and the Patriarchs was in reality nearly as old as Annius of Viterbo's commentary on Berosus, but it had

---

[1] *Athenae Oxonienses*, Oxford, 1692, vol. ii, cols. 90–91.
[2] *Heracles*, I, VI.
[3] op. cit., p. 36; *The Court of the Gentiles*, Part II, Oxford, 1671, p. 82.

hitherto received only the most perfunctory attention.[1] A few Continental scholars during the past century had mentioned Abraham and the Druids, and Selden briefly remarks on the Druids and Mamre in *Analecton Anglo-Britannicon*;[2] Dickinson's rhapsody marks the point where smouldering ideas suddenly burst into flame.

It was in the pages of the orientalist Thomas Smith's *Syntagma de Druidism Moribus*, 1664, that the subject received an attention so scrupulous as to leave room for no further improvement, or improvisation. The text is impressive to look at, for the quotations are printed in the original Greek, Syriac, Hebrew, and Arabic script. The boldness of Smith's contentions are to some extent disguised by a cautious and insinuating approach. The Brahmins of India, he says, took their name from Abraham. The oak religion of the Druids also originated with Abraham. But these statements are not made in a dogmatic or challenging manner. Nothing is taken for granted, and he makes a show of taking his reader into his confidence. Were the trees at Mamre, he asks himself, pine trees or terebinth?[3] He tests the ground at every step. Reluctant and hesitating in his advance, he arrives at conclusions which read rather like admissions that have been forced from him. To his readers it may have seemed that one of the deepest and most widely read of scholars had at last become convinced of the truth of what had hitherto only been a daring conjecture.

After *Syntagma de Druidum Moribus*, the serious student of Druidism became dissatisfied with displays of insight, with the kind of remark, brief, sage, and knowing, that Selden would drop: a word to the wise no longer carried conviction. If he wished to persuade, he was forced to argue his point. He then found himself in the predica-

[1] Conrad Celtes, op. cit., sig. m viii v.
[2] Frankfort, 1615, p. 22.
[3] op. cit., pp. 14 ff.

ment of a man who has something to say, who is certain that he is right, and whose case cannot in its nature be presented objectively. Henry Rowlands, one of the first antiquaries to write at any length on the Druids, felt this limitation strongly, and a notable feature of his work is that he invented his own technique of exposition. His preoccupation with method explains much that on the face of it appears to be merely fanciful in the literature on the Druids; paradoxically, its elaborate and wayward character often springs from a simple wish to demonstrate.

In all probability, *Mona Antiqua Restaurata*, 1723,[1] was inspired by the mention in Gibson's 1695 edition of *Britannia* of a few place-names in Anglesey which apparently went back to the Druids. Rowlands became Vicar of Llanidan in 1696, and he was evidently struck by the attention which his parish had attracted in the previous year. Tre'r Druw according to the new *Britannia* was Druid's town, and on looking about him, Rowlands could see many prehistoric remains which the antiquaries of his day thought were relics of the Druids; he also discovered in his locality further names whose 'Analogy . . . speaks something of Druidism'.[2] Convinced that he had inherited the Archdruids' seat, he went on to suggest that Mona was called, in the popular saying, 'the Mother of Wales' not because its corn had supplied the country, but because its relationship to the rest of Wales was like that of Canterbury to its suffragan dioceses.[3]

[1] Dublin, 1723, the year of the author's death. The original manuscript was sent to a bookseller 'some years earlier': British Museum MS. Adds. 14883, f. 180 v. This was lost, but a part of it seems to be preserved in Bodleian MS. Carte 10553. Another edition, in which the editor took liberties with the text but corrected the spelling of Welsh names, appeared in 1766: here Tre'r Druw, for instance, is spelled Tre'r Dryw. See also Bodleian shelfmark Gough Wales 76, p. 85; and Garel Jones, *The Life and Works of Henry Rowlands*, 1935, National Library of Wales MS. Theses 1936/14, p. 215.

[2] op. cit., plate II, fig. 1.

[3] ibid., pp. 70, 83.

When he set himself the task of writing a history of Anglesey from antediluvian times, Rowlands faced a peculiar difficulty. He lacked a model. *Britannia* and the county histories could give him no help. Rowlands, however, overcame this difficulty by naming the subject of his researches 'archaeology', thus avoiding the expectations normally aroused by the more familiar word 'antiquities'. His definition of archaeology then gave him plenty of room in which to develop his theories. Archaeology, he says,

> *or an Account of the Origin of Nations after the Universal* DELUGE *. . . admits of two Ways of Enquiry*, either beginning *at* BABEL, *the Place of Mankind's Dispersion, and tracing them downwards to our own Times by the Light of Records, which is* HISTORY, *and of Natural Reason, which is* INFERENCE *and* CONJECTURE.[1]

In the event, he had to depend almost entirely on conjecture. Since the Druids of Britain had been as reticent as those of Gaul, he was deprived of the light of records; he notices with chagrin that the Irish Druids had a library in their college at Tara in 927 B.C., for in Ireland

> *their Druids having less of Power and Authority among the People, became thereby, as more tractable, so more obliging, and kinder to Posterity than the British Druids were, as will appear hereafter, who humorously bigotted in their way, by their haughty disdain of Letters and contempt of Writing, treasured all in their own Noddles.*[2]

With so little documentary evidence available, he reflects that his history of Mona is for the most part 'meerly hypotheticall', but on second thoughts he admits that he had also some help from 'a few Testimonies of sacred Scripture' and 'the Assistance of Natural and Moral Evidence'.[3]

[1] op. cit., f. 5.
[2] ibid., p. 29. Matthew Kennedy, *A Chronological Dissertation of the Royal Family of the Stuarts*, Paris 1705, pp. 20 ff., discusses the learning of the Irish Druids.
[3] Bodleian MS. Carte, 10553, f. 59 v; *Mona*, 1723, p. 201.

Mona opens at a time when Anglesey was still untroubled by history, and adapting one of Thomas Burnet's
theories on the physical configuration of the world before
the Flood, Rowlands briefly describes the stage on which
his Druids were to appear. Burnet says:

We may take it for a well established truth, and proceed upon the
supposition, *that the Ante-Diluvian Earth was smooth and uniform,*
without Mountains or Sea, to the explication of the Universal
Deluge.[1]

Rowlands differs from Burnet only in thinking that there
had always been a sea, for he says that Mona was formerly
an antediluvian island: its soil contained no marine remains, and 'great bulky Trees buried in Slutch and Mud'
proved that it had once been inundated. He exhibits an almost featureless map of primeval Mona which shows that
the surface of the island had been quite level before 'that
great and mighty Deterration and Eluvies of the Universal
Deluge' created a less smooth and uniform landscape
when the subsiding waters made 'hideous *Eruptions* in
their Passage . . . and furrowed the Universal Quag, or
the dissolved and loosen'd surface of the Earth, into great
Gutts and Dingles'.[2]
  The first-comers to Mona arrived there within five
generations of those who had escaped the Flood. They
then spoke 'Celtish', which was 'very poor and barren' as
a result of the 'vagrant, loose unsettled Life' led by a
people who were only concerned about 'obvious Rustici-
ties', and their language at that time may have been 'a
gross heap of Monosyllables'. When 'Ease and Opportunity' permitted it, the settlers became 'more speculative
and thoughtful', and their speech grew more polished.
The purest language was spoken in Mona, the principal
seat of the Druids, and there 'the profound mysterious

[1] *The Theory of the Earth*, 1684, bk. I, p. 65.
[2] op. cit., p. 11.

Theorems of that learned Sect, flow'd in the choicest and most elaborate Language of the time'. Welsh, then, was the settlers' tongue when it had been enlarged by the Druids and 'modulated and sweetened' by the ancient Bards.[1]

Later on, the Titans overran Europe, but they, too, 'were of our own Race and Language, as appears by the *Names* of several of them'. Rowlands instances 'Saturnus, i.e., Saf-teyrn (*Imperator stabilis*)', 'Hercules, i.e., Erchyll (*horrendus*)', and 'Apollo, i.e., ap Haul'.[2] But Mona, remote and isolated, was not affected by these events. The settlers were of good Patriarchal stock and still thankful for their deliverance. In consequence

I may presume to affirm, that some of the first Planters of this Island, being so near in descent, to the Fountains of true Religion and Worship, as to have one of *Noah's* Sons for Grandsire or Greatgrandsire, may well be imagin'd, to have carried and convey'd here some of the Rites and Usages of that true Religion, pure and untainted, in the first propagating of them; tho' I must confess they soon after became . . . abominably corrupted.[3]

This is not hypothesis: Rowlands argues, surely on the best authority, that the original Patriarchal families would have erected altars, and on looking round his own Mona he finds, almost with a start of surprise, that there is a large primitive altar in the parish of Llan Edwen.[4] Confessedly he argues *a posteriori*, but he does not rely solely on prehistoric remains, these 'Marks and Footsteps of Antiquity to this day extant in many Places', to support his contentions: comparative philology also bears him out. Claiming that the name of these altars, or 'crom-lechs', would have survived the 'stupor' of Babel, he points out that '*cærcæm-lech*' yields the Hebrew etymology '*caerem-luach*, a devoted Stone'. What he calls 'coped Heaps of Stones', or 'Carnedde', also suggested to him that this

---

[1] op. cit., pp. 34 ff. [2] ibid., pp. 42–43.
[3] ibid., p. 45. [4] ibid., p. 46

word was derived from the Hebrew '*Keren Nedh*, a coped Heap'.[1] The similarity between Welsh and Hebrew showed that the former was one of 'the primary Issues of that sacred Fountain'. The oak, he adds, was venerated by both the Druids and the Jews, not because of its association with Mamre, but because the worship of both Druids and Jews 'follow'd a more ancient Copy, the *Mitzoth*, the sacred Patriarchal Rubrick'.[2]

At first, life was hard on Mona, and the settlers busied themselves with 'meer Necessities'. Their 'Primary Acquisitions', that is, their laws and religion, were originally simple, but in the course of time

these Acquisitions, these rational *Acts* of Human Life, began to open and display themselves, to scour off their original Rudenesses, and to appear here and there more prompt, useful and comprehensive: The *Languages* in a short Time became more Trim and Copious: The *Laws* more Nervous and Vigorous, justly suited to the Advantages of Communities: And *Religion*, the Mistress of all, variegated and set herself off, in multitudes of pompous Shews and Appearances.[3]

Druidism then came into being, for men arose 'whose chief Province was to enlarge the Bonds of Knowledge', men who already possessed the rudiments 'by oral Traduction from the Patriarchal *Cabala*', which is to say, the '*ante Diluvian* Knowledge'. The first steps towards the 'Improvement of Human Faculties' were

began and set on by a few thoughtful Persons here and there, who afterwards Consociating and Assembling together, began to settle Principles, and to form their little Platforms and Institutions, in a *Verbal* discursive way, to which they ever after cleav'd, neglecting the use of *Letters*.[4]

These were the Druids, who carried themselves ostentatiously, with 'Port and Authority', and who swiftly took

[1] ibid., pp. 46–48.   [2] ibid., pp. 39, 53–56.
[3] ibid., p. 54.   [4] ibid., pp. 59–60

over public offices, so that they ultimately had 'the chief Stroke, in the conduct of publick and private Affairs'.[1] The 'insinuating Priests' had excellent reasons for chosing Mona as their seat, and here, Rowlands's diction is more convincing than his arguments, for he says that Mona

> was a pleasant Island; every thing, as the Quality of the Soil and Temperance of its Air gives us to suppose, in the Flower and Vigour of Nature: It breath'd a chearful quick'ning Air: 'Twas a more plain and level Country than any of its neighbouring Regions, and yet variegated into a pleasing Diversity of Elevations and Vallies: It was plentifully purl'd with Springs, and sprinkl'd with Rivulets: It had a benign enlivening Sun, a pregnant fruitful Soil; enrich'd on all sides with the Bounties of the Sea . . . . In short, whatever contributed to maintain the Body in a sound *Athletic* Temper; to enliven the Soul in her briskest Operations; or to inform her with variety of Objects, was not wanting here.[2]

Passing over his special pleading in matters of detail, his headings and propositions: Rowlands adds that the ban on writing showed how old Druidism was, for to the conservative Druids letters 'were inconsistent with their original Establishment'. Their philosophy was 'Symbolical and Enigmatical . . . agreeing in that with the Traditional *Cabala* of the *Jews*', and Pythagoras advanced their methods until finally the imitative Greeks 'amus'd the World with their Mythologies and Riddles'. The principles of the natural philosophy of the Druids were either 'Corpuscularian, or Complex and Elemental', but more probably the former, agreeing as it did with 'the *Sydonian Philosophy*' of the Phoenician traders whom they met. In the course of time the Druids lapsed into idolatry and the worship of 'Medioxumate Gods', and thereafter Rowlands has little good to say about them.[3]

Now called 'infatuated Monkish *Druids*', they established themselves firmly in Mona and extended their

[1] op. cit., pp. 56 ff.   [2] ibid., p. 58.   [3] ibid., pp. 60 ff.

influence to Britain as a whole. But when their own island was threatened by the advancing Romans, 'these *Druids*, who before were every where sucking the Sweet of the Land, upon the Approach of the *Roman* Storm, were fain like Bees to rally home'. That Mona was their principal seat is certain, Rowlands argues, for their behaviour during the invasion showed that this was no ordinary battle. Too timid to be massacred and therefore extermi- nated, after the fighting was over the Druids came out of hiding and saw that everything they valued had been destroyed. 'These fearful slippery *Druids*' then went off to Man, Ireland, and Caledonia, and perhaps even to America, and with their disappearance, Mona was left 'expos'd to the Tumults of the Busy, and the Lust and Rapine of every Scrambler'.[1]

In the second part of his book a long commentary strengthens the weaker parts of Rowlands's reconstruction of Mona's past. He defends, for example, his Hebrew etymologies for words like cromlech and carnedd: how- ever poor and barren Celtish may have been as a result of their vagrant loose life, the settlers, he insists, would always remember the original names of objects which had been erected by their ancestors for religious purposes.[2] A solitary disputant, he contends, persuades and demon- strates, and he brings in still more material to give further weight to arguments which should refute the opponents who would sooner or later show themselves. By suggesting, like Edward Lhuyd, that Welsh gnomic poetry might be '*Druidical* Verses', he links the triads with the great body of verses which Caesar says the Druids had to learn and with the remarks of Diogenes Laertius on the riddles of the Druids. These 'triambicks' still preserved what was 'good and laudable' in Druidism.[3] Though he quotes some specimens of this poetry, he does not translate them, and English versions of the triads had to wait another

[1] ibid., pp. 80 ff.   [2] ibid., pp. 208 ff.   [3] ibid., pp. 267 ff.

fifty years before they appeared in some anonymous
author's *Description of Stonehenge*, 1776; there, a characteristic example, showing the typical introductory evocation of Nature and the sententious ending, runs:

> Mountain snow, swift deer,
> Scarce any in the world cares for me,
> Warning to the unlucky saveth not.[1]

As for the great learning of the Druids, it was easy for
him, within the framework of his theories, to trace this
back to its ultimate source. It was derived from Adam,
who had acquired his wisdom by 'Original Infusion' and
'hundreds of Years personal experience', and his 'true
knowledge . . . of the occult Nature' had then come
down through the Patriarchs and the Celtae 'to kindle
and diffuse itself into the oral Theorems and Placits of
the fore-mentioned *British Druids*'.[2]

But he defended positions that were rarely directly
attacked, and the scholarship of later centuries added,
without noticing it, another ruin to Mona. Yet he deserves
much sympathy. From his standpoint, where great bulky
trees emerging from the mud were visible reminders of
the Deluge, his foreshortened view of history gave the
Druids sufficient time in which to reach and settle down
in Mona. He could still see their remains, massive, simple
and rugged, as befitted an age before the birth of more
sophisticated arts. Place-names in his vicinity still preserved their memory, and the local tongue was still,
though modified by the effects of the damper climate on
the organs of speech, the venerable language of Noah.
He had collated not only records with 'a few Testimonies
of sacred Scripture', but with rocks, fields, and the everyday speech of his neighbours as well, and with this material
he had penetrated a past that was obscure to the classical

---

[1] Anon., *A Description of Stonehenge*, Salisbury, 1776, pp. 65–66.
[2] op. cit., pp. 268 ff.

historians themselves, and made it intelligible. His methods had worked:

And therefore where our Greeke and Roman Authors ascribe to these Druids or our ancient western philosophers, eminent skill in Astronomy, physiology . . . with other umbrages of revealed Knowledge, as the praeexistence and Immortality of Soules, eternal Beatitudes, the propitiation of Sacrifices, and other Dogm's transcending the reach of Meer Human sagacity, we may this way winde them up to their first bottome, and give the world a satisfaction in that particular.[1]

Mona Antiqua Restaurata not only has its place between the scattered comments of earlier centuries on the Druids and the longer essays of the eighteenth and nineteenth centuries, but it left its mark on what was to come. Even William Stukeley's works are less representative of the range of theories on the Druids than are the deliberations of the Vicar of Llanidan. His inquiries into the relationship between Welsh and the first language of men, the remains of the Druids, and Welsh poetry helped to establish these topics as distinct branches of studies of Druidism. His remarks on the mysterious 'Patriarchal Rubrick' —the original religion of both Druids and Patriarchs— anticipate Blake's ideas on a religion still more ancient than that of the Old Testament; even so fugitive a figure as Abaris, the Hyperborean servant of Apollo who caught the fancy of other historians of the Druids, did not escape Rowlands's notice, and in a footnote he suggests that his real name was ap Rees.[2]

Rowlands's kind of archaeology took root and helped to produce a vigorous growth out of which modern archaeology was to flower only after ruthless pruning. In the meantime, the subject of Druidism itself was attracting attention. Much was said about it that did not merely echo Caesar and Pliny, and though these floating conjectures

[1] MS. Carte, 10553, f. 93 v.
[2] op. cit., p. 76; Herodotus, 4, 36.

and asides are often little more than passing remarks, many of them have a place in a pattern which became increasingly clear during the course of the eighteenth century. Rowlands's *Mona* and Stukeley's *Stonehenge* stand well out from it, but they derive some of their arresting qualities from a background of related ideas which both sustained and were supported by the notion that the Druids were the heirs of the Patriarchs.

IV

SCRAPS OF DRUIDIC LORE

WHEN the origins of Druidism were discovered by reading between the lines of Holy Writ, it was, of course, taken for granted that in its nature, Druidism was a venerable faith. Those who did not lean so heavily on the Scriptures and who looked more closely into its nature and origins also thought that Druidism had started far outside the confines of Britain: it seems that once the Druids were no longer primarily thought of as philosophers, considerations of national prestige no longer prompted a strict interpretation of Caesar's remarks on the origin of their discipline. Its translation to the East was made easier because none disputed the antiquity of Druidism. Diogenes Laertius's comments on the barbarian origin of philosophy were accompanied by a suggestion that the Druids were as old as the Chaldeans: Christopher Helvicus therefore had some excuse for thinking that the Druids founded their College in 1823 B.C.,[1] and if few cared to commit themselves to so precise a date, nearly everyone agreed that Druidism was very ancient indeed. For this reason there was in the eighteenth century a tendency to link the Druids with theories on the origins of languages, of religions, even of mankind itself, thus helping to establish the Druids in a past remoter than that of classical antiquity. When Blake asserted that in its purest form, Druidism flourished before Adam, his theories on the Druids were carried on the same tide of opinion that floated the ideas of others.[2]

[1] *Theatrum Historicum*, Marburg, 1629, p. 11.
[2] 'All had originally one language, and one religion', *A Descriptive Catalogue of Pictures*, 1808, v.

The first inquiry into the origin of Druidism to be conducted on relatively rational lines was published in 1702. By comparing different religions, Thomas Brown pointed out that parallels for certain features of Druidism could be found in Eastern religions, but not in those of the West. Both the Druids and the Brahmins, he observed, believed in the transmigration of souls; like the Jews, the Druids started their day at dusk. Like the Egyptians, the Druids concealed their doctrine from the vulgar. Brown concluded that these close and significant resemblances between Druidism and Eastern religions indicated an oriental origin for the beliefs of the Druids.[1]

This idea received support later in the eighteenth century when the French astronomer Bailly claimed that the bearings given by ancient Indian astronomical data showed that the original home of man was in Asia. He also detected some similarity between the usages, philosophy and religion of the Chinese, Chaldeans, Indians, and others, and it seemed to him that their civilizations were derived from the institutions of a very ancient people with a sage and sublime philosophy which its emigrants carried with them. We cannot imagine, he protests, that the Druids left their forests two or three thousand years ago to learn from the Brahmins: rather, the Druids came from the earliest home of mankind when the cooling of the Earth drove them to seek a more congenial climate.

An indignant cleric at once replied:[2]

Dégrader ainsi nos ayeux & leurs Philosophes, dans leur propre Pays, à la face de leur postérité même, n'est-ce pas attenter en quelque sorte à la gloire Nationale?[3]

[1] 'A Short Dissertation about the Mona of Caesar',—W. Sacheverell, *An Account of the Isle of Man*, 1702, pp. 160 ff.
[2] *Lettres sur l'origine des Sciences*, Paris and London, 1777, pp. 488 ff., 123.
[3] N. Baudeau, *Mémoire à consulter pour les anciens Druides gaulois*, n.p., 1777, p. 6.

The promptness with which the Abbé Baudeau corrected
Bailly is impressive: both books were published in the
same year, and he must have had his learned answer at his
fingertips.

To give only some indication of the way in which his
argument goes: the Phrygians, he declares, were the first
of all peoples, and they were called the eldest sons of
Nature. Acmon, the father of Atlas, the founder of
Atlantis, lived in Phrygia; and so old was this people that
even the ancient Assyrians were merely a Phrygian colony.
The data supplied by the classical historians on the movements of ancient peoples showed Baudeau that the Phrygians originally came from Gaul: their home in Asia was
a colony. There, the Persians were their pupils. The Bri-
gantes of Britain were Phrygians. Their original name was
'Brigians', and Conon says that in the time of Midas and
Orpheus they took the name of Phrygians. Samothrace,
the seat of the mysteries of the mother of the gods, was
in Phrygia. Bailly had stated that the Atlantides were the
most ancient of peoples; the Abbé, seizing on this point,
retorted that Saturn, the brother of Atlantis, was impri-
soned in the British Isles, and the Atlantides had always
been associated with these islands. The oldest of peoples
were therefore the Celts, and the Druids, these 'très-
anciens, très-Sçavans & très-renommés Philosophes &
Astronomes', had been prominent among the Gauls,
Celts, Scythians, Hyperboreans, and 'Brigians' of Europe,
and they had founded the study of arts and science in
Asiatic Phrygia, Assyria, and Persia. But Baudeau's was
a lonely protest, and by 1777 even the British were no
longer paying much heed to 'disciplina in Britannia
reperta . . . existimatur'.[1]

Though none knew precisely what Druidism was,
nearly everyone held strong views on the subject, and
even the etymology of the word Druid was not a matter

[1] op. cit., p. 84.

on which all agreed. The etymology of 'druida' is derived from the same root as that of the Sanskrit 'vidya' (knowledge) and the Latin 'video'. In Welsh the word is 'derwydd', and Sir Ifor Williams says 'there is a strong probability that the second element in *derwydd* . . . is connected with the *vid-* in Latin *video* "I see", c.f. the Greek οἶδα "I have seen", then "I know", and the Welsh *gwyddbod, gwybod,* "to know", literally "be in a state of having seen".'[1] 'Derwydd' (its earliest meaning being 'prophet') is formed from the stem '*do-are-uĭd'. 'Darguid' is an Old Breton gloss on the Latin 'pythonicus.'[2] and the Irish 'druí' is derived from a stem '*dru-uid'. All these forms preserve the root from which 'vidya' is derived, but the prefix has given trouble to some philologists who are inclined to see in it vestiges of a word for oak preserved in Greek and the Welsh 'derw'; the strengthening prefix, however, is adequately explained by the prefixes '*do-are-' in the Welsh stem.

Because the Druids venerated the oak, Pliny suggests that their name was derived from the Greek word for this tree. It is hard to see why the Celts should resort to Greek in order to name their spiritual leaders. Pliny's suggestion may be based on analogy, for elsewhere he speaks of the Querquetulani, a tribe which lived near Rome and venerated and was named after the oak, and sacrificed white bulls to Jupiter.[3] His etymology was popular, but not everyone agreed with him, and as Simon Pelloutier's editor remarks, etymologies were discovered which varied according to taste. Perhaps the most unexpected are those which are derived from Teutonic roots. In Pelloutier's pages 'Druter', 'Druch', 'Trud', 'Trouwe', and 'Truchten' are collected from different sources.[4] J. Goropius Becanus thought that Druid was

---

[1] *Lectures on Early Welsh Poetry,* Dublin, 1944, p. 7.
[2] *Geiriadur Prifysgol Cymru,* Cardiff, vol. xv, 1960, 'derwydd'.
[3] *Natural History,* III, 269.
[4] S. Pelloutier, *Histoire des Celtes,* Paris, 1770, tom. VIII, pp. 334 ff.

derived from 'Tru-wijs', or 'True-Wise': this evolved into 'Dru-wis' and finally became 'Druis'.[1] Van Scrieck derived the word from 'De Rue-wys' or 'Rector Sapiens'.[2] Pontanus first suggested that it came from 'Try-wijs', or 'Tree-Wise'; later he thought it was derived from a root which he had found in 'druthines haus', or 'Dei domus'.[3] Keysler claimed that 'Druden' meant 'sagae, incantatores magi'.[4] Others found Hebrew roots: because the Hebrew for the Persian Magi was 'Drusim', Caesar Bulaeus thought that the root lay in the Hebrew 'Derulsim', that is, 'mediatores'.[5] The Welsh lexicographer and grammarian John Davies thought that 'Derwyddon' came from the Hebrew 'Darash',[6] but Edward Lhuyd derived it from 'Derwen', the 'British' word for oak.[7]

These etymologies, very broadly speaking, fall into two main groups which reflect contrasting views on the nature itself of Druidism. The school of Pliny, as it were, was disposed to see the Druids as simple, superstitious, bloodthirsty Nature lovers who worshipped oaks—though, of course, an author would select from these epithets. Those on the other hand who were more impressed by Caesar's account of the Druids were aware that Druidism still eluded them, and this gap in their knowledge gave them an incentive to further research. The distinction is not absolute; many authors made concessions to opposite points of view; but it helps to account for two very different kinds of interpretation of the classical texts. Not only was next to nothing known of the doctrines of the Druids, but the question of the status, so to speak, of Druidism

[1] J. Goropius Becanus, 'Hermathena', *Opera*, Antwerp, 1580, p. 112.
[2] A. Van Scrieck, *Monitorum secundorum libri quinque*, Ypres, 1614, sig. K3.
[3] I. Pontanus, *Itinerarium Galliae Narboniensis*, Leyden, 1606, p. 229, *Originum Francicarum*, Harderwijk, 1616, p. 587.
[4] *Antiquitates Selectae*, Hanover, 1720, p. 503.
[5] *Historia Universitatis Parisiensis*, Paris, 1665, p. 3.
[6] *Antiquae Linguae Britannicae*, 1621, sig. E3 v.
[7] Bodleian MS. Gen. Top. c 24, f. 192 v.

still remained to be answered. Was Druidism a primitive faith? Or was it in any way comparable to the great religions of antiquity?

It left no Luxor, no papyrus, no masks of gold, no inscriptions, no literature, no names of great men. Its groves are fields, and no one knows where the oaks of the Druids grew. Even their megaliths did not always arouse admiration—Samuel Johnson, for example, thought little of their temples.[1] Those who rejected Pliny's personal views on the Druids had little in the way of externals—though they were to make the most of Stonehenge and Avebury—to support their case. The question of the status of Druidism was nevertheless answered to nearly everyone's satisfaction when towards the end of the eighteenth century the study of comparative religion led to conclusions which for the time being were to give to the most divergent interpretations of Druidism a certain coherence. Blake's hardhearted priests of Urizen, Thomas Maurice's displaced Hindus, and Edward Davies's guardians of the Celtic mysteries have no resemblance to each other, but their creators were convinced that Druidism had its origin in primordial religion.

This belief evolved from earlier searches for a wider setting than that, say, of Caesar's narrative, into which Druidism could be placed. Once the standard sources of information on the Druids had been collected, the classics apparently had nothing more to yield. Sporadic attempts to add quite irrelevant material to the canon were soon abandoned, and later, students of Druidism took the opportunities offered by archaeology and comparative philology of exploring the past. But classical and patristic texts were then searched not so much for information as for guiding principles—for 'Truth is older than Errour'[2]

[1] *Boswell's Life of Johnson*, ed. G. B. Hill, 1950, vol. v, p. 132.
[2] Sir Matthew Hale, *The Primitive Origination of Mankind*, 1677, p. 169.

—which could throw further light on primordial religion. To some of the seekers the Christian and certain classical attitudes to the most distant past seemed much alike, for the conditions of the Golden Age as they are described or alluded to in Greek and Latin literature are in essence those of Eden. Cicero, for example, observes that in earlier ages, men were closer to the gods;[1] more strikingly, Lactantius, writing at a time when the Christian apologist might be expected to show hostility to the entire Roman pantheon, says that 'while Saturn reigned . . . God was manifestly worshipped'.[2] Passages in the literature of antiquity which mention Celtic worship gave them reason to believe that Druidism had its roots in the very remote past, and in particular, the remarks of Sotion might strongly confirm them in this belief:

There are some who say that the study of philosophy had its beginning among the barbarians. They urge that the Persians had their Magi, the Babylonians or Assyrians their Chaldeans, and the Indians their Gymnosophists; and among the Celts and Gauls there are people called Druids or Holy Ones.[3]

It was understandably taken for granted that any reference to Celtic religion was self-evidently a reference to Druidism. This testimonial, then, from Dionysius of Halicarnassus could be read as a tribute to the firmness with which the Druids had adhered to their beliefs:

no lapse of time has thus far induced either the Egyptians, the Libyans, the Gauls . . . or any other barbarian nation whatsoever to forget or transgress anything related to the rites of the gods, unless some of them have been subdued by a foreign power.[4]

[1] *Of the Laws*, II, 27.
[2] *Divine Institutes*, v, 5; see also Justin Martyr, *Hortatory Address to the Greeks*, xxxvi.
[3] *Lives*, I, 1; 'Holy Ones', or *semnotheoi*, is literally 'revered gods': cf. 'The barbarians signally honoured their lawgivers and teachers, designating them gods', Clement of Alexandria, op. cit., I, 15.
[4] *Roman Antiquities*, tr. E. Cary, 1937, VII, 70.

Aelianus says much the same when he declares

What manne, would not highly commend the wisedome of the
Barbarians? sithence none of them, at any time fel in to contempt
of yᵉ Gods, immortall, nether yet called this in question, whether
there were Gods, yea or nay. . . . No Indian, no Celtan, no
Aegiptian, harboured so hellish an opinion in their harts.[1]

St. Clement of Alexandria more explicitly places the
Druids on the same level as the priests of the oldest
civilizations, and he also implies that the Druids were the
contemporaries of the ancient Egyptians and the Chaldeans:

Thus philosophy, a thing of the highest utility, flourished in
antiquity among the barbarians, shedding its light among the
nations. And afterwards it came to Greece. First in its ranks were
the prophets of the Egyptians, and the Chaldeans among the
Assyrians, and the Druids among the Gauls . . . and the philosophers among the Celts.[2]

Diogenes Laertius twice mentions—though diffidently,
for he did not believe it—this claim that the barbarians
had studied philosophy before the Greeks, and the conci-
dence of these texts on this subject gave the student of
early religion some warrant for believing that Druidism
was of great antiquity. In the context of this passage, St.
Clement shows that his own view of the Druids was quite
incompatible with that of Pliny. Commenting on the
nature of barbarian and Hellenic philosophy, he says that
it had 'torn off a fragment of eternal truth not from the
mythology of Dionysius, but from the theology of the
ever-living Word'.[3] If Druidism possessed 'a fragment of
eternal truth', this endorsement provided a counterweight
to the charge that it was 'a dismal and confused heap of
superstition'. (St. Clement's gnosticism, it should be

[1] *A Registre of Hystories*, tr. A. Fleming, 1576, f. 23.
[2] op. cit., I, 15: *Works*, tr. W. Wilson, Edinburgh, 1876, p. 398.
[3] ibid., I, 13.

added, neither attracted nor repelled those of his readers who were primarily interested in the Druids. They do not seem to have noticed it, and their interpretation of this and like passages would not have conflicted with a most fundamentalist reading of Genesis.) Since St. Clement also states elsewhere in the same work, on the authority of Alexander Polyhistor, that Pythagoras had been 'a hearer of the Galatae',[1] he gives the impression that his high opinion of barbarian philosophy was partly founded on what he knew about Druidism.

Such remarks, then, which were consistent with Ammianus Marcellinus's statement that the Druids studied 'secret and sublime things', plausibly indicated, if only in the most general way, what kind of beliefs the Druids held. It thus became permissible to see, for example, in the architecture of Stonehenge a subtle expression of metaphysical principles: being open to the sky, and having no walls, it suggested that the illimitable could not be confined. 'Here', says the anonymous author of *A Description of Stonehenge* in 1776, 'is a Kebla, intimating, but not bounding, the presence of the Deity'.[2]

But not everyone regarded the distant past as a Golden Age. From another point of view, to visit primitive peoples outside the boundaries of the civilized world was in effect to return to the past, for there the traveller could see for himself the condition of his own ancestors. From this point of view the Druids might be looked down upon as the priests of backward tribesmen. Yet another factor militated against seeing the Druids as enlightened philosophers, for the classical historians who describe with distaste the inhabitants of pre-Christian Gaul and Britain had, if inadvertently, created the impression that the Druids were responsible for their plight, and Jeremy Collier's scorn reflects on the Druids when he calls the

---

[1] ibid., I, 15.
[2] Anon., op. cit., Salisbury, 1776, p. 22.

ancient Britons, 'low and unpolished in their under-
standings'.[1]

But he spoke for a minority. The references to the
Druids in patristic literature, few as they are—and it is
remarkable that there are any—received respectful attention from readers who went farther afield for their Druids.
St. Augustine of Hippo says that he felt himself nearest to
those philosophers who thought that God was the maker
of all things and the light by which all things are known;
were they Platonists or Pythagoreans, were they—among
others—the philosophers of the Gauls, 'we prefer these
to all other philosophers, and we confess that they approach nearest to us'.[2] Though he does not mention the
Druids by name here, he could have had no one else in
mind. As for hostile references in the early fathers, those
of Origen and Hippolytus did no harm to the reputation
of the Druids as philosophers: the former, in passing,
records the opinion of the learned Celsus that the Druids
were 'sapientissimas gentes antiquasque',[3] and Hippolytus places them on a level with Plato and Pythagoras in
his attack on the philosophies of the ancient world.[4] The
early Christians added nothing substantial to what was
already known of Druidism, but if the classics provided
the material for the study of Druidism, patristic literature
had some measure of influence on its interpretation.

A comment of the Abbé Antoine Banier's illustrates
in a rather striking fashion the effect of these relatively
secondary studies:

This antient Religion of the *Gauls* was at first of great Purity:
that People, especially the *Druids*, had much more just and spiritual
Apprehensions of God than either the *Greeks* or *Romans*. *Tacitus*,
Maximus Tyrius, and others inform us, that the *Druids* were

[1] *Ecclesiastical History of Great Britain*, 1708, p. 1.
[2] *Works*, tr. M. Dods, 1871, pp. 318–19: *The City of God*, VIII, 9.
[3] *Against Celsus*, I, 16.
[4] *Refutation of All Heresies*, I, ii; I, xxv.

persuaded that the supreme Being was to be worshipped no less by the silent Veneration of the Heart, than by external sacrifices.[1]

His authorities had said nothing of the kind, and it appears that Banier was so taken with the idea of the superiority of Druidism that his ideas, developed as they were from hints picked up from the background of his studies, then blinded him to the remarks of historians who had in fact described the Druids.

The theory that all religions had stemmed from a single source was also encouraged by the Latins' use of the *interpretatio Romana*. When Caesar said that the Gauls worshipped Mercury and Mars, he was, of course, using the names of Roman gods for their Celtic equivalents.[2] The practice suggested that this was possible only because the Greek, Roman, Celtic, and German gods were, when stripped of minor accidental differences, identical; in consequence, the *interpretatio Romana* was not only a useful literary convention, but it pointed to a time when the prototypes of these gods were worshipped. It was then left to the euhemerist to say exactly who these gods were.

Euhemerus argued that the gods were mortals who after death had been deified. During the Renaissance, his ideas were popular partly because the simplicity of this rationalization was in itself attractive, but mainly because they permitted a bridge to be built between the Bible and classical mythology. Taking, like Holinshed, the theories of Euhemerus a stage farther, Sir Walter Raleigh observes that 'out of the taking vp of *Henoch* by God was borrowed the conversion of *Heroes* . . . into starres', and he notes that there was a 'likelihood of name between *Tubalcain* and *Vulcan*'.[3] But the story which fascinated the anthropologist, the philologist, and the student of

---

[1] *The Mythology and Fables of the Ancients*, 1739, III, p. 218.
[2] *Gallic War*, VI, 17.
[3] *The History of the World*, 1614, p. 86.

comparative religion was that of Noah. Henry Reynolds claims that Bacchus was originally Noah: Noah was called Noachus, and later Boachus, and this name finally evolved into Bacchus.[1] Theophilus Gale, on the other hand, contended that Saturn was Noah, for under their reigns, he points out, everything was held peacefully in common, all men spoke one language, and both Saturn and Noah enjoyed wine.[2] Though he called his massive *Analysis of Ancient Mythology*, 1774-6, 'a new system', Jacob Bryant took his subject-matter from these early hints when he argued that beneath the mythology of the nations of antiquity a substratum of historical truth existed, all of it going back to the Flood:

And though the nations, who have preserved memorials of the Deluge, have not perhaps stated accurately the time of that event; yet it will be found the grand epocha, to which they referred; the highest point, to which they could ascend.[3]

Thus the method by means of which Euhemerus had attempted to rob the gods of much of their prestige finally led to their rehabilitation. It was accepted that the ancient gods were mere mortals—but these mere mortals were the great figures of the Old Testament. There was much disagreement in matters of detail: Annius of Viterbo identified Noah with Janus Ogyges, thus connecting him with the flood myths of the Greeks as the god who faced both past and future, the old world and the new; Dis, whom the Druids called the ancestor of the Gauls, was identified with Samothes by Holinshed,[4] with Noah by Lynche;[5] as the Lord of the Underworld, Dis was also identified with Adam, from whose darkness men were

---

[1] 'Mythomystes', 1633: *Critical Essays of the Seventeenth Century*, ed. J. E. Spingarn, Oxford, 1908, p. 175.

[2] *Court of the Gentiles*, Part I, Oxford, 1667, p. 112.

[3] op. cit., vol. i, p. xii. See also Holinshed, op. cit., f 8 v.

[4] op. cit., f. 8 v.

[5] *An Historicall Treatise of the Travels of Noah into Europe*, 1601, sig. Ciiij.

redeemed.[1] But in principle it was agreed that Euhemerus had been right, and his theories were then taken a stage farther and so adapted that they made a perceptible contribution to the theory of a Patriarchal origin for Greek and Roman religion.

Above all, comparisons between Druidism and other religions helped to encourage the idea that all religions had stemmed from a common source. These comparisons were often based on very flimsy analogies, and they were made in a rather offhand fashion. The Druids were likened to the bonzes of Japan and to the North American Indians as early as 1616,[2] and by the middle of the eighteenth century Simon Pelloutier was already protesting at the widespread tendency of authors to find traces of Druidism in the Jewish, Phoenician, Egyptian, Greek, and Roman religions.[3] This, however, did not stop Pelloutier from supplementing his own discussion of Druidism with pointed remarks on parallels between Celtic and Teutonic religion, for in order to further cultural relations between France and Prussia, he wished to prove the identity of their ancient faiths.

Those who were fond of making comparisons of this kind quite possibly took their cue from the classics, where the Druids are mentioned as though they were the equivalents of the Brahmins and the Magi. Suidas and Stephen of Byzantium describe the Druids as philosophers, but when the word Druid appeared in fifteenth-century printed editions of the classics, they were described in the margins as mages. Bodley's copy of the 1496 edition of *Pharsalia* printed at Leipzig, for instance, has for a gloss 'Drÿude Magij'.[4] Presumably this word had richer associations than 'philosophers' or 'priests'. This, however, was a synonym more often used by those who

---

[1] Caesar Bulaeus, *Historia Universitatis Parisiensis*, Paris, 1665, p. 10.
[2] P. Clüver, *Germaniae antiquae libri tres*, Leyden, 1616, pp. 204-5.
[3] *Histoire des Celtes*, Paris, 1770, tom. v, p. 16.
[4] Shelfmark: Auct. N.V. 42, sig. Cij v.

wrote in Latin than in English. But the comparisons which in the classics are handled with restraint were sometimes taken to extreme lengths, a tendency which is illustrated by the Cornish antiquary William Borlase. Like the Druids, he writes, the Persians had open temples before the time of Zoroaster; both wore white robes, lived and taught in caves, and venerated the serpent. Mithras was rock-born, and Borlase says that the Druids thought that divine intelligences lived in rocks; he had left his original sources far behind when he claimed that the Druids and Cyrus both had their white oracular horses.[1]

The parallels which had been drawn between the Druids and the Persians were also drawn between the Druids and the Hindus. According to Thomas Maurice, India was the former home not only of Druidism but other religions, and of the pinnacles of the Hindu temples he observes: '*the* Symbol *on their* Summits *exhibits the* Trident *of* SEEVA; *afterwards usurped by the* Greek NEPTUNE'.[2] 'The celebrated order of Druids, anciently established in this country,' he says, 'were the immediate descendants of a tribe of Brahmins' who mingled with a tribe of Celto-Scythians.[3] Their groves of oak recalled the groves of 'banian-trees';[4] they still had consecrated wands, they still venerated the serpent and the chacra of Vishnu, and the initiatic rites which were once held in the caves of Elephanta were then held in the subterranean recesses of Mona.[5]

Lieutenant Francis Wilford, who at the end of the eighteenth century was stationed in India and became a keen student of Sanskrit, suggests that Druidism was by no means derived from Hinduism. He appears to have

---

[1] *Observations on the Antiquities of Cornwall*, Oxford, 1754, pp. 139, 142.
[2] *Indian Antiquities*, vol. vi, pt. I, 1796, sig. B.
[3] ibid., pp. 19–20.
[4] ibid., vol. i, pt. III, 1793, p. 491.
[5] ibid., vol. vi, pt. I, 1796, p. 50.

studied James Macpherson on the subject of the monotheism of the Druids. The author of *Fingal* observes 'that
the primary ideas of the Druids concerning the Divinity
were the same with those of the ancient Brahmins of the
East; "that GOD is the GREAT SOUL, who animates
the whole body of nature",' or, as he transliterates the
Sanskrit, 'Pirrum Attima'.[1] In his 'Essay on the Sacred
Islands in the West' Wilford's remarks on the Druids
echo those of Macpherson,[2] but he found altogether
novel ties between the Druids and the Brahmins. He was
fascinated by constant allusions in his Sanskrit texts to a
remote island which was greatly revered by the Hindus,
and though he discovered that some of these texts had
been tampered with by his atypical 'Guru', he was satisfied that the forgeries did not materially affect his conclusions. 'The Sacred Isles in the West, of which . . .
the White Island, is the principal, and most famous,' he
writes, 'are in fact the holy land of the Hindus.' This holy
land 'is so intimately connected with their religion and
mythology, that they cannot be separated'. With the
evidence he placed in front of them, 'the learned have
little more to do, than to ascertain whether the White
Island be *England*, and the Sacred Isles of the *Hindus*,
the *British Isles*. After having maturely considered the
subject, *I think they are.*' His arguments are founded on
a misconception of the nature of Hindu cosmography;
nevertheless, his discovery of a Britain still remembered
and cherished in the scriptures of an alien faith might
have given his delusion an appropriate enchantment. But
his obsession did not affect his sense of values, and he
confesses that if his theory were proved wrong, he would
not particularly mind, 'for admitting my position to be
right, I am conscious that *Britain* cannot receive any

---

[1] *Introduction to the History of Great Britain and Ireland*, Dublin,
1771, p. 184. See also pp. 162–5.
[2] op. cit., *Asiatic Researches*, Calcutta, vol. xi, 1810, pp. 125, 129.

additional lustre from it'.[1] In this exotic paper, what he said of the Druids was not very remarkable; when he declared that their religion was identical with those of the Greeks, Romans, Goths, Egyptians, and Hindus,[2] his opinion would not have surprised contemporary students of comparative religion.

But even when it was accepted, to say the least of it, that Druidism had much in common with other ancient faiths, this did not necessarily enhance the reputation of the Druids: when William Francklin observes that 'the whole system of Pagan idolatry throughout the world carries with it a strong and striking affinity, collectively and separately', his tone is cool.[3] The great antiquity of Druidism did not always suggest the vanished glories of the Golden Age. All mankind may once have had a single religion, but John Cradock accounts for this by pointing out that 'there is a sameness in the primaeval state of every savage nation',[4] a remark which is elaborated by Bishop Percy when he observes that 'the more men approach to a state of wild and uncivilized life, the greater resemblance they will have in manners, because savage nature, reduced almost to meer brutal instinct, is simple and uniform'.[5]

Few shared this point of view: their Patriarchal connexions gave the Druids a certain venerability. Dom Martin, in a study of the religion of the Gauls published in 1727, dwells on the parallels he finds between the religion, discipline, and government of both Gauls and Patriarchs, and in such a context it was impertinent to see the Druids as pagan idolaters.[6] It was claimed that Jacob's pillar at Bethel was the equivalent of a British standing stone.[7]

[1] op. cit., vol. viii, 1805, pp. 246 ff.   [2] ibid., vol. xi, 1810, p. 122.
[3] *Researches on the Tenets of the Jeynes and Boodhists*, 1827, pp. 206–7.
[4] 'Remarks on North Wales', *Literary Memoirs*, vol. iii, 1828, p. 379.
[5] P. H. Mallet, *Northern Antiquities*, tr. T. Percy, 1770, vol. i, p. ix.
[6] *La Réligion des Gaulois*, Paris, vol. i, 1727, p. 52.
[7] W. Stukeley, *Abury*, 1743, p. 4.

The three stones of the 'trilithon', a word coined by
Stukeley for the double pillar with a lintel that still
stands at Stonehenge, corresponded according to John
Smith to the three seasons of the ancient Hebrews;[1] Sir
James Ware likened Samuel on circuit to the Druids'
assizes in the country of the Carnutes;[2] and Selden observed that, like the Levites, the Druids were exempt
from military service.[3] Even in their lapses the Druids
were apt to go astray in the same way as the Jews, for
their bowing stones still existed in Cornwall,[4] and like the
Jews, the Druids made idolatrous sacrifices under oaks.[5]
To picture the Druids as mere savages was to imply that
the Patriarchal communities were equally savage. Further,
these alleged similarities between the Druids and the
Jews were not based on data from the Old Testament
alone: at a royal entertainment in Paris in 1612, facetious
recipes for imaginary dishes were featured on the menu,
and they included 'Confection de la cabale des juifs, et
de la tradition des Druides'.[6] Theophilus Gale, after
censuring the Jews for 'growing weary of the plain and
familiar simplicitie of Sacred Revelations' and preferring
'that *Mythologic*, *Symbolic*, *Enigmatic*, or *Mystic* kind of
Philosophising, which they observed among the Grecians',
gave some hint of what he thought Druid doctrine was
like by calling it '*symbolick*, or *enigmatick*'.[7] Phrases like
the '*Cabbalistic Art*'[8] of the Druids and 'Druidical
Cabbala'[9] are not uncommon.

[1] *Choir Gaur*, Salisbury, 1771, p. 66.
[2] *The History and Antiquities of Ireland*, tr. W. Harris, Dublin, vol. ii,
1764, p. 120.
[3] *The Reverse of the English Janus*, 1683, p. 13.
[4] W. Borlase, *Observations*, 1754, p. 154.
[5] J. Ware, loc. cit.; Ezekiel, vi. 13.
[6] P. Lacroix, *Ballets et Mascarades de Cour*, Paris, 1868, vol. i, pp.
225–6.
[7] *Court of Gentiles*, II, Oxford, 1671, p. 79.
[8] J. Ware, op. cit., p. 125.
[9] E. Evans, *Some Specimens of the Poetry of the Antient Welsh Bards*,
1764, p. 18.

These scraps of Druidic lore, then, show rather like
the movement of jetsam the general drift of a literature
of single pages and paragraphs. They helped, in the end,
to create something more concrete than a climate of
opinion: 'the truth is', says Dr. Robert Henry,

> there is hardly anything more surprising in the history of mankind,
> than the similitude, or rather identity, of the opinions, constitu-
> tions, and manners of all these orders of ancient priests, though
> they lived under such different climates, at so great a distance
> from one another, without intercourse or communication. This
> amounts to a demonstration, that all these opinions and instruc-
> tions flowed originally from one fountain; the instruction which
> the sons of Noah gave to their immediate descendants, and they to
> posterity.[1]

By the last years of the eighteenth century this idea was
widely enough accepted for Edward King, a Fellow of
the Royal Society, to take it for granted that 'traces of
primaeval customs' among distant nations were still
survivals of the customs of 'the Patriarchal Residence'.[2]
Dr. Robert Henry's 'truth' was, after all, the outcome of
a very literal interpretation of what might be called the
evidence, and in all probability most of these students of
comparative religion quite missed the point of St.
Clement's remark that Plato was only Moses speaking
Greek.[3]

[1] *The History of Great Britain*, 1771, vol. i, p. 100.
[2] *Munimenta Antiqua*, 1799, vol. i, p. 223.
[3] op. cit., I, 25.

V

TEMPLA DRUIDUM

WHEN he lifted his eyes from the printed page and looked at the prehistoric remains of Britain, the English antiquary was slow to realize that there was still much to say about the Druids. In France, during the sixteenth century, it was being taken for granted that the more venerable antiquities of Authon and Dreux were relics of the Druids, and even a reference to a palace of the Druids can be met with at this time.[1] When in 1598 a coffer with 'Chyndonax' inscribed on its base was excavated, the urn it contained was readily identified as that of an Archdruid.[2] As early as 1502, the German poet Conrad Celtes thought that some large statues showing men with long forked beards, wearing cowled tunics, were of Druids,[3] and from his description comes the odd-looking Druid, sage and athletic, who illustrates the works of Rowlands and Stukeley.

It was only towards the end of the seventeenth century in England that the local antiquary began to suspect that the Druids had left their mark on his parish. Thereafter, he became very busy, and he left much for the modern archaeologist to repudiate. Yet it was the Druid who so greatly stimulated the curiosity which sharpened the wits of those who pondered over tumulus, dolmen, and menhir. The road which trampled down a segment of a Druid circle established a relative chronology, and the man who

---

[1] A. Alvernogenus, in Matago de Matagonibus, *Monitoriale*, Villeur-banne, 1594, p. 95.

[2] I. Guenebalt, *Le réveil de Chyndonax*, Paris 1623.

[3] 'Norinberga', op. cit., sig. m viii; John Selden, *The Reverse of the English Janus*, 1683, p. 15.

first noticed this had already given archaeology a method.
But it needed the dramatic impact of Stonehenge and
Avebury on their visitors to get this new science off to a
good start.

As he was talking about Stonehenge one morning, King
Charles II was told that John Aubrey had been heard
speaking about Avebury, where there were even more
impressive remains. 'His Matie admired that none of our
chorographers had taken notice of it',[1] but Avebury had
in fact been briefly described in Philemon Holland's
translation of Camden's *Britannia*.[2] During the eighteenth
century a number of its stones had been broken up by
farmers and a speculative builder—whose enterprise went
unrewarded, for his houses caught fire and ruined him.[3]
But it had been laid out on so vast a scale that at the
time when Aubrey saw it with its full complement of
stones its pattern did not always reveal itself to the
passer-by. After his audience with the King and the subsequent royal visit to Avebury, Aubrey surveyed the site
and later 'tooke a Review of Stonehenge' as well.[4] He
presented a description of the site to the King, but res-
pectfully declined the royal invitation to publish it until
he had studied some more monuments. Thirty years were
to pass before he was satisfied with his conclusions and
anxious to see them in print before he died.

Aubrey thought that the Druids had built Stonehenge
and Avebury. In 1663, however, his views conflicted with
everything that had ever been written on the subject.
Dr. Charleton's *Chorea Gigantum*, 1663,[5] in which

[1] *Monumenta Britannica*, Bodleian MS. Gen. Top. 24, f. 24 v. This
account of Aubrey's work is based on material taken from *A Revaluation
of the Writings of John Aubrey*, by Patricia Owen (unpublished).

[2] *Britain*, 1610, p. 255.

[3] This was Stukeley's enemy, Tom Robinson: see Charles Lucas, *A
Descriptive Account of Avebury*, Marlborough, 1801.

[4] Bodleian MS. Gen. Top. c 24, ff. 24 v ff.

[5] The name is taken from Geoffrey's *Historia*, VIII, 10, but this 'temple'
was in Ireland; it was first given to Stonehenge by Camden, *Brit.*, 1586,
p. 119.

Stonehenge was 'restored to the Danes', greatly provoked
Aubrey: he transcribed and annotated passages with
which he disagreed, not liking, for example, Charleton's
putting it out that the Danish chieftains used to stand on
the tops of the trilithons at Stonehenge in order to elect
their kings.[1] A more difficult argument to answer was
that of Inigo Jones. The eminent architect knew Italy
well, and there of course he had studied Roman architecture at first hand; his contention that the Romans had
built Stonehenge would carry more weight than the
theories of an obscure antiquary.

In *The Most Remarkable Antiquity of Great Britain,
vulgarly called Stone-Heng, Restored*, the notes for which
were written in 1620 and the text arranged by John Webb
and published in 1655, Jones advances the hypothesis
that the Druids had built Stonehenge, only to dismiss it
in order to clear the way for his own theory. They could
not have erected such a structure, he argues, because they
lacked the necessary professional qualifications: they had
no '*Academies* of *Designe*', no knowledge of mathematics.[2]
Further, he remarks, in the one place in the British Isles
where it is certainly known that the Druids had lived
there is no monument comparable to Stonehenge, nothing
to suggest that the two places had anything in common;
as he or Webb puts it:

Neither are we to wonder that they chose such an out-nook or
corner as *Anglesey*, to reside in; in regard, there, they lived remote,
and solitary; there, were store of caves, and dens to instruct their
Scholars in . . . and plenty of groves to perform their sacred
mysteries in.[3]

But Jones or Webb (who took a spade to Stonehenge)
completely falsified the plan of its stones: this showed
them forming a neat pattern of concentric circles. Far

[1] Bod. MS. Aubrey 11, f. 13 v.
[2] *Stone-Heng Restored* (1620), 1655, p. 3.
[3] ibid., p. 7.

from restoring Stonehenge, it seemed as though Jones
had remodelled it as though to force the structure into
conformity with his ideas. To Aubrey, who had surveyed
the site, it was clear that much still remained to be done,
and this, he says, 'gave me an edge to make more researches'.[1]

Aubrey remarks of Stonehenge and Avebury: 'These
Antiquities are so exceeding old that no Bookes doe
reache them',[2] and all that could be done was 'to make the
stones give Evidence for themselves'.[3] As it will be seen,
later antiquaries were to have their own notions of what
constituted admissible evidence: Aubrey looked for the
kind that would convince, as he says, a jury. Though he
presented his case unmethodically, and though his notes
give the impression that he was an undiscriminating
collector of trifles, the stones found in Aubrey a gifted
interpreter.

In the first place, he observed that stone circles were
to be found all over the British Isles. The extent to which
they were dispersed suggested that at the time when they
were constructed the same conditions might be met with
over the entire country, for political divisions did not then
exist. Neither the Saxons nor the Danes had extended
their rule to the whole of the British Isles, nor had the
Romans. By elimination, Aubrey inferred that the circles
had been built before the coming of the Romans.[4] He then
looked at the stones themselves. Holland's translation of
Camden speaks of 'Aiburie' as an 'old Campe', but
Aubrey points out that the 'Graffe', or ditch, would have
been outside the ramparts of the great circle if it had been
designed for defence. Since the ditch was inside the ramparts, he concluded that the structure had no military
significance.[5]

[1] Bod. MS. Gen. Top. c 24, ff. 23 v, 24.
[2] ibid., f. 26.
[3] *Proposals for Printing Monumenta Britannica* (1693).
[4] MS. Gen. Top. c 24, f. 80.   [5] ibid., f. 31.

Avebury, then, was a temple of the ancient Britons. Though he called these monuments 'Templa Druidum', in the light of the then available evidence the conclusion that the Druids were their 'Founders' was forced on him, but he regarded it as a probability rather than a certainty:

Now my presumption is, That the *Druids* being the most eminent Priests . . . among the Britaines: 'tis odds, but that these ancient Monuments . . . were Temples of the Priests of the most eminent Order, viz, *Druids*.[1]

Over the years he gathered much material for the study of ancient monuments. One item in particular engaged his attention: he had noticed that Camden mentions '*Cerig-y-Drudion*, id est, *Lapides Druydarum*',[2] and Aubrey evidently thought that these 'stones of the Druids' may have been arranged in a circle on the pattern of Stonehenge. He wanted to travel to North Wales to examine them, for in the past he had 'often been led out of the way, not only by common reports, but by Bookes'. He therefore decided to postpone publication of his theories until he had seen these stones for himself, and this might explain why he at first attached an altogether disproportionate importance to Camden's guess, for he says: 'The Hinge of this Discourse depends upon Mr. Camden's *Kerrig y Druidd*.'[3] Later, of course, he was to learn from Gibson that the only stones to be seen there were two specimens of the recently named 'Kist vâen'. Nevertheless, his inquiries were not entirely fruitless, for in *Britannia*, Gibson observes of their shape that these stones add 'not a little to Mr. *Aubrey*'s conjecture, that those rude Stones erected in a circular order, so common in this Island, are also Druid-Monuments: seeing that in the midst of such circles we sometimes find *Stone chests*.'[4]

[1] ibid., f. 26.
[2] In the 4th edition, 1594, for the first time: p. 519.
[3] MS. Gen. Top. c 24, f. 25.
[4] *Britannia*, ed. Gibson, 1695, col. 683.

Aubrey had other difficulties to contend with. Were the ancient Britons capable of erecting such monuments as Stonehenge? As his correspondent William Rogers remarks of conditions in the days of the Druids: 'All was then in yᵉ *Woods*.'[1] Indeed, the Britons in Geoffrey of Monmouth's pages may have come from Troy and built many fair cities, but when confronted with the more impressive monuments of the remote past, the antiquary might remember that Caesar had said that some of the ancient Britons wore skins. So, of Caerleon, the chronicler Ranulf Higden, as translated by John de Trevisa in 1387, observes:

The founder of this cyte is Vnknowe For Who that seeth the fou*n*damentes of the grete stones Wolde rather Wene that it Were Romayns Werke. or Werke of gyantes, than Were made by settynge of brytons.[2]

In compensation, however, Aubrey had one marked advantage: the others had already published their theories, and he was thus able to come 'in the Rear of all by comparative Arguments'.[3]

In order to find out more about these Druids who had built his temples, he collected as much information about them as possible. He notes with interest that an 'Irish Testament' he had seen in Dublin translates the word Magi as 'draoite'.[4] He learned that the starlings he observed roosting in Stonehenge are called in Welsh 'birds of the Druids'—which is untrue—and in a digression remembers a starling that could speak Greek.[5] The classical references to the Druids are copied out, and he transcribes a letter from his distant cousin, Henry Vaughan, on traditional Bardic learning: it contains a story about a shepherd who became a Bard after seeing in

[1] MS. Aubrey 13, f. 183.
[2] R. Higden, *Polychronicon*, tr. J. de Trevisa, 1482, f. lx.
[3] MS. Gen. Top. 24, f. 25.
[4] ibid., f. 31.   [5] ibid., f. 100.

a dream a young man carrying a hawk and whistling in several measures. The hawk flew into the dreaming shepherd's mouth, and he was afterwards possessed of the Awen, or 'rapture', and he became a chief Bard.[1] Here Aubrey was quickly collecting small items which were on the verge of being forgotten, and though his jumble of notes contains much that is useless, this was not entirely his fault: he was often at the mercy of his numerous correspondents. His flair for collecting apparently trivial but illuminating details, which gives so much vitality to his *Brief Lives*, does not show here, but his attitude to this miscellaneous material may perhaps be hinted at in his comments on a local tradition about Stonehenge. He had heard that Stonehenge harboured no birds, toads, nor snakes, but he accounts for the mysterious force that repelled these creatures by remarking that there was no shelter for birds there, and no water for toads, while snakes do not like open country.[2]

In 1692 his theory received further, if qualified, support from his correspondence with Dr. Garden, the Professor of Divinity at Aberdeen. Dr. Garden told Aubrey that, according to local traditions in Scotland, stone circles were places of worship and sacrifice in pagan times. This, of course, echoes Hector Boece, and much the same can be said about their being called 'chapels' in Dr. Garden's day. When he adds that according to local tradition, their priests had caused earth to be brought to these circles in order to make the land fertile, this is a piece of folklore which is quite consistent with what had in fact happened. The upshot of this correspondence was that while Dr. Garden had found no tradition which specifically connected stone circles with the Druids, Aubrey was satisfied that according to tradition they had been places of worship. Some thought that the 'Drounich' to whom they had belonged were Picts; Garden thought that the word

[1] ibid., f. 112. [2] ibid., f. 89.

alluded to the Druids.[1] This was his personal opinion,
but Aubrey valued Garden's testimony and judgement,
and he reasonably assumed, in the light of the then available evidence, that he had adequate proof that they had
been built by the Druids.

The time had come for him to publish. While gathering
material for 'Templa Druidum', he had also interested
himself in studies of other antiquities, and 'Templa
Druidum', with three appendices—'A Review of Stonehenge', 'Mantissa de Religione & Moribus Druidum',
and 'An Apparatus of the Bards'—thus became the first
of four parts of *Monumenta Britannica*. But Aubrey's
Proposals for Printing Monumenta Britannica, 1693, failed
to interest a sufficient number of suscribers in his two
volumes in folio. 'Templa Druidum' still remains in
manuscript, and during his lifetime his theories found
their way into print only through the remarks of others.
They are mentioned a few times in the 1695 edition of
Britannia—a most influential work which over the years
would keep Aubrey's name before the eighteenth-century
reader, even if in Gibson's list of theories on the origin
of Stonehenge, Aubrey's 'a Temple of the Druids' is
given only the second place.[2] In William Nicholson's
English Historical Library, 1696, the author remarks of
Stonehenge: 'Mr. *Aubrey* and others think they can
evidently proof 'tis *British*.'[3] But Aubrey had met and
impressed John Toland at Oxford, and Roger Gale's
transcript of the manuscript of 'Templa Druidum' was
shown to William Stukeley, who in turn copied out some
portions of Aubrey's text.

As the basis of these authors' ideas on the Druids,
Aubrey's contention that the Druids had built Stonehenge
was soon widely circulated. He would certainly have
disassociated himself from the use they made of 'Templa

[1] MS. Gen. Top, 24, ff. 119 ff.
[2] op. cit., pp. 636–7.   [3] op. cit., pp. 65–66.

Druidum', but time was to do this for him, and long after
the opinions of Toland and Stukeley had counted for anything, Aubrey's theory was still accepted on its own merits.
'DRUIDS. *See* CELTIC RACES: STONEHENGE',
says an entry for 1902 in a subject index of the books in
the library of the British Museum,[1] and if today only the
more kindly archaeologist concedes that the Druids may
have held ceremonies at a Stonehenge raised by the hands
of others, Aubrey's principal conclusions are still un-
shaken. Firmly committed to the theory that Stonehenge
and Avebury were temples of the Britons, he named their
'Founders' with a relative diffidence, and this also comes
out in the remarkable way in which he spoke of the
Druids. Nearly everyone who has written of them at any
length has written of Druids of his own making, and this
can be said not only of Drayton, Pope, Carte, and Stukeley, for example, but also of distinguished modern
scholars. It was with an air of detachment that Aubrey,
who spent twenty years with them, handled the Druids
like counters, and he left them just as he had found them.

Six years after Aubrey's death a young Scot published
his own remarks on megalithic remains, and on the face
of it, Aubrey's theory was vindicated. *A Description of the
Western Isles of Scotland* was published in 1703, and
Martin Martin, who purported to hand on a number of
genuine traditions about the Druids, called the great
stone circle at 'Classerniss', or Callernish, a temple of the
Druids. An ingenuous person who found eighteenth-
century polish rather slippery, his obvious awkwardness
must have disarmed his contemporaries' possible sus-
picions about his good faith. Even though his text does
not make good the promise of the title-page, which offers
readers an account of 'The Ancient and Modern
Government, Religion and Customs of the Inhabitants,
particularly of their Druids', the book was welcome:

[1] *Subject Index for 1881–1900*, 1902.

new information on the Druids had for some time been
difficult to come by. Martin's book was to give considerable support to the growing conviction of antiquaries that
the Druids had built Stonehenge.

In the most matter-of-fact way, Martin says that before
battle the Chief Druid would harangue the army with the
'Brosnichiy Kah', an oration in which he cited ancestral
valour and dispelled fear.[1] Every family had a Chief Druid
who foretold the future and 'decided all Causes Civil and
Ecclesiatical'. These remarks might be referred to a
slightly garbled version of Caesar for confirmation, but
Martin quickly introduces some very novel topics.
'Beltin', he says, was the day in May on which took place
'the custom practised by the *Druids* in the Isles, of ex-
tinguishing all the Fires in the Parish until the Tithes
were paid'.[2] Malefactors were burnt between two fires:
from this tradition he accounted for the origin of the
proverb: '*He is between two fires of Bel.*'[3]

He records a few practices of the Druids which, he
alleges, had survived the disappearance of Druidism
itself. The Orators, for example, had long continued to
keep pedigrees, and in order to compose their satires
they would retire and place a stone over their stomachs
and a plaid over their heads: 'indeed they furnish such
a Stile from this dark Cell, as is understood by very few'.[4]
This is reminiscent, in a rather distorted fashion, of what
is known of a practice of the medieval Irish Bardic
schools,[5] but what he says of the *locus classicus* shows that
in one verifiable instance his testimony is unreliable:
'*Caesar* says that they Worshipped a Deity under the name
of *Taramis*, or *Taran*, which in *Welsh* signifies Thunder.'
He also thought that the Druids 'wrought in the Night
Time, and rested all Day'.[6] His appeal to Caesar makes it

[1] op. cit., p. 104.   [2] loc. cit.
[3] ibid., p. 105.   [4] ibid., pp. 115 ff.
[5] See Robin Flower, *The Irish Tradition*, Oxford, 1947, pp. 95–96.
[6] op. cit., p. 105.

difficult to accept the parts of his description which cannot be verified, but, as it has been said, he writes in so guileless a manner that he gives the impression that he had faithfully reproduced only what he had been told. He was, after all, in an exceptionally favourable position for gathering traditions: the district was remote, the inhabitants had kept up old customs, and the Druids were not yet widely thought of as the builders of stone circles. His readers must therefore have been particularly interested in his remarks on the great monument at 'Classerniss':

I enquir'd of the Inhabitants what Tradition they had from their Ancestors concerning these Stones? and they told me, it was a place appointed for Worship in the time of Heathenism, and that the Chief *Druid* or Priest stood near the big Stone in the center.[1]

The classical descriptions of the Druids had become hackneyed; the classics had been carefully searched for the least hint which could throw some further light on Druidism; conjectures on the subject had multiplied. Then, after the passing of so many centuries, one hears of the Druids again, not from a text, but from a human voice.

Did Martin here record a genuine local tradition? The more cautious of his readers might well have wondered whether the inhabitants had actually mentioned 'the Chief *Druid*', for, as Aubrey's correspondence with Dr. Garden shows, the Scottish antiquaries were keeping a very sharp watch for anything which might have the least bearing on the Druids, and they had found no local tradition of any connexion between the Druids and megalithic remains. Though Martin's bibliography does not mention Gibson's edition of *Britannia*, he might have heard of Aubrey's theories at second hand: as it has been seen, Aubrey's ideas were being freely discussed in 1696. Martin's bibliography includes Boece, and Boece had

---

[1] ibid., p. 9.

paid much attention to these 'wise Clerkis'. In James
Wallace's *Isles of Orkney*, 1693, Martin would have read
of two stone circles in the Orkneys which were locally
regarded as having been 'High-Places in the *Pagan Times*,
whereon Sacrifices were offered'.[1] It is possible that Boece
and Wallace may have suggested to him that these sacrificers were Druids. Those of Martin's readers who quoted
him, however, were evidently satisfied that Martin was
recording verbatim just what he had heard.

Martin's book met with a mixed reception: James
Boswell, who does not here mention the Druids, states
that Martin is 'erroneous as to many particulars',[2] and
Lord Molesworth writes in the margin of Toland's copy:
'Your Author is a foolish pretending coxcomb.'[3] Yet
Toland, who also poked fun at Martin, was quite certain
that the other's material was authentic. Martin had a
substantial following and his name is found in the footnotes of a number of antiquarian works of the eighteenth
century. It may be a coincidence, but soon after the publication of *The Western Isles* the men who had eluded
Dr. Garden came at last to the fore. Sir Robert Sibbald
says in 1710 that 'many Vestiges' of Druidism still survived among the country people of the North and the
Isles;[4] by 1726, even the remains of large buildings were
being described as the remains of the Druids.[5] Not everyone, however, believed in this new folklore, and Sir
Walter Scott, for instance, did not think that stone circles
could be 'positively referred to the worship of the
Druids'.[6]

An unpublished commentary on the 'pagan monument'

[1] op. cit., ed. J. Small, Edinburgh, 1883, p. 27.
[2] *Journal of a Tour to the Hebrides*, ed. F. A. Pottle and C. H. Bennett,
1936, p. 3.
[3] See Bodleian shelfmark Gough Scotland 185, p. 92.
[4] *The History of Fife*, Edinburgh, 1710, p. 25.
[5] A. Gordon, *Itinerarium Septentrionale*, 1726, pp. 166 ff.
[6] 'Provincial Antiquities', *Miscellaneous Works*, Edinburgh, 1870, vol.
vii, pp. 14, 15.

at Callernish and its 'Chief *Druid* or Priest' is provided by the author himself. In an undated letter to Edward Lhuyd, who died in 1709, Martin says that its stones were wrongly called 'by some of the vulgar false men or centinels'. He goes on to explain that stones called sentinels are found only on high ground, while 'monuments' are found only on plains,[1] but it sounds as though, after all, local opinion was not unanimous in thinking that it was a temple, still less a temple of the Druids. Lhuyd's own notes on the Highlands mention no traditions of the Druids, and his transcript of 'Dominie Kirkwood's manuscript' on the subject of stone circles shows that they were associated with anyone but the Druids:

Some alledge them to be Burial places of the Giants; others the Giants Finger-Stones w[ch] casten from y[e] Hills. Others, y[e] places where y[e] Culdees conven'd.[2]

On the 9th January 1693/4 Edward Lhuyd wrote from Oxford to John Aubrey: 'One Mr. Tholonne is lately come hither . . . with a design to write an Irish Dictionary and a Dissertation to prove y[e] Irish a Colony of y[e] Gauls.'[3] Later, Aubrey and John Toland met, and compared notes; Aubrey showed him his correspondence with Dr. Garden. Toland carried on his further researches with some zeal, as is shown by his many unacknowledged borrowings from others. As he pointed out, no one had yet interpreted the classical fragments on Druidism who was also well acquainted with Celtic dialects. He knew of a little-touched repository of authentic testimony on Druidism; he thought that he had sufficient acumen to be able to interpret the significance of the mere data which his predecessors had supplied; and finally he intended to put the result of his studies to a use which he

[1] Bodleian MS. Ashmole, 1816, f. 342.
[2] 'A Collection of Highland Rites & Customs', undated: Bodleian MS. Carte 269, f. 12.
[3] MS. Aubrey 12, f. 125.

had very much at heart—the exposure of priestcraft, 'the designed abuse, and reverse of religion'.[1]

The title of Toland's work is misleading: his *History of the Druids* consists in reality of letters to Lord Molesworth, and it is not a history at all. They record his intention to write a definitive work and to 'leave no room for any to write on this subject after me'.[2] The self-confidence he showed in making this assertion is reflected in his own speculations on Druidism and in his bold interpretation of the evidence which Martin and others had supplied; he knew that much Irish material—'which gives such a lustre to this matter'[3]—was still in manuscript. He intended to use it. He died before he could carry out his plans, but his remarks to Lord Molesworth show sufficient evidence that he had studied at least two manuscripts.

He transcribed a Welsh antiquary's notes on the Bards, but Thomas Hearne anticipated their publication by including his own transcript in *A Collection of Curious Discourses* in 1720.[4] The other work to which Toland had access was a manuscript of Geoffrey Keating's *History of Ireland*. Much of this had been translated from the Irish by Dermod O'Connor and published in 1723—three years before Toland's *History*. It is clear, however, that Toland had worked independently of O'Connor; the promised book would certainly have been based on some original research, even if Toland had not looked very far for his material.

It is surprising that O'Connor's version of Keating made so slight an impression on those who were later to write on the Druids. He had a story to tell, and the anecdotes in which the Druids have a part and a setting are not unconnected. 'The second Tribe of the *Tuatha de*

[1] *A New Edition of Toland's History of the Druids*, ed. R. Huddleston, 1814, p. 159. It was first published in 1726.
[2] ibid., p. 79. [3] ibid., p. 65.
[4] op. cit., pp. 126 ff.—'Mr. Jones his Answers to Mr. Tate's Questions'.

Danans were called Dee, that is, *Gods*; these were Druids
or Priests':[1] from them emerge in the course of time the
Druids Trosdane, who was skilled at making antidotes for
venom, Bachrach, who interprets the meaning of the
'Convulsions in Nature' at the Crucifixion, and Maiolo-
geann, who kills King Cormac by magic.[2] Here, the
pattern of the degeneration of the Druids may be traced
until, finally, the Christian confessor inherits the derelict
functions of the earlier priests. But the eighteenth-century
reader obviously preferred the classical pictures of the
Druids, pictures which could be kept safely on the wall.
The Irish Druids are not only relatively exotic, but they
are also individuals; the eighteenth century student of
Druidism seems to have preferred anonymous figures,
and it is significant that Divitiacus was never made anything of, never allowed to step out of the frame.

Toland's version of Keating was more lively than
O'Connor's, and he supplies a few details that are lacking
in the longer and earlier translation. Keating's description
of the Ollamh's wand.is not in O'Connor;[3] Toland noticed
it, and states that it was 'one of the badges of their profession, the rod of Druidism', called the 'Slatnan Druid-
heacht';[4] and these rods of Druidism are 'the white wands'
which Wordsworth's Druids point to the sky in his description, in *The Prelude*, of the Druids on Salisbury
Plain.[5]

Toland had an exuberant fancy. On seeing some Irish-
men jumping over bonfires, he took it to mean that they
were still performing ancient rites of purification.[6] With
a rather pert facility, he found much to improve upon in
his sources, and by giving Martin's description of the

[1] op. cit., p. 48. (Túatha Dé Danann: the peoples of the goddess
Donu.)
[2] ibid., pp. 121, 186, 283.
[3] *The History of Ireland*, tr. P. S. Dinneen, 1909, Bk. II, p. 13.
[4] *Miscellaneous Works*, 1747, vol. i, p. 20.
[5] XIII, ll.345 ff.   [6] op. cit., 1814, p. 126.

temple at Callernish a novel 'explication', he initiated a
new phase of antiquarian speculation on Druidism.
Martin had merely recorded the number of stones he had
seen in the temple. Toland took a closer look at these
numbers: the stones, he declares, symbolized the twelve
signs of the zodiac, the four winds, and the cycle of nine-
teen years on which the calendar of the Druids was based.
He promised that in his proposed book he would prove
that this temple was dedicated to the sun, sea, and winds.[1]
Again, Martin's plan of the temple shows lateral exten-
sions projecting from the circle of stones; Toland called
them 'wings'—wings, that is, in the architectural meaning
of the word.[2] Almost by the association of ideas, he recalled that Erastothenes had said that Apollo's arrow was
kept in a Hyperborean temple made of wings—a winged
temple, in fact. Such a winged temple existed on Skye;
and on this island, Toland says, the tenantry still paid
rents by collecting feathers.[3]

He had much to say, and made little effort to organize
his material. He makes merry with Dickinson's suggestion
that Hercules Ogmius was the title given to Joshua after
he had slain Og the king of Bashan. 'Ogum', he points out,
was a Celtic word, the name of an alphabet in which each
letter was associated with a particular tree, and it was
clear that Hercules Ogmius was a Celt.[4] He gives a new
twist to well-known legends in order to expose the fraudu-
lent practices of the Druids:

the *Fatal Stone* so call'd, on which the supreme kings of Ireland
us'd to be inaugurated . . . was thought to emit a sound under the
rightful candidate (a thing easily managed by the Druids).[5]

A cromlech, he says, was a bowing stone—*crom* meant
'bent' and *lech* meant 'stone':[6] he added associations to
Martin's text where even that author had not found

[1] op. cit., p. 136. [2] loc. cit. [3] ibid., pp. 206–7.
[4] ibid., pp. 82 ff. [5] ibid., p. 150. [6] ibid., p. 143.

Druids. He lists with zeal example after example of invented superstitions of the Druids in order to prove

that no heathen priesthood ever came up to the perfection of the Druidical . . . as having been much better calculated to beget ignorance, and an implicit disposition in the people, no less than to procure power and profit to the priests.[1]

But these heterogeneous items had been collected for another purpose. His attack on Druidism masked a covert assault on the Church of England. He paid little attention to the human sacrifice of the Druids; rather, he preferred to lay more emphasis on more familiar failings, for these could be more easily insinuated into his parallels between Druidism and officially sponsored Christian institutions. It was more to his purpose to say that the Druids embraced Christianity quickly since it was financially profitable. Both Protestants and Catholics still circled cairns, and this, he implies, argues that Druidism and Christianity were equally based on superstition.[2] Such parallels, however, were not particularly provocative, and to give his oblique attack on Christianity more force, he adds that the aim of Druidism was to ensure 'plentiful eating and drinking, and variety of women'.[3]

His book came to the notice of a man who was impressed by Toland's remarks on megaliths, and deeply offended by his attacks on the Druids. William Stukeley started life as a student of law; in 1719 he took his degree of Doctor of Medicine at Cambridge, and practised in London, where he became a Fellow of the Royal Society and secretary of the Society of Antiquaries. In 1730 he became the incumbent of the living at All Hallows at Stamford. A many-sided man, Stukeley wrote extensively on numbers of topics, including *Earthquake in Islamabad, Flute Music, Saxon Burials at Chatteris, Embalming of Mummys, Origin of Cards, Pedigree of Queen Anne from*

[1] ibid., p. 56.   [2] ibid., p. 155.   [3] ibid., p. 200.
811602 D.–I

Noah, Medallic History of the Most Ancient Kings of Britain, Scheme for Repairs to Sinking Pier of Westminster Bridge, Corals, and *Turbinate Water Wheels.*[1]

Stukeley had a long career as a field archaeologist. By 1723 at the latest he came to the conclusion that the megalithic monuments of the British Isles had been erected by the Druids, and thereafter, his obsession with Druidism grew steadily. He signed some of his correspondence as 'Chyndonax, Archdruid', and under this name he dedicated his *Palaeographia Sacra*, 1763, to the Princess Dowager Augusta as 'Velida, Archdruidess of Kew'. A nobleman who invited him to dinner was called 'My Lord Archdruid Bathurst'.[2] The sight of a foxglove reminded him of the Druid's cowl, and he enthuses on the plant's 'great elegance, and duration, gradually aspiring on a noble stem', which made it the favourite of the Druids.[3] When moved to rebuke dignitaries of the Anglican Church for their worldliness, he reproachfully reminded them that they held the title, among others, of Druids:

But God's ambassadors, Druids, prophets, priests, spiritual persons, debase their high office, prostitute the sacred character, in too officiously running after the princes of Moab; in attending their levees: but especially on sabbath days.[4]

The very spontaneity of these utterances hints at the degree to which the Druids filled his thoughts, but his Druids were not the men whom Caesar had described. While no doubt he had his own kind of fondness for them, Stukeley particularly admired the Druids for their Christian orthodoxy, and he was firmly convinced that their teachings were still preserved in those of the Church of England.

[1] See S. Piggott, *William Stukeley*, 1950, pp. 193–200.
[2] Bodleian MS. Eng. misc. e 135 f. 14.
[3] *Palaeographia Sacra*, 1763, p. 15.
[4] ibid., p. 87.

By 1726 he had adopted the beliefs that he was then to hold for the rest of his life, and in his *Commonplace Book* he records what is already the gist of the message of *Stonehenge*, 1740, and *Abury*, 1743:

I went down in the Country intending to pass my days in finishing my studys upon the Druids, for which I had made vast preparations, diving into the tenets, and mysterys of those old philosophical priests of the patriarchal religion; I was surprised to find them so near akin to the Christian doctrin. Pursuing those studys to great length, and becoming enamourd therewith, I was moved to take the Gown.[1]

Three years earlier, he had described the results of his archaeological fieldwork in *Stonehenge*, which formed part of his unpublished *History of the Temples and the Religion of the antient Celts*.[2] He had already copied Gale's transcript of Aubrey's *Monumenta Britannica* in 1718, and he had in the meantime accepted Aubrey's conclusion that the Druids had built Stonehenge. But in that portion of the long manuscript of *Stonehenge* in his handwriting of 1723, there is no mention of the Patriarchal origin of Druidism.

The study of symbolism much appealed to Stukeley, who could swiftly detect intimate relationships between things that were only superficially like each other, who indeed could see farther into a stone than most. At some time before 1723 he had started to speculate on the meanings of Egyptian symbols, and it also occurred to him that the patterns made by the plans of Stonehenge, the Avebury complex, and other prehistoric monuments were huge ideograms. In spite of Caesar's remarks to the contrary, Stukeley thought that the Druids had, after all, used writing, but the page they wrote on was the surface of Britain. 'The Druids', he says, 'in Stonehenge have a

---

[1] *The Family Memoirs of the Rev. William Stukeley, M.D.*, ed. W. C. Lukis (Surtees Soc.), vol. i, 1882, p. 106.
[2] Cardiff Public Libraries MS. 4.253.

little more explicated their doctrine than elsewhere':[1] Stonehenge symbolized 'unformed matter which has an innate appetite or capacity to receive forms'.[2] Druid doctrine, expressed as it was in hieroglyphs, and which in 1726 was to be 'near akin to the Christian', was in 1723 'much the same as that of the Ægyptians'.[3] Their buildings as well had much in common, but this is not to say that he had confused Karnak with Carnac; he went back to a far earlier age to find a point of contact between the Druids and the architects of Egypt:

tis probable hermes trismegistus made his first temples of stones and obiliscs like ours before arts in the settled kingdom of Egypt rose to a considerable height and particularly that of architecture, so our druids followed still the most simple manner learnt from their master.[4]

Between 1723 and 1726 he revised his views on the Egyptian inspiration of Stonehenge, and thereafter he discovered that he had a surprise for the deists, and that he might extol the Anglican Church as the custodian of pure Patriarchal teaching untainted by Rome and without even 'the Mosaic dispensation, as a veil, intervening'.[5] Precisely what led him to change his mind is now unknown, but he left behind him a brief record of the moments at which the change was taking place. Between the leaves of the manuscript of *Stonehenge* of 1723 there is a loose sheet of paper on which is written an index and a note, 'Belongs to B.IV', in a later handwriting. Beneath the index the dawn of a surmise has its memorial in a scribbled 'the Druids of the patriarchal religion?' After that, the earlier version of *Stonehenge* was scrapped, and its Egyptian symbolism then reappeared in a modified and subordinate form in the work of 1740.

Stonehenge and *Avebury*, though published separately,

---

[1] Cardiff Public Libraries MS.4.253, p. 109.   [2] ibid., p. 106.
[3] ibid., p. 109.   [4] loc. cit.   [5] *Stonehenge*, 1740, sig. (a) v.

are parts of a larger study which was never completed. Their arguments are complicated. Stukeley sometimes writes as though he were a man who speaks and accompanies his remarks with gestures which have no apparent relevance to his subject, but who is being annoyed by a small fly. In order to follow Stukeley it is helpful to know that he was not only discussing the Druids but skirmishing with a *fashionable and audacious* enemy, deism. Toland was the original pest who provoked him, and in *Stonehenge* the foes of the priesthood were having their own arguments turned against them. The deists claimed that if the tenets of Holy Writ were wholly and self-sufficiently reasonable, and that if the unaided efforts of the reason could efficiently demonstrate the truth of religion, the conception of revelation was redundant.[1] The attendant nuances of their theory, however, hit their contemporaries like bricks, and they rightly answered that the deists wished 'under the cover of a zeal for religion, to attack Revelation'.[2] To eighteenth-century defenders of the faith, the deists must have seemed rather sly; Toland, for example, covertly assailed the Church of England by attacking the Druids. Stukeley, for his part, counter-attacked by replying that the Druids believed in revelation and in the Trinity, that they were quite capable of the subtlest ratiocination, and that the Church of England still preserved their teachings. He rightly declared that he intended to combat the deists from 'a quarter they least expect'.[3]

He had already done an immense amount of work on the sites of Stonehenge and Avebury, where he had taken thousands of measurements. He had wrested from the stones the secret of their builders' unit of measurement,

[1] See Matthew Tindal, *Christianity as Old as the Creation*, 1730, p. 199.
[2] Holograph comment of flyleaf of Bodleian shelfmark Godw. Pamph. 390.
[3] *Family Memoirs*, vol. i, 1882, p. 221.

the 'Druids' cubit'.[1] Accurate plans of the sites were now
to hand. He could now put the result of his industry to
use. But the very brilliance that he had shown in creating
his own equipment to solve archaeological problems was
then to turn against him. He had a special aptitude for
discovering similarities between things which have little
in common with each other, but when he came to theorize
on Druidism he detected significant affinities between
things which have nothing in common. He had a passion
for symbolism as the Hermetic philosophers understood
the word, but Stukeley's symbolism was a very subjective
matter, and he had no difficulty in reading into his symbols just what he wanted to see in them. Again, he was
addicted to metaphysical speculation; and though he
developed his ideas lucidly, he illustrated his principles
with particular instances to which they simply do not
apply. Further, since *Stonehenge* and *Abury* were merely
two sections of a work on Patriarchal Christianity, they
bear a relationship to a project which was never realized,
and their arguments were therefore not as straightforward
as they might have been in a more complete and self-
contained study. In addition, as it will be seen in passing,
he dabbled in etymology.

In 1740, with the publication of *Stonehenge A Temple
Restor'd to the British Druids*, the first steps were taken
to present what was to be 'an intire work' on Patriarchal
Christianity which, according to his plans in 1740, was
to include 'I. *An intire system of chronology from the
creation to the* Exodus'; 'II . . . *a delineation of the first
and patriarchal religion*' to show '*that the first religion was
no other than Christianity, the Mosaic dispensation, as a veil,
intervening*'; 'III. *Of the mysteries of the ancients, one of
the first deviations from true religion, to idolatry*'; 'IV. . . .
on the hieroglyphic learning of the ancients'; 'V. *The patriarchal history, particularly of* Abraham, *is largely pursu'd*;

[1] S. Piggott, op. cit., pp. 106 ff.

and the deduction of the Phoenician *colony into the Island of* Britain, *about or soon after his time; whence the origin of the* Druids, *of their Religion and writing; they brought the patriarchal Religion along with them, and some knowledge of symbols or hieroglyphics, like those of the ancient* Egyptians; *they had the notion and expectation of the Messiah, and of the time of the year when he was to be born, of his office and death'*; 'VI. *Of the Temples of the Druids in* Britain'; VII. *'Of the celebrated Stonehenge.'*[1]

Stukeley's message is conveniently summarized in this prospectus. His Druids came to Britain with the Phoenicians about whom Bochart had extensively written. Their leader was Hercules, and though Stukeley did not follow the road taken by the Celtic dynasts of Annius and by the Cimbri, he was nevertheless impressed by what the editor of Berosus had said about Noah. He took the other's euhemerism to even greater lengths, and Stukeley's Noah thus became Agroverus, Agrotes, Epigeus, Ouranos, and Titan; by his wife Ge, or Titea, or Vesta, Noah had Shem, Magus, Mithras, and Dis.[2] Believing that all men had once shared the same faith, Stukeley thought like Theophilus Gale that classical mythology preserved important elements of this religion, and he promoted the opinions of a number of authors who were not primarily interested in the Druids in order to support his own arguments. But it was principally on his interpretation of the patterns made by the plans and prospects of prehistoric remains that he based his exposition of the tenets of the Druids.

In the course of his surveys he observed that there were three kinds of 'temples'. There were temples which were simple circles of stones. A second class, 'with the form of a snake annext, as that of *Abury*, I shall call serpentine temples, or *Dracontia*'. The ancients, he points out, would 'analogize the form of the divine being', and

[1] op. cit., sig. (a) ff.
[2] *Abury*, 1743, p. 65.

by this means they produc'd a most effectual prophylact, as they
thought, which could not fail of drawing down the blessings of
divine providence upon that place and country, as it were, by
sympathy and similitude.[1]

Such a symbol was 'the sensible sign of an intellectual
idea'.[2] The Avebury complex also contained the third,
or winged, type of temple:

The whole figure is the circle, snake, and wings. By this they
meant to picture out, as well as they could, the nature of the
divinity. The circle meant the supreme fountain of all being,
the father; the serpent, that divine emanation from him which
was called the son; the wings imported that other divine emanation from them which was called the spirit, the *anima mundi*.[3]

The Druids revered the serpent for its mysterious egg,
and Stukeley also admired the snake for its beauty, its
godlike motion, its prudence. The sloughing of its skin
was a 'fit emblem of his resurrection from the dead'.[4]
Further, the snake and serpent symbol was used by both
Egyptians and Chinese, and it was a symbol for deity
among the Greeks.[5]

The symbolism of Avebury, then, conveyed a message,
an ancient message. But was it a Christian message? He
then attempted to answer this question by 'A metaphysical
disquisition upon the nature of the deity', showing how
the Druids, by the use of reason, might arrive at 'the
knowledge of a divine emanation or person'. This 'disquisition' was in the nature of a reply to Tindal's contention that it was possible to argue from such self-evident
premises as the Divine attributes of power and goodness,
and thus to found religious belief on pure reason. Stukeley
was here trying to show that the Druids were more than
a match for the deists at this kind of reasoning. Briefly,
his argument was that God could not be idle, and there-

---

[1] *Abury*, 1743, p. 9.   [2] ibid., p. 56.
[3] ibid., p. 54.   [4] ibid., p. 61.   [5] ibid., p. 78.

fore had to act. Stukeley here refers to the 'torpor' of
God; this use of the word suggests that the passage was
inspired by John Ray's metaphysical speculations: 'It
is not likely that Eternal Life shall be a torpid and unac-
tive state.'[1] 'The highest act of goodness which is possible',
Stukeley goes on to say, 'is the production of his like, the
act of filiation.' Thus Stukeley argued that the Druids
knew, in principle, of the 'divine emanation', of the
Nativity. He claims that the Druids might arrive at this
conclusion by reasoning, though

whether they would think in this manner *ex priori* I cannot say;
but that they did so think, we can need no weightier an argument
than the operose work of *Abury* before us.[2]

His metaphysical disquisitions, then, were founded on
his analysis of the symbolism of the Avebury complex,
the 'serpentine temple' with its head, coil, and tail. Yet
Stukeley has rightly been charged with a 'grave and
deliberate falsification' of his plan of the 'temple' on
Overton Hill: he had originally drawn it as a circle of
stones, but he changed the circle into an oval in order to
make it look more like a snake's head.[3] It is clear what he
had in mind, for he states that he regarded it as an oval
when seen from a distance, and it is true that he would
pay attention to perspective when surveying a site.[4] But
his lame comment on the actual plan of the 'temple', that
it 'consisted of two concentric ovals not much different
from circles', hardly exculpates him.[5]

Stukeley was self-deluded: not an uncommon state of
affairs, but in his case it is patent. His tampering with his
evidence, however, was a wilful act, and in consequence

[1] *The Wisdom of God manifested in the Works of Creation*, 4th edn.,
1704, p. 199.
[2] *Abury*, pp. 85–89.
[3] S. Piggott, op. cit., p. 129.
[4] *Abury*, p. 101.
[5] ibid., p. 32. His drawing shows the ratio of the longest and shortest
diameters as 7:6.

it might be asked whether he sincerely believed that the Druids were what he said they were. Yet it does not necessarily follow that he was hypocritical in his beliefs: the nature of his arguments in *Stonehenge* and *Abury* allow a distinction to be drawn between his firm conviction that the Druids were the heirs of the Patriarchs and the methods by means of which he tried to prove it, for his arguments were guided—with the help of his subdued and compliant mythology and etymology—towards a so-to-speak foregone conclusion. In one way or another, Stukeley was determined to demonstrate to others the truth of something which was evident to him.

To look at the beginning, end, and middle of his writings on the Druids: in a revealing passage from an early manuscript which may not have been meant for publication, he writes

Often when I have been in stonehenge have I been rapt up in Jacob's soliloquy, how dreadful is this place this is no other than the house of God and this is the gate of heaven.[1]

Later, he came to the conclusion that the Druids had brought the Patriarchal teaching to Britain. He was not alone in holding this belief; during the eighteenth century it did not clash with some widely held notions about antiquity, and if it may be likened to a mirage, it also had its own kind of credibility. Stukeley, however, had ambitious aims. He wanted to show, with the aid of what he thought was the equivalent of documentary proof, that his megaliths were so to speak formulations of Christian doctrine. It was between his response to the atmosphere of Stonehenge and his conclusion that the Anglican Church still taught the earliest Christianity that Stukeley found himself in difficulties with a weaker link than most in his chain of reasoning. Even so, Stukeley evidently did not think that this chain was broken when

[1] Cardiff Public Libraries MS. 4.253, p. 101.

he falsified his plan of the stone circle, for he relied very heavily on an elaborate argument to show that Overton Hill had on it a temple with a serpent's head.

The local name for the south ridge of Overton Hill was, he states, the 'Hakpen'. Phut the son of Cham—who was therefore Noah's grandson—was also called Apollo, who was also known as Python. He had planted the country round Parnassus. Stephanus Byzantinus says that the original name of Parnassus was Larnassus. But L, Stukeley observes, is not a radical in this word: it was therefore Harnassus. 'Har' meant 'headland', and 'nahas' meant 'serpent'. Parnassus was therefore, to restore the original meaning of the word, 'the Headland of the Snake'. Similarly, the name 'Hakpen' yielded the same meaning: 'Hak' came from the Hebrew 'Ochim', or 'serpents', and 'pen' is 'head' in 'British'. Pausanias, Stukeley points out, significantly mentions a like space 'fenc'd round with select stones which the Thebans call the snake's head'.[1]

Yet Stukeley's handling of etymologies and mythology was not entirely capricious, and in this case he was following a precedent, an already established method of showing how one name had evolved out of another. Bishop Richard Cumberland, wishing to show how the name of Osiris had grown out of Mizraim, had traced the stages of its transition by stating that Mizraim was the plural of Misor; since M was a 'Servile Letter', the original root was Isor. When the Greek termination is added, this produces Isiris. Thus only one further letter has to be changed in order to produce Osiris.[2] This method was, of course, not generally approved of, and William Webb calls it 'a chemical process',[3] but by Stukeley's standards it was valid.

So much for the serpent temples; it remained for Stukeley to interpret the third type, the *circus alatus*,

[1] *Abury*, pp. 67 ff.   [2] H. Street, *Leaves from Eusebius*, 1842, p. 55.
[3] *An Analysis of the History of Ireland*, Dublin, 1791, p. 54.

symbol of 'the *spirit pervading the universe*'. This was
based on a shape similar to that of the Egyptian symbol
'Cneph'. Claiming to find the etymology of this word in
the Hebrew 'ganaph', to fly, Stukeley says that it was like
the Aegis of Pallas, that 'great prophylactic hierogramm',
and he adds that Medusa's head was the same symbol,
but the 'delicate greeks new drest it'. The Greeks, he
complains, had 'improved the symbolical way of writing
. . . to that monstrous pitch, as to produce what we call
by the general name of mythology', and among other
things they had turned Cneph into Neptune by combining
it with 'Dunia', the Hebrew for circle, thus producing a
word which meant 'the winged circle'. This, Stukeley
claims, was the symbol of the spirit of God moving on the
face of the waters. He points out that the idea was anciently
known in Britain: a winged temple on the banks of the
Humber at Barrow had both fresh and salt water flowing
below it—'an agreeable picture of the sacred hieroglyphic'.[1]

From Stukeley's arguments, it may be inferred that the
Druids believed in revelation, and that they were also
capable of reasoning very acutely. The deists were
answered. But the deists had attacked the doctrine of the
Trinity, and to refute them once again, Stukeley claims
that the Druids also had their trinity of Hesus, Belenus
and Taranis. He describes a Druid grove with an oak in
the form of a *Tau* cross, with the names of the Druid
trinity inscribed thereon: the right branch of the tree
symbolized Hesus, the supreme God, the left Belenus,
or the son, and the trunk was the symbol of Taranis, the
equivalent of Thoth, Thor, 'Lord of the Air', the Spirit.[2]

He probably came across the suggestion that the Druids
had venerated the Trinity in Henry Bunting's *Itinerarium
et Chronicon Ecclesiasticum Totius Sacrae Scripturae*,

---

[1] *Abury*, pp. 92 ff.
[2] ibid., p. 99. See also G. Higgins, *The Celtic Druids*, 1827, p. 130,
and Cardiff Public Libraries MS. 2.370, f. 30.

1597:[1] apart from his notions on the Church of England and his analysis of the symbolism of prehistoric 'hieroglyphics', there is little that is entirely original in Stukeley on the Druids. Even his fondness for parallels and coincidences has a root in Henry Rowlands's maxims for archaeologists: 'Agreement and congruity of make, position, and peculiar circumstances, generally betoken identity of use and practice.'[2] Emending, dovetailing, amplifying, answering back, adapting, Stukeley made use of material gathered from several sources.

The ideas of others affected, but without deflecting, the tenor of his discourse, and he handled them adroitly. In presenting his case, it seemed to him that he had struck a nice balance between rationalism and enthusiasm. He wrote calmly and firmly: he would be, he says, 'as temperate as possible in multiplying conjectures'. He once relaxed and offered his readers a 'novel entertainment', never suspecting that they might be more bewildered than pleased when he put before them a 'Paraphrastic Translation of Horace: In Bacchum', in which he showed 'the Bacchus of the Heathen to be the Jehovah of the Jews'. Horace's nymphs are called Miriam's 'female throng', and like parallels are developed throughout the poem.[3] Stukeley here was not smuggling out some desperate message from some segregated cell of the imagination. Henry Reynolds had thought that Bacchus was Noah, and Bochart had found a Hebrew derivation for the name in 'Bar-chus', or 'son of Chus'.[4] Dickinson called Bacchus 'Deus excelsus',[5] and Theophilus Gale, in discussing the cry '*Io Bacchus*', pointed out that *Io* 'contracts of God's essential name'.[6] Stukeley had merely followed these signposts for part of his own journey, and

[1] op. cit., tom. I, p. 182.   [2] *Mona*, 1723, p. 51.
[3] *Palaeographia Sacra*, 1736, pp. 2 ff.
[4] *Geographia Sacra*, Caen 1646, p. 13.
[5] *Delphi Phoenicizantes*, Oxford, 1655, sig. M.
[6] *Court of Gentiles*, Pt. I, Oxford, 1669, p. 131.

what he saw so clearly was that Horace had written a hymn which in no way conflicted with its Anglican counterparts. When Stukeley referred to his paraphrase of Horace as a 'novel entertainment' he did not think that the idea was itself odd: rather, he was pleased that he could illustrate his main thesis in so unexpected a fashion.

Stukeley had a following, though it was selective and preferred some of his pages to others, and in the tributes that were paid to him there is little reference, for instance, to his thoughts on the route along which the original teachings of the Old Testament had been carried to this country: presumably that taken by Gomer and the Cimbri was more plausible. As for his attack on the deists, Stukeley never quite made contact with the enemy. His superiors in the Church evidently concealed their feelings at his roundabout way of demonstrating its orthodoxy, and he was addressed and spoken of with courtesy and indulgence. His claim that the Anglican Church was the heir of the Druids was waived by silence, but an echo of his ideas on the subject will be found in *A Descriptive Account of the Old Serpentine Temple of the Druids at Avebury*, which went into its second edition in 1801. The author, a curate, had been at Avebury for ten years, and in his spare time he would count the stones, watch with dismay their removal by farmers, and chat with welcome visitors to the parish. At Avebury there had been a long tradition of worship, but the changes were not all for the better, and the poet looks back with envy:

> Methinks I see the venerable Arch-druid
> Proceeding to the Fane, Thousands attend
> His solemn footsteps, or uncover'd crowd
> Along the spacious Way, and prostrate bow,
> As slow along he passes; See! he ascends
> The higher Cove, with awful silence
> The Multitude attentive stand without
> The Dike; within, his Brethren their allotted

Places take:—Each Word proceeding from his lips
The greedy Crowd devour; on him alone
All eyes are fix'd, all ears arrested wait,
His Word the only Truth, his Wishes Law.
But, shall I turn my eyes, and see, perhaps,
The lowly Pastor, on the sacred day
Urging his way to Church, the staring Group
Scarcely regard his coming, an hasty nod,
If any, meets his view, while every Child
Will lisp, ' 'tis but the Curate'; in the aisle
He draws the surplice on, the buzzing noise,
Within, without, is heard.—The Service opens,—
And to and fro in churchyard or the porch
The gauking Clowns are loitering: now clash
The gates, or screak the doors, the voices now
Are heard without, and drown his humbler tone.[1]

The Reverend William Borlase, who was presented to
the living of Ludgvan in Cornwall in 1722, found himself
like Henry Rowlands surrounded by the remains of the
Druids. Though like others he assumed that Genesis
threw some light on conditions in prehistoric Britain, he
saw nothing to link the Druids with the Patriarchs. In his
Observations on the Antiquities of Cornwall, 1754, he pronounced at length on the significant parallels he had found
between the Druids and the ancient Persians, but he
called Druidism a superstition. It had preserved none of
the antediluvian wisdom. It was a manifestation of the
general decay of primeval religion, and he dealt with the
earliest ages of mankind in a sharply critical fashion,
saying that under the Druids, instead of the 'true fear of
God, a gloomy kind of awe, and religious dread, consisting
of Grove, and Night-worship was introduced . . .' and
'instead of the true purity of heart, a false superficial
purity was introduced, consisting of ablutions, white
garments, outward sprinklings, and lustrations'.[2]

[1] C. Lucas, op. cit., Marlborough, 1801, p. 24.
[2] *Observations*, Oxford, 1754, pp. 60–61.

The Celts, he said, were undoubtedly of great antiquity. The many Hebrew roots in Celtic showed that they
left the East soon after the collapse of Babel, before the
language had much altered. It may be noticed that instead
of mentioning Noah, Borlase claims that Druidism started
in ignominious circumstances. He concluded that the
universality of the doctrine of the immortality of the soul,
of the practice of consecrating places for worship and
propitiation by sacrifice, and of erecting monuments to
the dead show that mankind held these ideas in common
before the dispersal.[1]

The oldest monuments were those which bore the
greatest resemblance to those of the East, 'as being nearest
of kin to that simplicity with which monuments were
erected in the first ages of mankind'.[2] It appeared, then,
that in the first ages, Druidism acknowledged 'the same
Deities, us'd the same worship and therefore must have
the same original as the customs, tenets, rites and superstition of other gentile nations'.[3] Borlase, it is clear, could
agree with the thesis of the original unity of religion, but
he had little use for its hidden secrets; he also found that
what subsequently happened could be traced to the same
root: 'one and the same principle, Polytheism, will produce a multitude of corruptions in all places'. Grove
worship—the result of worshipping the sun—produced
debauchery, and moon worship produced prostitution.
Where others had cited the general prevalence of human
sacrifice in order to excuse the Druids, Borlase mentioned
it to attack the entire ancient world.[4]

Alert and inquisitive, Borlase had a fondness for analogy
which sometimes gave his comments a narrow but lively
channel. An acute if occasionally erratic student of the
classical historians, he saw in their work patterns of ideas
that gave his interpretation of hackneyed material a

[1] *Observations*, pp. 17 ff.   [2] ibid., p. 24.
[3] ibid., p. 54.   [4] ibid., pp. 62 ff.

welcome freshness. In his description of the dolmen, which he calls 'a large Orbicular stone, supported by two Stones', he observes:

One thing is remarkable, which is, that these Tolmens rest on supporters, and do not touch the Earth, agreeably to an establish'd principle of the Druids, who thought every thing that was sacred, would be profan'd by touching the ground, and therefore order'd it so, as that these Deities should rest upon the pure Rock, and not be defil'd by touching the common Earth.[1]

The surprising reference to a hitherto unheard of 'establish'd principle' is explained in his notes: the Druids, he points out, took care never to allow mistletoe, 'selago' and 'samolus', and the 'anguinum' to touch the ground when they were being gathered. Though a dolmen does not illustrate his 'establish'd principle', there is some perception in his reading of Pliny. But more characteristic of his methods is the way in which he identifies the idols that were scattered over Cornwall, the weathered rocks which he claims had been roughly carved by Druids in order to fashion crude images. There were, he explains, many places called Trefadarn in the county, and this he translates as the place or house of Saturn, to whom human sacrifices were offered; he thinks it significant that the Druids' 'age' or cycle corresponded to one revolution of the planet Saturn.[2] The Druids, he also says, 'had a rite of cursing . . . and as every thing among them was to be done in a solemn manner, they turn'd this religious mystick round towards the left, in order to pour out their imprecations more efficaciously'. This suggestion of witchcraft and widdershins was not pure invention: Borlase had seen something in Tacitus which had escaped other readers. The historian writes: 'Druidaequae circum, preces diras sublatis ad caelum manibus fundentes' ('All around, the Druids, lifting their hands to heaven and

[1] ibid., pp. 166–7.   [2] ibid., p. 164.
811602 D.–K

pouring forth dreadful imprecations'), and Borlase gave
the word 'circum' in this context a novel meaning.[1] Since
Druidism was 'a branch of the first general, and most
ancient idolatry', he argues that 'purification by washing
and sprinklings', so well attested to in other religions, was
one of the rites of the Druids: the declivities which he
had noticed on the tops of great stones must therefore
have been rock basins which held water for lustrations.[2]

Borlase's perspicuity was akin to that of the modern
archaeologist, for in his own way he was prepared to
justify his assumptions as well as his conclusions, and
when he left analogy alone, his comments were not particularly fanciful. The absence of a roof at Stonehenge has
inspired some subtle speculation on the metaphysics of
the Druids; Borlase merely suggests that in an edifice
where sacrificial fires were constantly lit, a roof would be
undesirable.[3] He disagreed with those who thought that
cromlechs were Druid altars, for in his opinion the 'lintels'
were so thin that they would crumble if heat were applied
to them. Further, he adds, their size made it unlikely that
they were used as such by the Druids; to illustrate the
point, he says:

There is also one in Pembrokeshire, of which the middle, or covering Stone, is eighteen feet high, and nine feet broad towards the
Base; now what kind of Altar could this be?[4]

Stonehenge, he declares positively, could not have been
built by the Romans. 'Let it only be considered', he urges,
'that the Roman ways cross and mangle these Circles (as
see Tab, IV. of Dr Stukeley's Stonehenge), and it can
never be true, that the Romans would errect and dis-
figure the same, and their own works.'[5] Intermittently,
but more and more cogently, the stones were giving
evidence for themselves.

[1] *Observations*, p. 127.
[2] ibid., p. 238. Gibson speaks of a duct in the top of a large stone in
Britannia, 1695, col. 638.
[3] ibid., p. 185.   [4] ibid., p. 213.   [5] ibid., p. 186.

When reading Martin Martin's description of the temple at Callernish in *The Western Isles* he carefully studied the accompanying plan and took the trouble to count the stones. There were, he remarks, fifty-two stones in the avenue and circle, and twelve of them standing apart. But what might be deduced from this, he says, 'I submit to the learned'.[1] This suggestion of a calendar anticipates yet another interpretation of the significance of the arrangement of megaliths, one so striking that it finally resulted in the convergence today of the costumed figures who, in the darkness on Salisbury Plain, gather at Stonehenge at the summer solstice to honour the rising sun.

Some twenty years after the publication of Borlase's *Observations*, a Dr. John Smith travelled about Wiltshire following his occupation:

As an innoculator of the Small-Pox, I rented a convenient house in the parish of Boscombe, Wilts, by consent of those who called themselves the principal inhabitants: which I had no sooner done, but was prevented by every act of violence, in pursuit of my business, by these malevolent villains, NOYSEY WRETCHES! who actually partake of the nature and quality of that Brute they daily feed on.[2]

To divert himself, he went to Stonehenge and with the help of an ephemeris surveyed the site. There, in the stone then called the Friar's Heel, he discovered 'the Key, or Gnomon, by means of which I propose to unlock this Ambre, or Repository of Druidical secrets'.[3] He claimed that the Archdruid by standing against his stall and looking over certain stones—as though they were gunsights—would find himself looking along an axis which pointed at the midsummer sunrise. He also observed that if the thirty stones he counted in the outer circle were multiplied by twelve, the number into which the zodiac was divided,

[1] ibid., p. 190.
[2] *Choir Gaur*, Salisbury, 1771, sig. A.3.   [3] ibid., p. 63.

this would give the number of days in a lunar year. The stones in the inner circle provided a guide to the phases of the moon, thus enabling the Druids to cut mistletoe at the proper time. Choir Gaur, the earlier name of Stonehenge, was derived from the Celtic word for church and the Irish for a 'he-goat': it therefore alluded to the sun's leaving Capricorn for the winter solstice.[1]

Smith's observations later inspired the theory that the orientation of Stonehenge had left a permanent record of the date of its erection, for owing to the fact that the Earth's axis is not constant in its relationship to the sun and the midsummer sunrise slowly moves to the East along the horizon's rim in the course of a cycle lasting about forty thousand years, a fixed and accurate sighting of any midsummer sunrise leaves behind it evidence of the date at which it was made. Thinking that 'the axis of Stonehenge was aligned accurately by its builders upon the point of midsummer sunrise at the date of its construction', Sir Norman Lockyer made observations in 1901 which led him to conclude that the date of the construction of the sarsen circle at Stonehenge was 1680 B.C., plus or minus two hundred years. His 'basic assumptions', however, 'are archaeologically unsound', and though his figures, emended by more accurate astronomical tables, give approximately the date of the first arrangement of the earliest structure at Stonehenge, this is a coincidence. As for Smith's own theories, they still survive in the admission that the second and third stages of Stonehenge's construction 'were aligned *roughly and approximately* on the midsummer sunrise. This is a fact; but it does not tell us either why or when it was done.'[2] The Gnonom was indeed turned, but as far as the Druids were concerned, the Ambre was empty.

In the early years of the nineteenth century the

[1] *Choir Gaur*, pp. 60 ff.
[2] R. J. C. Atkinson, *Stonehenge*, 1960, pp. 94 ff.

antiquary as such disappeared, taking with him his pictures in the fire of the Druid, and the word archaeology then began to acquire its modern meaning. Yet earlier literature on the Druids carries with it its own lessons, and in so far as the Euclidean procession of his thoughts is towards demonstrably valid conclusions, the archaeologist today still shares the anxieties of Henry Rowlands and checks the impulses of William Stukeley. But the Druid did not only attract the attention of men of a speculative turn of mind, of the antiquary, the philologist, the student of early Welsh poetry: he touched the imagination of the lover of Nature as well, and the fancy of those who sometimes indulged in a taste for the sensational; and the defender of Mona's coastline also became a patriot who in spirit was to defend far wider boundaries.

VI

THE FEARLESS BRITISH PRIESTS

IN *The Decline and Fall of the Roman Empire*, Gibbon says of the Roman conquest of Britain: 'Neither the fortitude of Caractacus, nor the despair of Boadicea, nor the fanaticism of the Druids, could avert the slavery of the country.'[1] The Druids had little appeal for Gibbon, and his half-reproachful acknowledgement of their patriotism also accommodates a stricture on their calling. But the historian was speaking of a Druid unknown to history.

The notion that the Druids were militant patriots probably arises from Caesar's comment that their teaching supplied 'the greatest incentive to valour', and it is supported by Tacitus's description of a brief battle in which the Druids died facing their enemy. That the Bards sang their songs in praise of heroes undoubtedly made this notion attractive to poets; possibly it was also recalled that the precepts of the Druids which are quoted by Diogenes Laertius end with an adjuration to maintain 'manly behaviour'. The classical historians, however, say nothing about the Druids as prominent leaders of resistance to the Romans. Exempt from conscription and the payment of war-taxes, and famous for their ability to stop intertribal hostilities simply by appearing on the battle-field, the Druids are seen by Lucan as men who flourish in times of peace; Caesar also notes that they generally 'hold themselves aloof from war'.

As it is evident from the reports of Pomponius Mela and Valerius Maximus on some effects of the Druids'

[1] *Decline and Fall of the Roman Empire*, ed. J. B. Bury, 1913, vol. i, p. 4.

teaching, Caesar's comment touched on only part of the significance which it had for the Gauls. In the only description in the classics of a battle in which the Druids clashed with the Romans, they are not shown fighting in defence of Britain, for by this time much of the country was occupied by invaders who had landed twenty years before; the Druids were, in fact, sought out and cornered on Mona when Suetonius Paulinus took his forces into North Wales. In the context of Diogenes Laertius's summary of their ethical precepts, the Druids' adjuration sets not so much value on physical courage as on the manliness of which valour is a part. When the imperial measures against Druidism grew harsher, the Druids are described not as conspiring against Rome, but as living in remote forests where they still followed their principal interests. Nevertheless, they were regarded by poets, antiquaries, and historians as zealous defenders of the island's freedom.

Unlike the majority of the inhabitants of Gaul and Britain, the Druids never came to terms with Rome. On Mona they gave shelter to fugitives, but if theirs was a defiant isolation, there is no documentary evidence to show that they took an active part in the defence of Britain, nor is there any record of their being involved in risings against the Romans. In Gaul, they did not resist Caesar, and it is nowhere plainly implied that in Britain they were sufficiently important to be attacked for political reasons. Suetonius, by massacring the Druids, was implementing normal Roman policy towards Druidism. If his purpose in seeking them out is primarily thought of as a measure taken against a vital threat to Roman security, this complicates interpretation of the known facts, for gossip in Rome itself attributed his action to a jealous desire to emulate another general's success, and Tacitus defends the massacre not on the grounds of political expedience, but by reminding his readers that the Druids

had sacrificed men. In Britain in A.D. 60 the centre of
disaffection was elsewhere, and when Suetonius faced the
Druids he had turned his back on political realities.

   If the historian was not justified in thinking of the
Druids as fanatical defenders of British freedom, the
poets had some excuse for portraying them as patriots.
Roman bureaucracy attempted to control all departments
of a subjugated people's life but the Druids refused to be
assimilated. It was their intransigence that impressed
Drayton and the poets who followed him, and while the
Druids had their own reasons for wishing to keep the
Romans at arm's length, the image of the Druid as patriot
was an approximation which was consistent with their attitude to Rome and with their Bards' praise of heroes. They
then kept an unsleeping watch over the island's liberty:

> What native Genius taught the Britons bold
> To guard their sea-girt cliffs of old?
> 'Twas Liberty: she taught disdain
> Of death, of Rome's imperial chain.
> She bade the Druid harp to battle sound.[1]

They may have been massacred on Mona, but true to
their teaching on the immortality of the soul, in spirit
they still guarded the shores of Britain. A fresh wave of
invaders arrived, and when 'crafty *Hengist* with his
Saxons came', William Diaper shows him deceiving the
unsuspecting Britons easily enough:

> But Druids taught by Nymphs repining sate
> And saw the coming Ills, and knew Britannia's fate.[2]

Thomas Maurice, in the course of a poem in praise of a
farm yielding 'a considerable traffick in Bacon', also
describes how, at the coming of Hengist and Horsa

> In vain, the Druid smites the magic String.[3]

[1] Thomas Warton, *Poetical Works*, 1802, p. 125.
[2] W. Diaper, *Dryades*, 1713, p. 32.
[3] *Netherby*, Oxford, 1776, p. 10.

Even King Alfred, in Robert Holmes's *Alfred*, has mysterious communings with the Bards—whom Holmes
regarded as the only respectable branch of the Druids—
and they inspire him in his struggle against the Danes.[1]
And when, in Gilbert West's *Masque*, King Edward III
instituted the Order of the Garter, the spirits of the
Druids were still watchful in 1349:

> Sage Druids, Britain's old philosophers,
> Who still enamour'd of their ancient haunts
> Unseen of mortal eyes they hover round.

They ask why they have been called from 'our sequester'd
vallies', but when they learn the purpose of the gathering,
the Chief Druid declares:

> Our country's weal, ev'n from the bliss of heav'n
> Can charm down patriot souls.

They thoroughly approve of the institution of the new
Order, the 'plan of glory' which will turn Britain's
'monarchs into judges of mankind'.[2] In 1758 the Druids
were called on to support the foreign policy of Pitt the
Elder. The 'Genuine BRITISH MUSE, Nurs'd amidst
the *Druids* old' is begged to rouse the Bards and bid them
leave inglorious themes:

> But when War's tremendous roar
> Shakes the Isle from Shore to Shore,
> Every Bard of purer fire
> *Tyrtaeus*-like should grasp the Lyre.[3]

But the conception of the Druids as fervent patriots
placed the poets who cherished it in a dilemma; oddly
enough, it was not recognized as such until Pope wrote
his notes for *Brutus*.[4] '*In* Britain', Thomas Hearne re-

---

[1] op. cit., Oxford, 1778, p. 12.
[2] Gilbert West, *The Songs . . . of the Masque called The Institution
of the Garter*, 1771, pp. 3 ff.
[3] W. Whitehead, *Verses to the People of England*, 1758, pp. 10, 11.
[4] British Museum MS. Egerton 1950, ff. 4–5 v.

marks, '*the State of* learning *was* very mean *and* incon-
siderable (*being* ingrossed *by the* Druids, *who had themselves originally received it from the* East) '*till the Arrival
of the* Romans':[1] here the antiquary plainly regards the
Roman invasion not as an act of aggression but as the
prelude to civilization. Edmond Howes, on the other hand,
calls Caesar's invasion a part of the 'vniuersall vexation
of the world at this time for sinne . . . prophesied by
Daniel', and in adding that it made 'a free people seruile,
tributary and vassall', he makes an equally pertinent
comment on the Roman conquest.[2] Admiration of the
patriotic Druids further complicated these deceptively
simple issues: to see them solely as the champions of
liberty was in effect to condone their resistance to the
bearers of civilization. Two points of view had somehow
to be reconciled, and Pope went to some pains in his
rough draft of the plot of *Brutus* to show the Romans in a
favourable light without at the same time discrediting his
Druids. William Mason's sympathy with both sides im-
perilled the unity of *Caractacus*, but it was precisely at
the point of greatest danger that he skilfully brought his
drama to a convincing and satisfying conclusion. William
Cowper took Alexander's sword to the problem, but his
solution—on the face of it so one-sided that it conceals a
plausible reconciliation of the two points of view—was so
drastic that rarely again, after 'Boadicea', were the Druids
thought of as the champions of liberty.

His work on the *Iliad* had caused Pope to postpone the
writing of an epic poem of his own. Its 'matter', he said
shortly before his death in 1744, was 'digested & prepar'd',[3] and the manuscript of *Brutus* bears this out. A
collection of notes and jottings, it shows how sensitive
he was to the implications of apparently trifling details.

[1] John Leland, *Collectanea*, ed. T. Hearne, Oxford, 1715, vol. vi, p. 59.
[2] 'An Historical Preface', J. Stow, *Annales*, 1631, sig. 4 v.
[3] Edward Young, *Complete Works*, Edinburgh, 1854, vol. i, p. 569.

In particular, it shows how greatly he had modified his mental picture of the Druids in order to give them a more discreet role in his story, one that would not throw his plot out of balance, for long before his thoughts were to turn to *Brutus*, Pope wrote of the Druids as the priests of heroic barbarians, men who would have hurled themselves on Brutus's landing parties. In *The Temple of Fame*, which was written in 1711, he describes an ornate building whose four gates face the four quarters '*as an Intimation that all Nations of the Earth may alike be receiv'd into it*'.[1] The west wall is in a Greek style, and

> Of *Gothic* Structure was the Northern Side,
> O'er-wrought with Ornaments of barb'rous Pride.
> There huge Colosses rose, with Trophies crown'd,
> And Runic Characters were grav'd around:
> There sate *Zamolxis* with erected Eyes,
> And *Odin* here in *mimick* Trances dies.
> There, on rude Iron Columns smear'd with Blood,
> The horrid Forms of *Scythian* Heroes stood,
> *Druids* and *Bards* (their once loud Harps unstrung)
> And Youths that dy'd to be by Poets sung.[2]

These Druids and Bards who rub shoulders with Scythian heroes—or who themselves may be Scythians, for the place of the verb 'stood' in the sentence suggests such a reading—owe their association to Pope's interest in Sir William Temple's essay 'Of Heroick Virtue'. Here Temple says that the Getae whom Herodotus describes were Goths of Scythian descent, and he thinks that the Goths owed their indifference to death to the teachings of Zamolxis or of Odin.[3] Herodotus says that the Getae thought they were immortal, and that after death they would go to Salmoxis, and he diffidently adds that it was also thought that this Salmoxis was a slave of Pythagoras who after regaining his freedom taught that the soul did

[1] op. cit., 1715, p. 47.   [2] ibid., pp. 15–16.
[3] *Works*, 1720, vol. i, pp. 212 ff.

not die.[1] Pope, in his notes to his poem, refers to this latter story; Temple does not mention it. (Hippolytus says that the same Zamolxis who was the slave of Pythagoras taught the doctrine of the immortality of the soul to the Druids, and his name thus links the Druids with the Getae;[2] neither Pope nor Temple, however, alludes to this.) Temple draws the Druids and Goths together by quoting Lucan on the Druids' beliefs. Lucan says:

they teach that the soul does not descend to the silent land of Erebus and the sunless realms of Dis below, but that the same breath still governs the limbs in a different scene. If this tale be true, death is but a point in the midst of continuous life.

He then exclaims: 'Truly the nations on whom the Pole star looks down are happily deceived: for they are free from that king of terrors, the fear of death.'[3] These last lines are quoted by Temple as though they applied to the Goths, and he also says that the Goths believed 'That Death was but the entrance into another Life', which is in effect what Lucan says of the Druids.[4] Pope certainly knew that this sentence from Lucan alluded to the teaching of the Druids, and he may therefore have thought that the Druids were the priests of these Scythians and Goths who lived beneath the Bear. In his notes to the 1715 edition of *The Temple* he says 'Zamolxis *was the Disciple of* Pythagoras, *who taught the Immortality of the Soul to the* Scythians', thus echoing Temple rather than Herodotus, and he explains that Odin was the hero of the Goths. Immediately following his mention of the Scythians and Goths, he writes: '*Pag.* 16. *ver.* 5. Druids *and* Bards, *&c. These were the Priests and Poets of those People, so celebrated for their savage Virtue.*'[5] This suggests

---

[1] IV, 93–95. He speaks only of the Getae, and not of Goths and Scythians.

[2] *Refutation*, I, xxv.

[3] *Civil War*, I, II. 454 ff., tr. J. D. Duff, Cambridge, Mass., 1951, p. 37.

[4] op. cit., p. 215.   [5] op. cit., p. 49.

that Pope was indeed under the impression that the Druids were '*Scythian* Heroes'. If so, this was a simple error; but whether he discriminated between the Druids and Scythians or not, the Druids he admits to his temple are celebrities not because they are philosophers, but because they are the priests and poets of '*heroick Barbarians*' who would rush '*to certain Death in the Prospect of an After-Life, and for the Glory of a Song from their Bards in Praise of their Actions*'.[1] But the Druids on iron columns smeared with blood were not the men whom Brutus met.

The hero of Pope's epic sets sail from Greece. 'Benevolence' was the 'First Principle and Predominant in Brutus', and when after passing the Pillars of Hercules he reaches the Canaries, he refuses to settle them: they were uninhabited and therefore afforded him no opportunity 'of extending Benevolence, & polishing & teaching Nations'. On reaching Britain, it was his intention to see that the 'whole island submits to good government wch ends ye Poem'. The stage is thus set for a clash with the Druids. None, however, takes place. 'Druids, meets y^m at an Altar of Turf in an open place offering fruits & flowers to Heaven',[2] Pope notes. Far from resisting the invader, they evidently recognize the purity of his motives and welcome him. Pope also keeps the future well in mind. If Brutus succeeds in his mission, a model government will be set up; why, then, should Caesar invade Britain? But while Pope had no intention of branding the Romans as aggressors, he also makes it clear that the Druids will not resist this new encroachment on their liberty. They are still seen as patriots, but these patriots take a very long view of the island's welfare, and when as soothsayers they look into the future, what they see there meets with their

[1] loc. cit.
[2] Possibly taken from Elias Schedius, *De Diis Germanis*, Halle, 1728, p. 528, a reprint of the 1648 edition published in Amsterdam and mentioned in E. Bohun's translation of D. Wheare's *Method of Reading Histories*, 1694, p. 137.

approval. Pope wonders what happened to Brutus's re-
forms, and his hero therefore hears a

Prophecy delivered to him by an Old Druid that the Britons
shou'd Degenerate in an Age or Two, and Relapse . . . but that
they shou'd be Redeemd again by a Descendant of his Family out
of Italy, Julius Caesar, under whose Successors they shou'd be
Repolishd.

The climate of Britain 'is described to be free from the
effeminacy of the southern climes, and the savageness of
the northern'.[1] The inhabitants are correspondingly temperate: they are uncorrupted in their manners and need
only the Arts and government to make them happy, and
they 'are represented worshippers of the sun and fire', a
harmless form of belief which without calling for severe
correction leaves room for improvement, and they are of
'good and gentle dispositions, having no bloody sacrifices
among them'. If they have a fault, this is possibly a lack
of moral fibre, for Brutus intends to introduce 'Love of
Liberty . . . the Martial Spirit, and other Moral Virtues'
to the islanders.

These Druids, then, do not sacrifice men, place little
value on liberty, and certainly preach no doctrine which
inculcates bravery. On closer acquaintance, Brutus 'finds
yᵉ Druids Doctrine tending to a nobler Religion'. Since
the inhabitants of Britain are to be modelled on 'yᵉ best
Savages', it would be pointless, as Pope recognizes, to
subdue an already docile people, and incongruous for him
to land fingering his sword. But Pope had indeed up to a
point digested his plot, and he managed to justify Brutus's
intervention by noting that some parts of Britain were
suffering from 'False Policies', which he identifies as
Superstition, Anarchy, and Tyranny; accordingly, Brutus
is given an opportunity of exhibiting the virtues he

[1] See also Owen Ruffhead, *Life of Alexander Pope*, 1769, pp. 418–19,
where an outline of *Brutus* is given.

possessed in such abundance, but which needed tactful handling if they were not to harm both his own reputation and the inoffensive Britons.

Here, however, Pope's scheme breaks down. The peaceful priests are clearly called Druids, but it is Mona that is 'under *Superstition* gover[ne]d by Priests', and these anonymous superstitious priests are, as his reference to Tacitus shows, none other than the Druids themselves.[1] Pope does not indicate how he would have resolved this contradiction. As it is, by representing his invasions as visitations which would have polished and repolished the ancient Britons, Pope so far managed to manoeuvre the details of his plot into a consistent whole, and *Brutus* should not have antagonized either the patriot or the admirer of Rome. Nevertheless, he had completely falsified everything that the classical historians say about the Druids, and it was left to William Mason to show what could be done by keeping more closely to the classics.

As the embodiment of the spirit of 'Independency', the Druids of *Caractacus* have a central part in the most outstanding heroic drama of the eighteenth century. Mason found his theme in his reading of the histories of Caesar and Tacitus, and though he championed the cause of the defeated, he was not at all hostile to Rome. But while he was sympathetic to both the invaders and the defenders of Britain, unlike Pope, he made no attempt to reconcile the enemies. This unresolved conflict of values might, at a most critical moment, have caused the play to collapse. Mason's handling of the situation, however, turned a real danger to advantage. As a writer of verse, he was aware of his limitations, but his was a poet's feeling for the relationship between the different parts of his drama.

He drew heavily on his sources not only for material which gave credibility and local colour to his scenes, but also for details which helped to develop his plot. When,

[1] British Museum MS. Egerton 1950, ff. 4–5 v.

for example, Caractacus invoked the gods, this permitted
Mason to introduce a rocking-stone from Gibson's
edition of Camden, and at the same time, his wish to display a rocking-stone called for an appropriate crisis in
which it might be resorted to. Though he was interested in
what British and Continental antiquaries had said about
the Druids, he went only slightly farther afield than the
classics for his inspiration, for Thomas Gray kept him as
closely as he could to the established authorities.[1] Gray,
whom Mason frequently consulted during the writing
of *Caractacus*, had no particular feelings about the Druids:
Druidism was for him merely 'the Druid-Stock . . .
those half-dozen of old fancies, that are known to have
made their system'.[2] But he was interested in the proprie-
ties, and of the classical descriptions of the Druids he
points out:

they leave an unbounded liberty to pure imagination, & fiction
(our favourite provinces) where no Critick can molest, or Antiquary gainsay us. & yet (to please me) these Fictions must have
some affinity, some seeming connection with that little we really
know of the character & customs of the People.[3]

Mason accepted this in principle, and he greatly profited
from Gray's constant supervision. Some very fanciful
passages were burned in the other's 'Critical Colossus'.[4]
Caractacus has no Patriarchs or Cabbalistic nuances, but
the sword Trifingus slipped past the censor.

Briefly, the plot is based on the efforts of a Roman
general to capture the great British chief who had
countered the military tactics of the Romans with new
and disconcerting measures. When the play opens,
Caractacus is thinking of retiring from the world in order

---

[1] He knew J. G. Keysler's *Antiquitates Selectae*, Hanover, 1720, and
he possessed Simon Pelloutier's *Histoire des Celtes*, La Haye, 1740, but
this edition says very little about the Druids.

[2] *The Correspondence of Thomas Gray*, ed. P. Toynbee and L. Whibley,
1935, vol. ii, p. 568.

[3] ibid., pp. 528–9 (Sept. 1757).   [4] ibid., pp. 467, 554, 607.

to become a Druid, but events are moving too swiftly for
the ageing soldier, and he feels that he has to return to the
battlefield once more. The play ends with his capture.
The growing threat of the Roman advance gives Caractacus's struggles to find his proper course of action a background of tension and urgency. A minor plot, unfolding
its story between Caractacus's clashes with grave and
censurious Druids, gives the play momentum and helps
to carry the drama towards its climax.

Mason turns his limitations to advantage: though his
characters are rather thin, this only concentrates the attention on the play's theme. His Druids give the drama its
philosophical background, and in their firmness Caractacus's resolution is deeply rooted. The Bards with their
songs enrich the play's emotional atmosphere, and Thomas
Arne's music represents 'by corresponding sounds and
rhythms' such themes as the spirits of Snowdon 'lamenting the approaching fall of Mona' and the souls of
'departed Druids personified by the harp, interceding to
avert the impending danger'.[1] In effect, then, Mason takes
his material as he finds it in the classics, and builds up the
play with an inspired competence.

The Bards enter and purify the ground with vervaine.
The Druids are approached by Caractacus, who wishes to
abdicate, and they advise him:

> Prince,
> Bethink thee well, if ought on this vain earth
> Still holds too firm an union with thy soul,
> Estranging it from peace.[2]

Sage and weighty, they accuse Caractacus of being at war
with himself, and wish

> that Resignation meek,
> That dove-ey'd Peace, handmaid of Sanctity,
> Approach'd this altar with thee.[3]

[1] J. S. Shedlock in *The Musical Times*, 1 Feb. 1899, p. 89.
[2] W. Mason, *Poems*, 1764, p. 190.   [3] ibid., p. 195.

Instead of these, they notice that he is accompanied by

> gaunt Revenge, ensanguin'd Slaughter,
> And mad Ambition, clinging to thy Soul.[1]

The Bards are then ordered to purge his unhallowed bosom, and they start the ode 'Mona on Snowdon calls'.

The Roman advance on Mona causes Caractacus to reconsider his decision to go into retirement as a Druid. The soothsayers are consulted, and the rocking-stone warns Caractacus not to return to the field. Nevertheless, he is defiant, and the Druid is forced to reassert his authority:

> Thou art a King, a sov'reign o'er frail Man;
> I am a Druid, a servant of the Gods.[2]

But even this austere Druid changes his attitude to the apparently rebellious chieftain when Caractacus declares that he is going to fight for Liberty. The atmosphere changes at once. Caractacus and the Druids are reconciled. The chorus declaims that

> Destiny and Death,
> Thron'd in a burning car, the thund'ring wheels
> Arm'd with gigantic scythes of adamant

are drawing near, and the theme of Freedom is then extolled by the Bards. Britain is eulogized, an island that was once mute except for the sound of running water, wind and wolves, that was silent until the coming of the harp. Britain was from the beginning chosen and plucked from the deep as the throne of Freedom. At this point, a traitor is unmasked, and the patriotic sentiments of the Bards are given an even more vehement expression:

CHORUS   Say, thou false one!
    What doom befits the slave, who sells his country?
ELIDURUS   Death, sudden death!
CHORUS   No, ling'ring piece-meal death.[3]

---

[1] *Poems*, 1764, p. 196.   [2] ibid., p. 206.   [3] ibid., pp. 256 ff.

Hasty preparations are made for battle. Lustrations are performed with dew from the May-thorn blossom, and Caractacus is given the sword Trifingus. But the Britons are overcome, and the Romans force the pass. They make their stage entrance, and they are found, after all, to be reasonable people: their general, Aulus Didius, declares

> The Romans fight
> Not to enslave, but humanize the world.[1]

Here, *Caractacus* might have gone on to anticlimax. If Mason had attempted to stress the benefits of the Roman occupation, the Druids, seen in retrospect, would have appeared as obstacles to the progress of civilization, and this would have particularly reflected on their cult of Liberty. But Mason does not compromise. Aulus Didius and Caractacus face each other, and in this final clash between the two leaders Caractacus is at a further disadvantage. He is still defiant; but chilly, laconic, and rather too reasonable, the Roman general carries himself with the bearing of a conqueror who has more than physical force on his side. Nevertheless, Caractacus's outpourings are convincing. Both the battle and logic have gone against him, but if the Roman point of view is given in the general's brief remarks its own kind of justification, Caractacus's appeal is, on the other hand, to yet another category, as it were, of human values. The deadlock is complete. The Roman case, resting as it did on imposition, was quite incompatible with that of Caractacus and the Druids. By refusing to foist an arbitrary solution of the dilemma on the play, Mason's acceptance of the deadlock tacitly applauds the intransigence of the Druids and the chieftain who has their blessing. In this last scene the catastrophe which overwhelms the Britons only reaffirms and strengthens the theme of the play.

The poet may not have been conscious of this problem,

[1] ibid., p. 281.

but if justice were to be done to Rome as well, it spontaneously posed itself when the Druids were presented as
patriots. In 'Boadicea' Cowper solved it partly by ignoring
distracting notions about liberty: as a prophet of empire,
his Druid set no absolute value on national independence.
Cowper then confronted imperial Rome not so much
with a Britain on the defensive as with a Druid's vision
of an even greater empire. Partisan as he was, Cowper
was not indifferent to Roman civilization, but in his scales
the Roman virtues were by implication transferred to the
opposite pan: his verdict thus came down heavily on the
British side. With great spirit he opens the poem:

> When the British warrior queen,
> Bleeding from the Roman rods,
> Sought, with an indignant mien,
> Counsel of her country's gods,
>
> Sage beneath the spreading oak
> Sat the Druid, hoary chief;
> Ev'ry burning word he spoke
> Full of rage and full of grief.

Others were reluctant to condemn an invader whom
Milton and Hearne, for instance, clearly regarded as a
benefactor, but Cowper was untroubled by hesitations,
and his Druid replies:

> Rome shall perish—write that word
> In the blood that she has spilt;
> Perish, hopeless and abhor'd,
> Deep in ruin as in guilt.

Since, in Cowper's view, the Roman Empire and its
values were to be superseded by the greater British
Empire, he felt no clash of loyalties. Looking into the
future, his Druid tells Boadicea:

> Then the progeny that springs
> From the forests of our land,

> Arm'd with thunder, clad with wings,
> Shall a wider world command.
>
> Regions Caesar never knew
> Thy posterity shall sway,
> Where his eagles never flew,
> None invincible as they.

Cowper thus consistently saw Rome solely as an aggressor, and when the queen returned to the field, she denounced not only the mercenaries who had provoked the Iceni into rising but Rome itself:

> Ruffians, pitiless as proud,
> Heav'n awaits the vengeance due;
> Empire is on us bestow'd,
> Shame and ruin wait for you.

Though the poem was inspired by Cowper's indignation at the story of Boadicea, it is also based on a passage in Tacitus's *Histories* in which the burning of the Capitol is described. The writer adds: 'The Druids declared with the prophetic utterance of an idle superstition that this . . . portended universal empire for the Transalpine nations.'[1] Cowper's Druid replies with the answer of history, and he meets the historian's scorn of his fellow Druids with a quiet irony that is concealed by the poem's vigorous diction.

After 'Boadicea', the poets apparently felt that the picture of the Druid as the defender of Britain's shores was out of date, and that the new Druid had been adequately portrayed. Cowper had few imitators. The phrase 'the Empire on which the sun never sets' is implicit in the Druids' prophecy in James Mylne's *The British Kings*, where 'old seers' foretell

> that Britain's pow'r shall stride
> From the sun's rising to his setting place,[2]

[1] IV, 54.
[2] *Poems*, Edinburgh, 1790, p. 238.

and William Mickle's Druids wear chaplets of red, white, and blue flowers.[1] The poets, incidentally, were not alone in thinking of the Druids as patriots: when John Fletcher's *Bonduca* was revived in 1706, Henry Purcell added the following libretto to the original text:

> 1ST DRUID. (Alto.) Hear us great, great Rugwith, hear!
> 2ND DRUID. (Tenor.) Defend, de . . . fend thy British Isle.
> 1ST DRUID. (Alto.) Revive our hopes, disperse our fears.
> 1ST DRUIDESS. (Soprano.) Nor let thine Al . . . tars be the Roman's spoil.
> 3RD DRUID. (Bass.) De . . . scend in Chariots of e . . . therial flame . . . and touch, and touch the Al . . . tars you de . . . fend.[2]

A later composer who once interpreted 'the mysteries of the Druids'[3] in his music is better known for his 'Land of Hope and Glory'. But the figure of the Druid as the guardian of British liberty made only sporadic appearances, and if he was never generally accepted as a patriotic symbol, this may well have been because his name, honoured as it was as a philosopher's and as that of the pupil of Nature, also carried with it sombre associations.

[1] *Poems*, 1794, p. 101.
[2] J. Genest, *Some Account of the English Stage*, Bath, vol. ii, 1832, p. 339; Henry Purcell, *The Music in the Tragedy of Bonduca*, 1842, pp. 6–7.
[3] *Grove's History of Music*, ed. H. C. Colles, 1927, vol. ii, p. 151.

VII

THE POMP OF BLOODY ALTARS

I N the course of a facetious description of a journey into seventeenth-century Wales, William Richards remarks:

The Study of *Wizzardism* hath also been famous amongst them; one Goodman *Druis* was well accomplished in that kind of Learning; hence formerly a *Wizard* was stil'd a Drue. This fellow (they tell us) was the *School-master* of Pythagoras, into whose Breech ('tis said) he infus'd by Birch the Opinions of *Transmigration*. He was dextrous at a Fortune, and *Old-Dog* at Augury; and the only thing we dislike in him, is, he sacrific'd Men, and so divin'd by Butchery.[1]

This was probably the opinion of many an admirer of the Druid. Few were so frank as to admit that 'the only thing we dislike in him, is, he sacrific'd Men, and so divin'd by Butchery': the human sacrifice was a provocative subject to bring up, and likely to arouse high feelings.

Their oblations and sacrifices in these their dayes of blindnesse, were performed with such inhumane and ungodly fashions, with the effusion and shedding of human bloud in that lamentable and cruell manner, as is too straunge to be reported:[2]

this, from Richard Lynche's *Travels of Noah into Europe*, 1601, was to the writer's contemporaries the language in which murder was described, and the Jesuit Father Galtruchius, plainly calling the sacrifice murder, declares that the Druids had a 'Spirit of cruelty, natural to the Devils of Hell'.[3] Yet it was by no means universally

---

[1] *Wallography*, 1682, p. 96.   [2] op. cit., sig. G iii v.
[3] *Poetical Histories*, tr. M. d'Assigni, 1671, Bk. III, p. 32.

execrated, and Pedro Mexia, speaking for those who could see two sides to a question, both took the Druids to task and admired their sacrifice 'as truely declaring admirable Religion, and meruailous perswasion of the Gods might and power'.[1] This accorded with the views of the author of the long romance *Astrea*, 1657–8, which is set in early Gaul and which has for its climax a dramatic description of preparations for a human sacrifice. The hero, Silvander, about to be immolated by the benign Druid Adamas, was saved only because the Druid recognized the youth as his long-lost son. Nevertheless, before the discovery of his identity, Silvander was not at all perturbed: he willingly accepted his fate, and 'protesting, with abundance of alacrity, that the minute of the death, was the sweetest minute of all his life, he opened his brest to receive the blow'.[2]

Between these extremes of condemnation and approval, room was found in which to meet and, as far as possible, disarm hostile criticism of the Druids as sacrificers of men. Among the earliest and most common of methods was the listing of precedents and parallel practices in the ancient world, as though a wide dispersal of odium would make it less obnoxious in particular instances. Selden's artifice was brevity: calling it an error of judgement, he passed hastily on to other matters.[3] Franciscus Irenicus perhaps made an unintentional defence of the Druids with his pungent remark: 'Hi homines mactabant & mortem contempserunt.' As he puts it, the Druids' sacrifice is plausibly related to 'with grand contempt for mortal lot they proclaimed the immortality of the soul'.[4]

It was in sixteenth-century France that the Druids' sacrifices were most vigorously defended, and this without

[1] *Ten Following Books to the Former Treasurie of Ancient and Moderne Times*, 1619, p. 47.
[2] H. d'Urfé, *Astrea*, 1657–8, vol. iii, p. 452.
[3] N. Bacon, *An Historical Discourse*, 1689, p. 2.
[4] F. Irenicus, *Germaniae Exegeseos*, Haguenau, 1518, f. XXIX v.

any suspicion of misanthropy on the one hand, or of apology on the other. Their eulogists then showed an entirely consistent attitude to the Druids. Guillaume Postel, for example, thought that they worshipped 'le Dieu souuerain & impossible de nomer'. He found marked parallels between Druid and Christian doctrine, saying that the Druids' ideas on the future life showed that they thought it would compensate for injustices suffered in this life. Far from trying to avoid any mention of the sacrifice, he boldly brought the subject to the fore in order to support his views. The wicker figure in which men and beasts were burned was in effect, he says, a symbolical affirmation of the Catholic Church's teaching on Purgatory:

ilz enseignoint non seulement que il hauoit enfer & purgatoire, mays que depuys la purge du feu il failloit que les vicieuses ames passassent dedans les bestes aulxquelles en penchant se rendoint plussemblables.[1]

Jean le Fèvre and Noël Taillepied also thought that the Druids' attitude to human life was compatible with the attitude of 'la foy catholique' to 'le vil corps'.[2] In the Hermetic poem *La Galliade*, the Druids are regarded as men who anticipated the Nativity: the sacrifice was a form of prophecy, an anticipation of the coming of the Archetypal Man whose death would redeem the world.[3] Three centuries later, this interpretation was offered, presumably quite independently of *La Galliade*, and more hesitantly, by William Francklin:

this sanguinary immolation, it would seem, was by many understood to be a mystical sacrifice, and a typical representation of the great vicarial sacrifice that was to come.[4]

[1] *L'histoire mémorable des expéditions depuys le déluge*, Paris, 1552, ff. 47 ff.
[2] *Les fleurs et antiquitez des Gaules*, ed. A. de Montaiglon, *Recueil de poésies françoises des 15e et 16e siècles*, Paris, 1858, tom. VIII, p. 187; *Histoire de l'Estat et République des Druides*, Paris, 1585, I, f. 48.
[3] Gui le Fèvre de la Boderie, op. cit., Paris, 1578, f. 53 v.
[4] *Tenets of the Jeynes*, 1827, p. 55.

The same thought occurred to Stukeley: 'their crucifying a man at one of their great Festivals in the temple', he writes in his earlier *Stonehenge*, 'is a wonderful tho' horrid notion of the Sacrifice of the Messiah'. In the published *Stonehenge*, he discarded this interpretation in favour of one which more nearly accorded with his theories on the Druids and the Patriarchs: calling the sacrifice 'a most extravagent form of superstition', he accounts for it by saying that the Druids had misunderstood the story of Abraham and Isaac.[1]

In England, the defence of the Druids was conducted rather diffidently. Aylett Sammes merely observed that the Druids had made their huge wicker figures in commemoration of the Phoenicians, who, themselves large men, became the giants of later legends.[2] William Mason claimed that only the Druids of Gaul sacrificed human beings.[3] John Cleland suavely pointed out that 'the most polished nations in Europe' were still sacrificing men.[4] Pope's Druids brought only fruit and flowers to the altar. A late eighteenth-century archaeologist took practical steps to discount all stories of the Druids' holocausts by heating a fragment of a 'Druids' altar' in a crucible: the stone, he said, quickly turned to powder, and since it could not bear heat, he concluded that there could have been no human sacrifices.[5]

The most effective defence was that offered in *The Misfortunes of Elphin* (1829) by Thomas Love Peacock, who liked little in Druidism and disliked much that he saw in front of him; he shielded the Druids simply by holding up a mirror to magistrates:

These human sacrifices have done much injury to the Druidical character, amongst us, who never practise them in the same way.

[1] Cardiff Public Libraries MS. 4.253, p. 111: *Stonehenge*, 1740, p. 54.
[2] *Britannia Antiqua Illustrata*, 1676, p. 106.
[3] *Works*, 1811, vol. ii, p. 160.
[4] *The Way to Things by Words*, 1776, p. 69.
[5] John Smith, *Choir Gaur*, Salisbury, 1771, p. 68.

They lacked, it must be confessed, some of our light, and also some of our prisons. They lacked some of our light, to enable them to perceive that the act of coming, in great multitudes, with fire and sword, to the remote dwellings of peacable men, with the premeditated design of cutting their throats, ravishing their wives and daughters, killing their children, and appropriating their worldly goods, belongs, not to the department of murder and robbery, but to that of legitimate war, of which all the practitioners are gentlemen, and entitled to be treated like gentlemen. They lacked some of our prisons, in which our philanthropy has provided accommodation for so large a portion of our own people, wherein, if they had left their prisoners alive, they could have kept them from returning to their countrymen, and being at their old tricks again immediately. They would also, perhaps, have found some difficulty in feeding them, from the lack of the country rates, by which the most sensible and amiable part of our nation, the country squires, contrive to coop up, and feed, at the public charge, all who meddle with the wild animals of which they have given themselves the monopoly. But as the Druids could neither lock up their captives, nor trust them at large, the darkness of their intellect could suggest no alternative to the process they adopted, of putting them out of the way, which they did with all the sanctions of religion and law. If one of these old Druids could have slept, like the seven sleepers of Ephesus, and awaked, in the nineteenth century, some fine morning near Newgate, the exhibition of some half-dozen funipendulous forgers might have shocked the tender bowels of his humanity as much as one of his wicker baskets of captives in the flames shocked those of Caesar; and it would, perhaps, have been difficult to convince him that paper credit was not an idol, and one of a more sanguinary character than his Andraste.[1]

The hostile critic of the Druids always had the advantage of being able to take the initiative: it was not necessary for him to defend his attitude to the ritual taking of human life. The Reverend James Foot, in a long poem which exposes 'the Impieties and Folly of Heathenism', advances on the Druids in the confident expectation that

[1] op. cit., ed. R. Garnett, 1891, pp. 67–69.

his readers will endorse all that he has to say. The hero of *Penseroso*, a 'pensive sage', visits

> The drear remains of once pronounc'd a fane
> Fram'd for the Druids' use.

He looks around and appreciates the symbolism of Druid architecture: the fane, he notices, was

> by Heav'n
> Sublimely roof'd.

Giving the Druids their due, he acknowledges that

> some useful truths charm'd in the song
> Of Druid wisdom.

But this reflective approach serves only to contrast with the vigour of his denunciation, and he calls

> their groves
> The bloody shambles of misguided zeal,
> And the vile priests the butch'ring tools of Heav'n.[1]

Still more censurious, even if their hostility shows itself only in brief outbursts, were those to whom the sacrifice was merely one example among others of Druid depravity. Pliny observes that after the Druids had cut down the mistletoe, they would hold a feast. William Borlase takes this to mean that 'after Sacrifice, Luxury and Debauch ensued'.[2] 'However incredible the imputation,' Thomas Maurice says, 'it is not without reason suspected that they proceeded to even more criminal lengths, and finished their horrid sacrifice with a still more horrid banquet';[3] and Jacob des Moulins, after charging them with 'incestuous concubinage', adds that they 'gave specimens of an absurd and impolitic carriage'.[4]

Less indiscriminate in their accusations, but more

---

[1] op. cit., 1771, pp. 161 ff.   [2] *Observations*, p. 61.
[3] *Indian Antiquities*, vol. vi, part 1, 1796, p. 128.
[4] *Antiqua Restaurata*, 1794, pp. 44, 53.

intense, there were those who dwelt on the sacrifice with relish. 'The altars of Druidical worship, which smoaked with the blood of human victims'[1] had an attraction for poets who wished to exploit the artistic possibilities of the ceremony: John Walters frankly admits

> CAMBRIA, I love thy genius bold;
> Thy dreadful rites, and Druids old.[2]

Seen by the light of their holocausts, the Druids became 'the subtle priests with venom'd breath',[3] and Robert Holmes attacks them with even greater energy:

> When rous'd by Mona's bloody-mantled Priest,
> Impatient Homicide, his Druid-crew
> With eyes of madness, watch the midnight spell,
> And drown with deaf'ning yell
> The scream of captives stretch'd in furnace blue.[4]

Consequently, in poems of this kind, including Richard Llwyd's 'Mona', 'where Immolation heap'd the pile', and with its

> Groves where Rome, affrighted, hear'd
> The Druids' oral stores[5]

attention is easily diverted from their subject to their diction.

But the classical descriptions of the sacrifice also made their influence felt in less striking ways. They haunted the very name of the Druids, and the sombre associations which were attached to them and the atmosphere which surrounded them—the atmosphere which was so strongly felt by William Pearce on his walks in their countryside:

> Ye walks of despondence! ye groves! awful vales!
> Where Druids prophetic erst mutter'd their tales—[6]

[1] Richard Warner, *A Second Walk through Wales*, 1800, p. 298.
[2] *Poems*, n.p., 1780, p. 9.
[3] Michael Woodhull, *Poems*, 1772, p. 30.
[4] Robert Holmes, *Alfred*, Oxford, 1778, p. 10.
[5] Richard Llwyd, *Beaumaris Bay*, 1800, p. 21.
[6] *The Haunts of Shakespeare*, 1778, p. 11.

made it impossible to portray the Druids consistently as mere philosophers or lovers of Nature. They are remote not only in time and the forest.

It might be expected that their aloofness, their antiquity, and their Celtic background—not to look too closely at their qualifications—entitled them to a place in Ossian's poetry. A contemporary reviewer of *Fingal*, 1762, remarks the absence of sinister figures from this work, and thus suspects its authenticity: 'the total silence of the poem with regard to the grosser parts of the druidical religion, and the retaining what was more pure and poetic . . . induce a suspicion of more art than simplicity in the poem'.[1] (James Macpherson was, over a decade later, to write of their religion at length; drawing for some of his ideas on Simon Pelloutier's revised edition of his history of the Celts, and reinforcing his arguments with material collected from wide reading in the classics, he showed that the Druids were worshippers of the 'INCOMPREHENSIBLE SOMETHING'.)[2] But though there are no recognizable Druids in *Fingal*, there were Druids on estates which marched with Fingal's. John Smith, the Gaelic scholar, states that he had spent about twelve years collecting the manuscripts which he published in *Galic Antiquities*, 1780. As their editor, he claims that he had found distinct references to Druidism in these poems.[3] There can be no better authority, for he had himself first written the poems in English, and after translating them into Gaelic, he then published the translations as originals, and the originals as translations.

In the context of his prose poems, then, the Druids are called 'the gray sons of other times', and 'the gray-musing son of a rock'. When Sithama says 'We wither as a grass of the mountain' he is identified as a Druid,

[1] *Annual Register*, 1761, p. 278.
[2] *Introduction to the History of Great Britain*, Edinburgh, 1773, pp. 209, 243, 347.
[3] op. cit., Edinburgh, 1780, pp. 127 ff.

because, as Smith points out, the Druids uttered their wisdom in the form of 'enigmatical apophthegms'. The phrase 'enwrapped in meteors they came' seems to be at first sight nothing more than a flamboyant image; it is, however, an allusion to their use of gunpowder, with which, he explains, they intimidated the people in the proximity of their grove near Marseilles.[1] In this amorphous landscape, the Druids are fittingly vague figures, yet even here they are pursued by their reputation, and in 'Dargo the Son of Druivel' they are still ominous:

A SOUND comes by halves to my ear. It is like the voice of a wave that climbs, when it is calm, the distant rock. It is the voice of Struthandorcha's stream, murmuring, deep, in the vale of oaks. In the bosom of its grove is the circle of stones. Dim unfinished forms sigh, within their gray locks, around it. The sons of the feeble hear the sound; and, trembling, shun the awful shadowy spot. 'The haunt of ghosts', they say, 'is there.'[2]

It is surprising to find that Wordsworth, who was much interested in the Druids, was particularly fascinated by their sacrifices. He mentions the Druids more often than any other English poet, though rarely in his best work. He held them in sufficiently high regard to call them 'auxiliars of the Cross',[3] and they were in his thoughts on his walks, when he would sometimes allow his fancy to play round 'Druid stones' and

> Altars for Druid service fit;
> (But where no fire was ever lit,
> Unless the glow-worm to the skies
> Thence offer nightly sacrifice).[4]

He knew of Stukeley's theories: he refers in his poetry to the 'hieroglyphic round' of a stone circle, and to the Druids' knowledge of 'Diluvian truths and patriarchal

---

[1] ibid., pp. 74–75.   [2] ibid., p. 277.
[3] *Ecclesiastical Sonnets*, x.
[4] 'The Pass of Kirkstone', ll.136 ff.

lore'.[1] But unlike Stukeley, he thought that their religion
had degenerated, and this might explain why he both
admired the Druids and indulged in lurid descriptions
of their holocausts.

They also had one interest in common:

> Though in the depths of sunless groves, no more
> The Druid-priest the hallowed oak adore;
> Yet, for the Initiate, rocks and whispering trees
> Do still perform mysterious offices![2]

The romantic suggestion of kinship and continuity is here
made lightly, yet at one time he thought seriously of
picturing himself in *The Prelude* as the heir to the secrets
of the Druids. At Cambridge, Wordsworth found it
difficult to adjust himself to undergraduate life, but in
describing this troubled period, he is not entirely on the
defensive: he wishes to say that Cambridge had its own
shortcomings. There was much that the university could
not teach him. Searching for an image which would be
apt and striking, he dramatizes himself as

> A youthful Druid taught in shady groves
> Primaeval mysteries, a bard elect
> To celebrate in sympathetic verse
> Magnanimous exploits.

Therefore, he asks, why should he grieve

> who was a chosen Son
> Why should he languish with a student's gown
> Depress'd, when would more fitly had been clad
> In vernal green, like an Aspirant youth.

On his second attempt, he tidies his grammar and makes
the imagery more concrete, and he asks why

> aught of self-respecting fear
> Should plague the young Initiate who had seen

[1] *Ecclesiastical Sonnets*, IV.
[2] 'Humanity', ll.7–10.

Thrice sacred mysteries mid Druid groves
Or where grey Temples stood on native Hills?
Why should he droop who fitliest had been clad
Like an Aspirant in cerulean Robes
Adress'd to celebrate with harp and voice
Magnanimous exploits.[1]

It is quite certain that Wordsworth had not thought this of himself, in so many words, at Cambridge. His Druid garb, and the title of Aspirant in this context come from a book which was published a year after he had left Cambridge. His 'vernal green' and 'cerulean Robes' are taken from William Owen's *Heroic Elegies of Llwyarç Hen*, 1792,[2] and by substituting 'cerulean Robes' for 'vernal green', Wordsworth was showing a little harmless vanity: he had promoted himself, on second thoughts, to what Owen calls the highest of the Bardic classes. The portenteous allusion to 'thrice sacred mysteries' may also come from this source. Wordsworth later recognized the intrinsic falsity of this image, and he rightly rejected it. Yet in spite of its incongruity, he had made his point: dissatisfaction is no less powerful because it cannot be described, and the pretentious image which he discarded shows rather touchingly how he had struggled in vain to explain himself.

The allusions to mysteries and to shade in these quotations are significant; in a number of poems in which he mentions the Druids he treats mysteries and the mysterious as though they were synonymous, to go by such phrases as 'that fabric of mysterious form'; 'The mystic ring'; 'Pile of Stonehenge! So proud to hint yet keep /Thy secrets'; 'That mystic round of Druid fame'; 'Where once the savage viewed mysterious fires'; 'Perform mysterious offices'; 'Mysterious rites'; 'Primaeval mysteries'; 'Thrice sacred mysteries'; 'The Druids

---

[1] *The Prelude*, ed. E. de Selincourt, Oxford, 1950, pp. 74–75.
[2] Owen, op. cit., 1792, pp. xxxvii, xli.

811602 D.–M

covertly expressed'.[1] Wordsworth was convinced that
Druidism had its esoteric side, but he also had—to
adapt the title of one of his sonnets—a trepidation of the
Druids, and a weakness for the melodramatic vulgarized
his notion of what is both meant and implied by the word
mysteries. The background of shade and darkness which
attends many of his allusions to the Druids was intended
to supply them with an appropriate setting, but this
emotional local colour was also tinged with the macabre.

This is more evident in his drafts than in his finished
poems; in an early version of *Guilt and Sorrow*, when a
hollow voice cries to a wanderer who comes upon Stonehenge, Wordsworth is obviously assaulting his readers'
feelings:

> 'Fly ere at once the fiends their prey devour
> 'Or grinning, on thy endless tortures scowl
> 'Till very madness seems a mercy to thy soul
>
> 'For oft, at dead of night, when dreadful fire
> 'Unfolds that powerful circle's reddening stones
> 'Mid priests and spectres grim and idols dire,
> 'Far heard the great flame utters human moans.'[2]

In the published version of these lines, the revised passage
shows nothing of this striving after effect, but in writing
of the Druids, Wordsworth quite often felt an impulse
to appeal to what he calls 'coarse sympathies'. A touch
of the sensational attaches itself to his Druids in the first
written of his poems as well as in the last published. In
his *Juvenalia* they roll their eyes and threaten him:

> At noon I hied to gloomy shades
> Religious woods and midnight glades . . .
> And hark! the ringing harp I hear

---

[1] *Guilt and Sorrow*, xv; *Ecclesiastical Sonnets*, iii; *Guilt and Sorrow*,
xiv; *River Duddon*, xvii, l.12; 'Evening Walk', ms.B, l.199, *Poetical
Works*, ed. de Selincourt, vol. i, p. 20; *Humanity*, l.10; *Excursion*, ix,
l.690; *Prelude*, ed. de Selincourt, p. 75; ibid. (1805), xii, l.345.
[2] *Guilt and Sorrow*, xiv; ed. de Selincourt, i, pp. 100–1.

And lo! her druid sons appear.
Why roll on me your glaring eyes?
Why fix on me for sacrifice?[1]

In *The Prelude*, they are the same Druids; only the
presentation is more discreet:

I called on Darkness—but before the word
Was uttered, midnight darkness seemed to take
All objects from my sight; and lo! again
The Desert visible by dismal flames;
It is the sacrificial altar, fed
With living men—how deep the groans! the voice
Of those that crowd the giant wicker thrills
The monumental hillocks.[2]

They thrilled Wordsworth as well; elsewhere he lingers
over the flame that uttered human moans, the 'horrid
shrieks', the groans, and the voices of victims that could be
heard above the sounds of storm and cataract. Curiously
enough, since he was interested in Druid stones, in the
Druids who knew the secrets of Nature, the Druids who
had known the Patriarchs, the Druids who lived in
Drayton's 'darksome groves', and the Druids who waved
Toland's white wands in his vision on Salisbury Plain
of the long-bearded teachers, his only point of contact
with the Druids as they had been described in the original
sources is with the sacrificers of men.

In the nineteenth century, the Druid continued in a
typically unconvincing fashion to meet a demand for
blood and thunder; in the early Victorian theatre, he
became a stage villain. In Thomas Cromwell's tragedy,
The Druid, the play is little more than an extension of the
implications of the stage directions:

*A Circular Area, in the Middle of a thick Grove of Oaks. —Within
the Area a Double Enclosure of vast Pillars of Stone . . . —A
gloomy Twilight over-spreads the Scene. —Thunder.*[3]

[1] 'Vale of Esthwaite', ll.25 ff.
[2] op. cit., XIII, ll.327 ff. [3] op. cit., 1832, p. 1.

This melodramatic treatment of the Druids had long been hackneyed when Harrison Ainsworth reproduced in *Windsor Castle* the kind of writing that had been current a hundred years earlier:

'Nuptials!' echoed Mabel.
'Ay, at that altar,' he cried, pointing to the Druid pile of stones —'there you shall vow yourself to me before terrible witnesses. I shall have no fear that you will break your oath.'[1]

Literature at this level, however, gives no real indication of what must have been more widely felt of the Druids. They had studied secret and sublime things. They were of 'definite account and dignity'. 'The Druids', says Strabo, 'were considered the most just of men'; and had this fairly summed up all that had been said of the priests, philosophers, poets, and judges of the Celts, far more might have been made of the Druid. In his white robes and with his golden sickle he might have displaced in popular fancy the skin-clad Festival of Britain ancient Briton as the representative of this island's prehistoric inhabitants. But the historians had more to say, and it is plain that approval of men who were once called 'revered gods' must be relatively restricted. For, as Diodorus Siculus remarks, 'they practice a strange and incredible custom'.

[1] *Windsor Castle* (1843), Bk. 5, Ch. 3; Collins edn., n.p., n.d., p. 340.

VIII

SAGE BENEATH THE SPREADING OAK

NOTHING is known of the everyday life of the Druids. As they are described in the classics, they are untouched by the commonplace, and none mingle with them on terms of equal ostentation. The centre of interest wherever they appear, they officiate at sacrifices, sit in judgement, and halt armies. For the rest of the time they are in the background, apparently indifferent to the course of current events: 'the innermost groves of far-off forests are your abodes'.

Though, on the evidence supplied by Pomponius Mela, it is possible that the Druids in Gaul had retreated to remote districts only after the Roman conquest, they seemed on the face of it to have 'that enthusiastic Love and Admiration of the Beauties of Nature' which, as a contributor to the eighteenth-century *Monthly Review* observes, 'are generally the concomitants of a virtuous and feeling Mind'.[1] Their veneration of the oak lent plausibility to the assumption that they were lovers of Nature, and it also made them popular with a wider public than the admirers of the picturesque. The oak had almost the status of a national symbol, and its associations then attached themselves to the Druids: Thomas Warton was not the only poet to notice that England's 'future navies' had grown in the Druids' 'oaken bowers'.[2] The interest which they roused as Nature's priests showed itself in many ways. Aubrey records a Star Chamber case of about 1631 in which a man who had felled 'an oake, under which

[1] *Monthly Review*, Dec. 1798, p. 423.
[2] 'On the Marriage of the King', *Poetical Works*, 1802, p. 41.

Sir Jeofrey was wont to sitt, called *Chaucer's-oake*' was harangued by an angry judge with 'topiques from the Druides'.[1] The author of *The Modern Druid*, 1747, giving 'instructions for the much better culture of young oaks', expected that the point of his joke would at once be seen. The esteem in which the Druids had held 'the hallowed parasites'[2] led an eminent physician of the eighteenth century to prescribe, with results that gratified him, powder of mistletoe for Hereditary Epilectical Distemper.[3] Rooted as they were in the country, the Druids came to the notice of early students of folklore, and the Reverend Luke Booker describes how the Druids were shaded by a 'nicely balanc'd rocking-stone' in summer, and how in winter they still contrived to sit under their boughs by bringing branches indoors, thus incidentally starting the custom of Christmas decorations.[4]

But even where the charm of their environment was acknowledged, they were not permitted to sit back and take pleasure in the scenery. From the seventeenth-century editors of Caesar to the most facile of versifiers, nearly everyone agreed that by retreating to their groves the Druids sought or were subject to edification. Georges de Brebeuf, in his translation of Lucan gives in 1670 the woods of the Druids a character that would have surprised the Latin poet: in their countryside, Brebeuf says

> Au milieu du silence et des bois solitaires
> La Nature en secret leur ouvre ses Mystères.[5]

By the eighteenth century their surroundings were in turn beginning to show more markedly the effects of this long association: trees were themselves openly speaking

---

[1] Bodleian MS. Aubrey 8, f. 27.

[2] Anon., *Stonehenge*, 1792, p. 10.

[3] John Colbatch, *A Dissertation concerning Mistletoe*, 1719, pp. 5 ff.

[4] Luke Booker, *A Sequel to the Hop-Garden*, Newport, Salop., 1799, pp. 84 ff.

[5] *La Pharsale de Lucain*, Paris, 1670, p. 27.

in dark prophetic numbers,[1] while groves became 'pensive'[2] and the mistletoe 'sage'.[3]

At first, the Druid's forests were thought of as secluded places where they could follow their studies undisturbed, and James Howells in 1645 simply observes that the Druids were

> So *call'd*, because they commonly did use
> On God and Nature's workes, 'mongst *Trees* to muse.[4]

Later, Nature came to be regarded as a force which actively worked on them and helped to mould their characters. 'They had preferred for the exercise of their Religion', says the Abbé Banier, 'solitary and solemn Woods, whose very Aspect inspires with something of religious Awe.'[5] The Reverend John Whitaker in his *History of Manchester*, 1771, hints that 'the Druidical species of heathenism' took a strong tone from its background:

The rudely majestic cincture of stones . . . the huge enormous Cromlech, the massy tremulous Logan . . . and the magnificent amphitheatre of woods, all must have very strongly laid hold upon that religious thoughtfulness of soul which has ever been so natural to man amid all the wrecks of humanity, the monuments of his former perfection.[6]

Even William Mason's Roman general, the enemy of Caractacus, is susceptible to the Druids' environment, and he observes:

> Surely there is a hidden power that reigns
> 'Mid the lone majesty of untam'd nature
> Controuling sober reason.[7]

---

[1] W. Lipscomb, *Poems*, Oxford, 1784, p. 5.
[2] G. West, *The Garter*, 1771, p. 4.
[3] W. Mason, *Poems*, 1764, p. 98.
[4] *Dodona's Grove*, 1645, sig. ¶ 4 v.
[5] *Mythology and Fables of the Ancients*, 1739, p. 219.
[6] *History of Manchester*, 1771, pp. 395–6.
[7] *Poems*, 1764, p. 174.

It was under its sway and beneath the consecrated boughs of their oaks that, as the same poet says of them in another context,

> the holy Druids
> Lay rapt in moral musings.[1]

They were becoming sages to whom Wordsworth might have listened, and in this particular instance, he not only shared Aulus Didius's appreciation of their background, but his language, for in these lines from Wordsworth's *Descriptive Sketches* there is a perceptible echo of *Caractacus*:

> And sure there is a secret Power that reigns
> Here, where no trace of man the spot profanes.[2]

Within the narrow context of this special relationship between the Druids and Nature—if only within its limits —Wordsworth aptly called himself 'a youthful Druid'.

A more lighthearted feeling prompted Andrew Marvell to liken himself to 'some great Prelate of the Grove' as he walked among the oaks near Appleton House:[3] he much admired Brebeuf's poetry, and he was evidently taken with the Druids of *La Pharsale de Lucain*. More strikingly, the Druids also link the names of James Thomson and William Collins, and this is at first sight surprising, for the author of *The Seasons* does not introduce them into his reflective poetry on Nature. He may possibly have been thinking of them in his lines on the forest:

> These are the haunts of meditation, these
> The scenes where ancient bards the inspiring breath
> Ecstatic felt, and, from this world retired,
> Conversed with angels and immortal forms.[4]

The mention of angels here weakens the possibility that the 'ancient bards' he had in mind were Druids, but this

[1] 'Elfrida', *Poems*, 1764, p. 98.   [2] op. cit., ll.424–5.
[3] 'Upon Appleton House', LXXIV, LXXXXIII.
[4] *Summer*, 1746, ll.522 ff.

is recognizably the kind of country in which they were being placed, a landscape which was open to larger skies than the natural. When, however, Collins in his *Ode Occasion'd by the Death of Mr Thomson*, 1749, called Thomson himself a Druid, he placed his poet-philosopher of Nature in a setting which, tinged with sadness though it is, noticeably lacks brooding overtones. In its evocation of atmosphere, the ode looks back over a hundred years to that surrounding Sir William Temple's Druids, whose 'Lives were simple and innocent, in Woods, Caves and hollow Trees'.[1]

Collins's ode starts:

> In yonder Grave a DRUID lies
> Where slowly winds the stealing Wave!
> The *Year*'s best Sweets shall duteous rise
> To deck *it*'s POET'*s* sylvan Grave!
>
> In yon deep Bed of whisp'ring Reeds
> His airy Harp shall now be laid,
> That He, whose Heart in Sorrow bleeds,
> May love thro' Life the soothing Shade.
>
> Then Maids and Youths shall linger here,
> And while it's Sounds at distance swell,
> Shall sadly seem in Pity's Ear
> To hear the WOODLAND PILGRIM's Knell.

Finally, as though to insist that this was a considered and significant choice of an epithet for Thomson, the poem ends:

> Long, long, thy Stone and pointed Clay
> Shall melt the musing BRITON's Eyes,
> O! VALES and WILD WOODS, shall HE say
> In yonder Grave YOUR DRUID lies!

The skill with which Collins controls its gentle elegiac mood gives the poem all the appeal of the artless, and its

---

[1] 'An Introduction to the History of England', *Works*, 1720, vol. iii, p. 531.

feeling perhaps makes comment rather intrusive. Nevertheless, this epithet is most arresting, and Collins himself
invites a second look at it. It is intended to epitomize
Thomson, and yet it cannot mean that Collins thought
that Thomson was the equivalent of the Druid as he had
been described in the classics. Nor does Thomson re-
semble any contemporary picture of the Druid: there is
no trace in him, or in the ode, of Toland's superstitious
and crafty priest, of Rowlands's and Stukeley's custodians
of Patriarchal wisdom, of Carte's accomplished Hyperborean Highlander. Even the more casual of Augustan
references to the Druids have little in common with
Thomson: Addison uses their name as humorous slang
for a priest,[1] Mrs. Pendarves as slang for a singer,[2] and
Leonard Welsted calls himself a Druid apparently because
he likes wine.[3] The word suggests no stock figure which
can be recognized as the early or mid-eighteenth century
Druid.

Collins, in fact, seems to have heard nothing about these
authors and their Druids. Only a year before he wrote
the ode, he described what he thought was a characteristic
or ideal temple of the Druids, and there is a reminiscence
of Pope's *Temple of Fame* in Collins's architecture:

> In *Gothic* Pride it seems to rise!
> Yet *Graecia*'s graceful Orders join,
> Majestic thro' the mix'd Design.[4]

But if Collins had dipped into Toland and the others he
would have seen that they held at least one belief in

[1] *Tatler*, No. 255, 1710.
[2] *The Autobiography and Correspondence of Mary Granville, Mrs.
Delany*, 1861, vol. i, p. 229. 'Holy Druides composing songs' appear in
Fletcher's *Bonduca* (*Works*, ed. A. R. Waller, 1908, VI, p. 81), which was
again staged in 1706 with music by Purcell; in Thomas Coke's *The Bath*,
1726, Britain is called 'Thrice happy land, 'tis here the Druids sing,
(quoted by T. D. Kendrick, *The Druids*, 1928, p. 25.); they are shown as
singers in Thomas Carew's masque, *Coelum Britannicum* (*Poems*, ed.
R. Dunlop, Oxford, 1949, p. 177).
[3] *Oikographia*, 1725, p. 4.   [4] 'Ode to Liberty', *Odes*, 1747, p. 28.

common: he would have been left in no doubt that they all thought that temples of the Druids were circles of megaliths.

A third possibility is that for Thomson himself the word had a special meaning, and that Collins had this meaning particularly in mind when he was writing the ode. A footnote in the original edition referring to *The Castle of Indolence* shows that Collins was thinking of this poem at the time, and here there is a significant clue to a meaning which is both pointed and yet general enough to comprehend Thomson as a philosopher and a poet. In *The Castle*, the Knight of Arts and Industry sets out to stem the tide of lethargy which threatens to overwhelm the country. His spokesman is a 'Druid-wight',[1] and though he has a strange appearance, Thomson insists that his soul is fair. Playing on his harp, this Druid—now called a Bard—exhorts his fellow countrymen to cast off their sloth; but what is more significant, the Druid's message expounds Thomson's own philosophy of life, and in the circumstances in which *The Castle of Indolence* appeared—for Thomson died shortly after its publication —the Druid's message is also Thomson's spiritual testament.

In Thomson's philosophy, the doctrine of the Great Chain of Being was united with the Pythagorean doctrine of metempsychosis. He saw the Great Chain rising from the bedrock of the world, from

> the mineral strata there;
> Thrust, blooming, thence the vegetable world;
> Over that the rising system, more complex,
> Of animals; and, higher still, the mind,
> The varied scene of quick-compounded thought,
> And where the mixing passions ever shift.[2]

---

[1] op. cit., 11, xxxiii.   [2] *Autumn*, ll. 1358 ff. See also G. R. Potter, 'James Thomson,' *Englische Studien*, Leipzig, 1926. pp. 57 ff.

With these ascending states the human faculties had a
kind of hierarchical correspondence: 'plain perception'
observed the physical world, and the fancy perceived 'fair
forms'; higher again, the human reason reigned; above
the 'world of spirits' where life is 'unfettered and un-
mixed', a 'cloud' was placed between ultimate reality and
human awareness. Yet the mind could still go

> up-tracing, from the dreary void
> The chain of causes and effects to Him,
> The world-possessing essence, who alone
> Possesses being.[1]

By itself, the idea of metempsychosis evidently appeared
to Thomson to lack direction; at the same time, the fixed
hierarchy of the Great Chain seemed from his point of
view to be static. The fusing of the two doctrines which
produced Thomson's own philosophy thus gave rein-
carnation a direction, and it turned the Great Chain into
a ladder. Within its own terms, this philosophy is not only
logical but persuasive, and Thomson congratulates himself on going a stage farther than Pythagoras, whose
doctrine, he says, would have been a

> Delightful truth!
> Had he beheld the living chain ascend,
> And not a circling form, but rising whole.[2]

Once he had found what he calls this delightful truth
he never abandoned it, and it is possible to see his belief
growing on him. Where, for example, he alludes to it in
these lines from *The Seasons*, he shows some hesitancy:

> Heaven forbid the bold presumptuous strain,
> Whose wisest will has fixed us in a state
> That must not yet to pure perfection rise:
> Besides, who knows, how, raised to higher life,
> From stage to stage, the vital scene ascends?[3]

[1] *Summer*, ll. 1745 ff., 1782 ff.   [2] *Liberty*, III, ll.68–70.
[3] *Spring*, ll.374 ff.

The Druid of *The Castle*, speaking on the same subject, is far more sure of himself:

> Up from the unfeeling mould
> To seraphs burning round the Almighty's throne,
> Life rising still on life in higher tone
> Perfection forms, and with perfection bliss.[1]

The poetry in which Thomson first expounds his philosophy is rather flat, as though his response to this belief is not yet complete. His Druid, however, after reciting some tendentious stanzas in praise of initiative and exertion, reaches a peroration in which this belief is expressed in an appreciably altered tone, and he apostrophizes his hearers as

> Heirs of eternity, yborn to rise
> Through endless states of being, still more near
> To bliss approaching, and perfection clear.[2]

Here, then, is a Druid who not only shares Thomson's personal convictions, but speaks for Thomson with the force of a man with a ministry. Collins may have known very little about the Druids, but he knew their 'cardinal doctrine', he knew Thomson's philosophy, and he was all too aware that it had received its final expression in the Druid's message. In the interpretation offered here, Collins's use of the word has a very pointed meaning, and as it will appear, this was recognized by one of Thomson's readers later in the century.

Yet this probing into Collins's intention may be over-curious. The poem's imagery is compact, and its pastoral idiom sufficiently defines the meaning of the word Druid by restricting its scope. 'Woodland pilgrim' (unknowingly, a happy translation of 'silvivagi', as Johannes Textor calls the Druids)[3] and 'meek Nature's child' sufficiently modify it, and simply to regard this Druid as

[1] op. cit., II, xlviii.   [2] ibid., lxiii.
[3] *Epithetorum Jo. Ravisii Textoris Epitome*, 1664, p. 95 (Textor died in 1524).

a poet-philosopher of Nature accords with the feeling of the poem.

It was reprinted with a small alteration in *The Poetical Calendar*, 1763,[1] whose editor, William Woty, also collaborated with John Tait in writing *The Druids' Monument*, an intended tribute to the recently deceased Oliver Goldsmith. In these verses a poet wandering near the Isis is accosted by a strange figure, and he learns that the other's fellow Druids have raised a monument to the memory of Goldsmith. They often meet in order to discuss Goldsmith's works; they are particularly fond of the story of Angelina and Edwin:

> 'O! say what beauties grace the song,
> 'What heavenly Ardor warms,
> 'When ANGELINA, lost so long,
> 'Is lock'd in EDWIN's arms.

> 'This strain the *Druids* oft repeat
> 'In some sequester'd grove,
> 'Where with the *Fairy* train they meet,
> 'To hear the rules of love.'[2]

If Collins's editor had little idea of what the Druids were, he had at least gathered from the ode that they lived in the country.

With the appearance of Wordsworth, the evolution of the Druids to whom Nature had secretly revealed her mysteries came to an altogether unexpected end. But though they had been superseded, the Druids in their forests were not entirely forgotten; when they are next met with, however, the forests themselves had only a few acorns between them and Eden, and the Druids are here mainly of interest to the philologist as men who made an early and picturesque contribution to the development of language.

[1] op. cit., p. 104. In the first line, 'grove' is substituted for 'grave': surely an abrasive editorial touch rather than the poet's emendation.
[2] op. cit., pp. 7 ff.

IX

BEFORE BABEL

DURING the eighteenth century there was much speculation on the origins of language, and the discovery of the relationship of Sanskrit to the major tongues of Europe was almost incidental to a search which was inspired by a fallacy, which followed the directions of the misguided, and which ended far short of its object. The commonplace of today was then attacked by men of marked common sense: 'Upon what grounds', Bishop Percy asks, 'can it be pretended that the ancient languages of Gaul and Germany flowed from one common source? Or who will believe so improbable a fact?'[1]

The similarity between words in different languages which are now known to be cognate had early been remarked, and the inference that they had 'flowed from one common source' was supported by the Bible. 'The whole earth was of one language' at a not very remote period, and for some philologists, comparative philology was in effect an inquiry into the implications of a verse in Genesis. Their dependence on 'a few Testimonies of sacred Scriptures'[2] thus led them to assume that the attempt to build Babel, or the postdiluvian dispersal of the Patriarchal families gave the approximate dates at which the 'primitive tongue' was last spoken before it disintegrated and produced the different languages of the world. Some thought that Celtic had evolved along the route taken by the kings of Annius or Camden's Cimbri from Ararat to Britain: 'Japhetic', according to Adrian

---

[1] P. H. Mallet, *Northern Antiquities*, 1859, p. 18.
[2] H. Rowlands, *Mona*, p. 201.

Van Scrieck, was nothing other than Celtic.[1] The English
language, says the Elizabethan grammarian John David
Rhys, had evolved from the Hebrew by way of Chaldean,
Arabic, Slavonic, and Saxon, but Welsh, he declares, 'sed
haec nostra Cambrobrytannica adeo est (ut ita dicam)
aboriginate'.[2] Welsh, claims a Jacobean historian, was so
old that no one knew anything about its origins, but his
eighteenth-century editor insists that it was Gomerian,
the parent of the European tongues. 'By our Author's
leave, we have proved', he adds, 'that the Gomerians were
in their Time the most Polite Nation in Europe.'[3] The
reader of Pezron's *Antiquities of Nations*, 1706, would
learn that the Welsh had preserved their language 'after a
Revolution of above Four Thousand Years'.[4] The alleged
affinity between Welsh and Hebrew is discussed at length
in Charles Edwards's *Hebraicorum Cambro-Britannicorum
Specimen*, 1675, 'wherein the learned Author observes,
that the Resemblance is so great between the *Hebrew* and
Welsh, that he could not forbear thinking when he read the
Hebrew Bible at any time, but that he heard those old
Patriarchs and *Israelites* talk *Welsh* together';[5] the similar
arguments of Henry Rowlands and William Cooke[6] also
helped to encourage the notion that there were originally
the closest of links between the Druids and the Patriarchs.

But the more ambitious inquirer was not primarily
interested in comparative philology. His aim was to discover, by recovering and analysing their language, the
lost lore of the Patriarchs. John Webb, in the introduction
to *An Historical Essay Endeavouring a Probability that the*

[1] Quoted in J. de Long, *Bibliotheque Historique*, Paris, 1719, p. 28.
[2] *Cambrobrytannicae Cymraecaeve Linguae Institutiones*, 1592, sig. **2.
[3] J. Lewis, *History of Great Britain*, ed. H. Thomas, 1729, pp. 27–28.
[4] op. cit., p. xii.
[5] Myles Davies, *Athenae Britannicae*, 1716, vol. i, pp. 300–1, who
records the title *Hebraismorum*, &c. Part of the text is given in *The
Cambrian Quarterly*, vol. iv, 1832.
[6] W. Cooke, *An Enquiry into the Druidical and Patriarchal Religion*,
1754.

Language of the Empire of China is the Primitive Language,
1669, shows what he had at the back of his mind:

This ESSAY *pretends to advance the* DISCOVERY *of that*
GOLDEN-MINE *of* Learning, *which from all* ANTIQUITY
hath lain concealed in the PRIMITIVE TONGUE; *whether*
Religion, *Famous* Examples *of the* Wisedom *of Old, Politique*
Rules *for* Government, *or what ever else advantageous to* Mankind
be respected. And wherein no doubt, so great Mysteries *are involved,*
as nothing hitherto in all the Learning *of the* World *can either excel*
or equal.[1]

Webb detected many similarities between the ancient
Hebrews and the Chinese, and he inferred that the two
peoples had a common ancestry. In his view, the Chinese
had disassociated themselves from the attempt to build
Babel:

which can admit of no other construction, than that the Language
of *These*, that were THERE, that is, at that place in *Babylonia*,
not in *India* or elsewhere was confounded. So in like manner
THEIR Language, *i.e. Their* Language that were with *Nimrod*,
and of this Western Colony; not the Language of *Noah*, and his
Plantations in the East. Again also, That THEY, to wit, those
children of men, that built the Tower; not those generations that
had no hand in building of the same, might *not understand one*
anothers speech.[2]

That is, the conservative Chinese still spoke the 'primitive
tongue', and Webb's thesis, then, was that a thorough
investigation of their language would reveal '*the* Wisedom
of Old'. Needless to say, he did not claim to have discovered it: like others, he was mainly concerned with
supplying incentives to further research, though today
they read as though they were promoting dubious enter-
prises.

These remarks apply to no more than a portion of the
extensive literature on the origins of language that
flourished in the eighteenth century; references to the

[1] op. cit., sig. A2 v.   [2] ibid., p. 33.

Druids are found only where it is rooted in uneasy ground. Here they are quite at home, for as custodians of ante-diluvian lore they conserved the most ancient wisdom, and they also spoke a modified form of Japhet's Celtic. Even more could be said about them in this context: they had taught 'secret and sublime things' in 'dark sayings', and they never committed their doctrines to writing. Such striking features of their teaching suggested that a search in the Cabbala—which means 'oral tradition'—might lead to the discovery of the secrets of the Druids, and this partly explains why, with the publication of *The Origin of Language and Nations* in 1764, Rowland Jones attempted an analysis of the structure of English words in terms of Cabbalistic teachings, claiming that this would lead to the discovery of the secrets of the Druids.

He fought long to win acceptance for his ideas, and nine years were to pass before he was defeated by 'the uncommon discouragement and opposition he has met with'.[1] The Critical Reviewers remarked of his works that 'the author soars too high to be the subject of their approbation or censure', and their perplexity is under-standable.[2] His aim was to sketch 'the plan of an universal philosophical lexicon, which shows the English language to be the most capable of an universal one';[3] far from anticipating the future status of English as a world language, he looked back to the past, and he proposed not so much to discover as uncover the language of Adam, which, he thought, still lay hidden in modern English.

To start with his first principles: 'I think', he says, 'that language ought not to be considered as mere arbitrary sounds', for 'the deity appears to have made use of a form of speech, previous to the formation of Adam.' Therefore, by finding 'those primary signs transmitted from Adam amongst his posterity, and preserved at all

---

[1] *The 10-Triads*, 1773, p. 49.
[2] *The Philosophy of Words*, 1769, p. 45.   [3] ibid., p. 11.

times in some corner of the world', we 'might again recover a rational scheme of speech'. The antediluvians, he goes on to say, each lived to a very ripe old age, and in consequence they accumulated much knowledge; this was then transmitted to Noah, Japhet (whom he calls a Druid), Gomer, and the succeeding Druids.[1] An examination of Druidism would therefore lead to an understanding of the fundamentals of religion and government. Jones's immediate concern, however, was with English, which was originally Celtic, the language of the Druids: this he had reduced to its basic elements, thereby discovering hidden meanings which other lexicographers could not see.

He found these hidden meanings both in the 'particles' of words and in the typographical appearance of the letters themselves. Letters, he says, took their shape in the first place from the division of the globe, or O. The letter a, which should be written in the form of two parallel semicircles, ∞, was the symbol of subterranean water. In E, or rather, ε, water is symbolically shown as springing forth and producing 'surface water'. The letter C by itself implied motion, and L implied length and breadth. He also invented—or adapted from Plato's *Cratylus*—a more elaborate method of analysis: after isolating in a rather arbitrary fashion the separate components of a word, he assigned meanings to these 'particles' and then put them together again in such a way that a single word became in effect a phrase. The word Druid for example, thus yields the etymology 'di-riu-id', or 'a dark or divine sort or kind'.[2]

To return to his more general remarks: the Druids, he says, thought that a human being had two souls. One was animal, and its faculties could only receive impressions from the outside world. The other soul was furnished with free volition, intelligence, and the divine

---

[1] *The Origin of Language and Nations*, sig. B [2] ff.
[2] ibid., sig. [A] 3 ff.

language. Because of their knowledge of the divine language, the Druids' doctrines were 'the most compatible of any of the philosophical sects with revealed religion', for Adam was 'endued with a living soul by God himself; which could supply him with no intuitive knowledge of evil, nor with words to put a negative to the divine command'.[1] Having made this very subtle but telling point, he argues that to adopt his linguistic principles, 'to purify our expressions', would finally lead to self-purification in the highest sense of the word.[2]

The English language was, he says, originally Celtic, and it was carried to this island by the migrating Titans, whom Pezron had described, and their Druids. Deeply rooted in the remotest past, it still retained features which pointed to its great antiquity: the original and esoteric significance of the shape of the letter i, for example, was that it symbolized 'man in his state of innocence'—the dot represented his head and the line his body. 'This lettering was the sacred character made use of by the Druids to preserve their original, ancient, and secret knowledge'.[3] Its distinguished ancestry thus made it the fittest language for universal use. In his final works, he produces novel transliterations of the Hebrew name of God, showing how the symbols for the physical elements had been incorporated into their Creator's name. A most striking illustration of his methods is seen in his analysis of the symbolism of the letters of the word Jove. Writing it EUOI, and thus reading from the right to the left, he explains that it starts with the dot over the i; from this 'dark point, or intelligent omega' came its 'fluxion, or ilation in a line'; this then expanded to form a circle which, as the next letter shows, burst and erupted into the solar system before it finally separated and produced matter.[4]

[1] *The Origin of Language and Nations*, pp. (7) ff.
[2] *Hieroglyfic*, 1768, sig. A2 v.   [3] ibid., pp. 15, 84.   [4] 10-*Triads*, pp. 8 ff.

Pezron had charted the course taken by the Patriarchal ancestors of the Celts, and Jones was satisfied that it was along this road that the Druids had preserved and carried their knowledge of ancient symbolism. Given that the earliest wisdom had been transmitted through Noah to his descendants the Celts, given that English was originally Celtic, given that the conservative Druids had tenaciously preserved the earliest language and learning among the Celts, it followed that the English language still preserved the pristine roots. And given this, it followed that Druid symbolism might be explained in terms of the esoterism of the Cabbala, and what Jones says about the dot and its 'ilation' might now be read in the light of this quotation from *The Universal Jewish Encyclopaedia*: 'The mystics declared that . . . God had even created the entire universe by means of two letters of his name, Yod [which looks rather like the raised comma of an apostrophe] and He, of which the word of creation, *yehi*, "let there be", is composed.'[1]

Enough has been said here to give a general idea of the contents of a few books which are not without a certain pathos. Wholeheartedly dedicated to his task of setting 'the present confused, deluded or enchanted state of language and knowledge in a right direction',[2] Jones tried to remedy matters by treating modern English as though it had exactly the same character as a Hebrew text, and if it never occurred to him that what he was doing was meaningless, this was only because he thought that in essentials English was the language of Adam and the Druids, and therefore susceptible to such reverential treatment. Persuaded that he had discovered the secret principles of Druid philology, he applied them, as it has been seen, to his analysis of the name of the supreme god of the Romans as though to show that the Latin word

[1] op. cit., New York, vol. v, 1941, p. 7.
[2] *Hieroglyfic*, p. 15.

would then yield the same kind of 'etymology' as its Hebrew equivalent, as though to demonstrate that all languages and religions had a common origin. The message was never listened to. To the general reader it was incomprehensible, and Jones may well have alienated the sympathies of those who were able to follow him, for they might easily have been affronted by his unintentional parody of what to the devout reader of the Cabbala is a sacred science.

Yet he may have had one appreciative reader: the student of Blake will find much to interest him in the works of Rowland Jones. Both men had common aims, and by calling Japhet a Druid, Jones anticipates Blake's contention that the Patriarchs were Druids. Blake's Urizen is foreshadowed in Jones's remarks on idolatry. Jones thought that Druidism and Cabbalist doctrine were the same, and Blake had only to take a single step farther when he claimed that the Jews had been taught their Cabbalist doctrine by the Druids.

Among Rowland Jones's rival etymologists was John Cleland the novelist, who was not the kind of man one might expect to be interested in the Druids. Yet he held strong views about them, and he had one particular advantage over the philologists who were still tied to Genesis, for to show that Celtic was the parent of the European languages was all that he wanted to do. Celtic, he decided, must 'in the simplicity of its origin have been purely monosyllabic', and he therefore proposed 'to discover those Celtic primitives precisely at their point of divergence into other languages' such as Greek, Latin, and German. He based his researches on 'a multitude of concurrences of sense, of sound, of analogy, and of history', and he also considered 'the significant radicals' in the proper names of heathen mythology.[1]

---

[1] *The Way to Things by Words*, 1766, pp. ii ff.

Mythology, he explains,

is demonstrably founded on the Druidical plan of fiction: the Druids not only gave any other sense than an allegorical one, to their most ingenious inventions, but annexed the strongest ideas of horror to the prophanation of them, in erecting those impersonations into objects of religious worship.[1]

He did not get very far with his inquiries into the hidden meanings of myths and legends, but a general history of early Europe emerges from his studies. When the rest of the world rejected the wisdom of the Druids and turned to idolatry, Britain alone, he says, stood firm: the legend of Atlantis simply meant that the scandalized British Druids were isolated morally and geographically from the Continent. One Odin or Woden revolted, escaped from Britain, and went to Prussia. After extirpating Druidism there, he joined forces with the Saxons, 'so that the *Saxons* might properly be said to return to originally their own country'.[2] The name of the goddess Frea, he adds, meant Liberty—'allusively to the shaking off of Druidism'.[3]

Christianity came to Europe, and the Cross took the place of the Druids' maypole. But much of the ancient faith survived, either by taking new forms or by being adapted to suit the new circumstances. The Freemasons, he points out, took their origin from the Druids, and as the May's sons they kept their old title of the sons of the May.[4] The Mass was not derived from 'missa est', but from the 'missletoe'.[5] Whit Sunday was the Druids' day of Apollo. Ash Wednesday commemorated the burning of criminals in the Druids' colossus.[6] Twelfth Night was the Yule of the Druids.[7]

These 'specimens of an etymological vocabulary' were

---

[1] ibid., p. 10.   [2] ibid., pp. 12 ff.
[3] ibid., p. 40.   [4] ibid., p. 120   [5] ibid., p. 14.
[6] *Specimens of an Etymological Vocabulary*, 1768, pp. 33, 90.
[7] *Way to Things*, p. 97.

produced by little more than a free association of ideas. Cleland sometimes reads as though he were parodying his fellow philologists, but he was serious. He was convinced that the languages of Europe had a unity that was hidden and even belied by appearances. If any man ever had the answer on the tip of his tongue, it was Cleland. He shows that he was tantalized by something that he had seen but had not recognized for what it was, for he knew the one language that would have helped him to prove his case. He had at one time lived in India, and there he had picked up enough Sanskrit to be able to say: 'The grammar of the Bramins may be justly put in the rank of the most beautiful Sciences', for he had noticed that the Hindus had 'by analysis, reduced the richest language in the world to a few primitive elements'.[1] He was interested in etymology, he was certain that European languages had a common origin, he knew Sanskrit, and he was particularly impressed by its 'significant radicals'. The truth was before his eyes, and to go by some of his excited remarks, he must have known that he was constantly on the verge of making an important discovery: he very nearly anticipated by twenty years Sir William Jones's announcement that Sanskrit and most European languages are cognate.[2]

But his deeper interests were elsewhere: for him, the Greek or Roman myth was a secular parable, as it were. Mythology, once 'cleared of that contemptible adulteration' which populated it with gods, was 'demonstrably the production of the Druids'.[3] He never found the universal truths which his myths concealed: such matters do not reveal themselves to men of his urbanity. It was not for him to say that at the end of the road, 'so great Mysteries are involved as nothing in all the learning of the

[1] *Way to Things*, pp. 91–92.
[2] *Discourses delivered before the Royal Asiatic Society*, 1824, p. 28. (24 Feb. 1785).
[3] *Specimen*, p. 152.

World can either excel or equal'. Instead, he remarks that
the Druids' way of teaching was 'one of the noblest efforts
of the human genius for giving . . . to very solid truths
. . . the passport of instructive amusement'.[1]

By the beginning of the nineteenth century the etymologist who sought the roots of the primitive language
approached his goal in the spirit of a man who is content
with knowledge for its own sake. The Reverend Edward
Davies may have gone back to a time and place where
the modern philologist would feel an intruder, but Davies
pursued his inquiries into the origin of language in the
most sober fashion, even if they led him to a time and
place where the incoherent emerged explosively from the
inarticulate.

Celtic Researches was published in 1804, and it owes more
than he admits to a book which had appeared some forty
years earlier. James Parson's *Remains of Japhet*, 1768,
offers a new interpretation of the relationship of Welsh
to Hebrew. He calls Welsh Gomerian, and Irish Mago-
gian, the latter being reminiscent of the Celtic passage
through Scythia,[2] and his main point is that since the
order in which the letters are arranged in the Beth-Luis-
Nion alphabet of the Irish differs greatly from the order
in which they follow each other in the Hebrew alphabet,
Irish and Welsh are not derived from Hebrew: Irish and
Hebrew both come independently of each other from the
same source.[3] His arguments are based on studies of
Biblical genealogies and on a comparison of other alpha-
bets with the tree alphabet of the Irish. These lines of
inquiry run through *Celtic Researches*, but Davies places
far more emphasis on the important part played by the
Druids in conserving the ancient language.

Davies insists that the simpler a language is, the earlier
it is.[4] The language of savages is elaborate, and this argues

[1] loc. cit.   [2] op. cit., pp. 31 ff.
[3] ibid., pp. 244 ff.   [4] op. cit., p. 379.

degeneration.[1] The earliest of men (since, presumably,
they had been in existence for a short time, and degeneration had not yet set in) were not savages, and their
language must have been very simple. In the course of
time, this early simplicity was lost:

That any living language, whatsoever, should have remained in
the same state from the Creation, to the time of Moses, is a thing
in itself of the utmost improbability. During this period of 2500
years, human society had undergone the greatest changes imagin-
able.[2]

By then, Hebrew had become sophisticated: in Davies's
linguistic cosmogony, it was a dialect of the primitive
language.

The Druids were more resistant to change:

Their studies embraced those elevated objects which had engaged
the attention of the world in its primitive state—the nature of the
Deity—of the human Soul—of the future State. . . . Their
conceptions were great and sublime, their speculations comprehensive in their sphere. . . . Perhaps there was no order of men
amongst the heathens, who preserved the history and the opinions
of mankind, in its early state, with more simplicity, and more
integrity.

The religion of the *patriarchs* had, indeed, been deformed with
various superstitions, by all nations. But this order, notwithstanding their many and gross errors, appears to have retained
many of its vital and essential principles.[3]

Moving slowly towards his point by way of a long discussion of some features of classical mythology, and on his
way noting that the maxims of the Druids recorded by
Diogenes Laertius form a triad, a form of poetry which
still existed in Welsh, and claiming that the Druids were
Hyperboreans, for no island north of Britain could produce the two annual crops which Hecataeus mentions in
his description of the island of the Hyperboreans,[4] Davies

[1] op. cit., p. 103.   [2] ibid., p. 91.   [3] ibid., p. 119.   [4] ibid., p. 181.

concludes that the simple and straightforward Irish was not derived from Hebrew, and that the only difference between Irish and Welsh was that while Irish was the primitive, Welsh was the 'cultivated, or *Druidical Celtic*'.[1]

So great was the antiquity of Druidism that the language of the Druids went back to Nature herself for its alphabet. The many references to trees in the literature of the Celts were not literary images:

Our Druids possessed a kind of alphabet which was formed upon the system of their symbolical sprigs, or hieroglyphs, cut . . . so as to represent the first principle, or elementary sounds of their language.[2]

And so,

The *Sage* of *Druidism* could express, or convey his ideas, by *a mere sprig* of the *fir*, the *birch*, the *ivy*, and the *oak*, arranged upon a string. A *Chaldean* or the ancient *Hebrew*, could not, so conveniently, do the same[3]

for by using symbols such as an ox's head, for example, they had to resort to a relatively elaborate 'delineation'. Hebrew, then, was not the primitive language,[4] not the source from which Welsh flowed, and Davies 'can scarce hesitate in yielding to the force of such evidence, and concluding, that *our* ancestors, in the western continent, have presented us with a most authentic transcript of the general alphabet employed by the *Noachidae*'.[5]

A painstaking scholar, quite unlike the more timid Selden, who would drop an oracular hint and then keep his silence, Davies did not hesitate to illustrate, to exemplify. The letter A, he says, had in the Druidical alphabet 'the general idea of *proceeding*', and its 'symbolical plant, which represented this power, was the *fir-tree*'. Other languages still retained in their use of A traces of a similar meaning which was derived from the primitive language itself. In Latin, the sense in which the Druids

[1] ibid., p. 234. [2] ibid., pp. 266–7.
[3] ibid., p. 334. [4] ibid., p. 103. [5] ibid., p. 336.

used this letter existed in 'Ai-o, *I affirm*'; in Greek, alpha suggested honour, and precedence; the Hebrew aleph implied direction and guidance.[1]

He went even farther back in his researches, and arrived at the ultimate context itself of language in the garden of Eden. Here, he describes how the root of the word which finally evolved into 'behemoth' came into being. The day of the grandiose claim, the dangerous incentive was over; it is in a more temperate intellectual climate that he says:

Let us put the case, that *Adam*, the first man, would inform his new-created bride, of the *elephant*. The character which he had already described in this animal, in the act of naming him, was, probably, his enormous bulk. This description he is now to repeat. Being an inexpert orator, he would not trust entirely, and exclusively, to the powers of his voice. His arms would be elevated, and spread abroad,—in order to intimate the comprehension of gigantic space.

This descriptive gesture would be added by an immediate, and spontaneous inflation of his cheeks, till his breath would find a passage through his nostrils. This natural description of a huge bulk would produce the sound B,—M; and that sound, rendered articulate by the intervention of a vowel, would describe bulkiness, and might be appropriated most happily, to the *elephant*, or great beast.[2]

[1] op. cit., pp. 408 ff.   [2] ibid., p. 382.

X

DEEP DRUIDIC LORE

THOUGH 'these gownsmen among the Gauls'[1] were once highly praised for their devotion to learning, it was never forgotten that they had studied more than the liberal arts, for those of the Druids who were 'loftier in intellect' had studied 'secret and sublime things'. Lucan's sneer that to the Druids 'alone it is given to know the truth about the gods', for instance, and scattered references in later literature to Celtic mysteries continued to attract the more curious student to the arcana of the Druids, but if he suspected that classical mythology or the Cabbala held the keys to Celtic esoterism, he did not follow these lines of inquiry very far; possibly the clues they offered were, if anything, more mystifying than the secrets they pointed to.

There was yet another direction in which to look. Holinshed and Sir Philip Sidney remark that the Welsh had had their Bards for a very long time,[2] and Sir John Price observes that

those who now cultivate poetry among the Britons are no Doubt Imitators of those Bards, since the Name, after so many Ages, is not yet relinquished.

He goes on to say that the Welsh

much cherish and esteem their Poets and Bards, whom by another name they call Pryduids, the same, I imagine, as by the Antients were stiled Druids; that by this Means they might preserve and

---

[1] J. Selden, *Reverse of the English Janus*, 1683, p. 12.
[2] *Apologie for Poetrie* (1595), ed. J. Arber, 1868, p. 22.

guard the Authority and Genuiness of the *British* Language and Antiquity.[1]

To a man still eager to learn more about the Druids, these brief remarks take on other shades of meaning, and it was as though to warn him that the trail was long cold that Maurice Kyffin, writing in 1595, says that he did not believe that any part of Druid doctrine had 'come down to the Welsh poets for many an age'.[2] Nevertheless, precisely two centuries later, the poet and antiquary Edward Williams—who is better known in Wales under his Bardic name of Iolo Morganwg—not only asserted that the original teachings of the Druids had been passed on in an unbroken sequence from generation to generation of Bards in Wales, but that he had documentary proof of his claim, and he also stated that the poems of Taliesin 'exhibit a complete system of DRUIDISM'.[3]

Much of what might be said of Williams's 'bardic mysteries' lies outside the scope of this book; here, it will only be asked if Williams's was indeed 'deep Druidic lore'. Briefly to describe some of the circumstances in which it was revealed: it was in July 1761 that Thomas Percy, whose *Reliques* were to appear three years later, started to correspond with the most eminent Welsh scholar of his day. *Fragments of Ancient Poetry, Collected in the Highlands of Scotland* had recently been 'imported', as Percy puts it, into England, and he tells the Reverend Evan Evans, then a curate in Denbighshire: 'I am verily persuaded an elegant translation of some curious pieces of ancient British Poetry would be as well received, if executed in the same manner.'[4] Evans had already in 1758

[1] *Historiae Brytannicae Defensio*, 1573, p. 11; translation from British Museum MS. Adds. 14, 925, ff. 23–25. The Welsh for poet is 'prydydd'.
[2] *Deffyniad Ffydd Eglwys Loegr a Gyfieithwyd i'r Gymraeg* (1595), ed. W. P. Williams, Bangor, 1908, p. xi.
[3] *Poems, Lyric and Pastoral*, 1794, vol. ii, p. 194.
[4] *The Correspondence of Thomas Percy and Evan Evans*, ed. Aneirin Lewis, Louisiana, 1957, p. 3.

started to translate 'ancient British Poetry', and with encouragement and help from Percy, he published *Some Specimens of the Poetry of the Antient Welsh Bards* in 1764. In this work and in his correspondence he alludes to some of the difficulties which then faced the student of early Welsh poetry: 'for want of a thorough knowledg of their language,' he tells Percy, 'wherein there are many obsolete words, not to be found in any dictionary or vocabulary, I cannot translate some of the best pieces of the Bards of the sixth century without great pains and study.'[1] In his book he also complains of the negligence of transcribers. Some of the works of Taliesin, he says in a letter, 'I ingenuously confess I do not understand'. He thought that they contained 'Druidical Cabbala', a remark that must have greatly impressed Williams;[2] but when Williams speaks of the 'complete system' which he finds in Taliesin's poetry, he implies that he had mastered the meaning of texts that had baffled Evans—an achievement that in itself would have satisfied most Welsh scholars—and that where Evans had seen little more than a number of poems 'about the transmigration of souls',[3] he had discovered an organized body of belief.

Evans had intended to publish a scholarly edition of early Welsh texts, an enterprise that had a melancholy ending. Years later, when *The Myvyrian Archaiology of Wales* appeared in 1801–7, the problems raised by this collection of early texts and those as yet unpublished were complicated by the forgeries of Edward Williams, who had already contributed forged poems to an edition of the fourteenth-century poet Dafydd ap Gwilym. Dedication, learning, self-delusion, mischief and error characterize this phase of Welsh studies, and under cover of its attendant obscurity Williams smuggled his 'Aboriginal' and baptized Druids into early Welsh literature. For Edward Davies, who learned Welsh in difficult circumstances,

[1] op. cit., p. 7.   [2] See *Specimens*, p. 53.   [3] op. cit., p. 37.

early Welsh poetry was an enigma which by yielding to
him intelligible meanings here and there, lured him on
until he found in Druidism the key to all its secrets. His
Mythology and Rites of the British Druids helped to make
this renaissance even more colourful, but, unlike Williams's inventions, it placed no very heavy burden on the
scholars who replaced the antiquaries. The kind of reader
for whom Williams and Davies wrote might also be
remembered here. 'Dear Bob,' writes W. Griffith in 1762
to a friend on behalf of an inquisitive 'Oxford Acquaintance' who desired to know the name of the author of
the triads, 'I am to trouble you to make enquiry, not after
hounds or horses, but after venerable very excellent
British Bards, that have been dust and ashes some twelve
hundred year ago.'[1] At about that time, a brother clergy-
man was asking Evans for further clarification of some
finer points of a translation from the Welsh.[2] Between
these poles, there were many whose curiosity about
venerable very excellent British Bards had been roused by
poems such as those of Thomas Gray's on Welsh themes,
but those who knew no Welsh were not alone in being
largely dependent on the scholarship and good faith of
editors and translators, and they gave Williams and
Davies a captive audience.

A *'self-tutored Journeyman Mason'*, as he called himself,[3]
for years Williams followed his studies and acquired a
reputation for learning which earned him the respect and
friendship of Welsh scholars in London. This friendship,
however, did not survive his persistent championship
of the cause of a quite unfamiliar version of 'Bardism',
but later, when he was much older, his reputation was
revived by members of a new generation of Welsh
students. To draw on Dr. Thomas Parry's brief description of his activities in middle age: Williams asserted that
the Bards of his native Glamorgan had refused to follow

[1] op. cit., p. 166.   [2] ibid., pp. 163–6.   [3] *Poems*, vol. i, p. xiii.

the precepts laid down at an important Eisteddfod held in Carmarthen in about 1450, and by adhering to the older metres, they preserved the traditional metres in Glamorgan long after they had been forgotten elsewhere. None of Williams's contemporaries had heard of these Bards, and to support his contentions, he invented metres, the names of poets, and examples of their work in the older metres. 'But the strangest of all Iolo's fabrications is the Gorsedd of the Bards'; between 1780 and 1790 Williams added to his romantic story of 'the customs of Glamorgan' some further details which completely altered the nature of his claims: he stated that 'the succession of Bards had been maintained unbroken in that part of the country from the ages before Christ to his own day, but that there now remained none of the ordained bards but himself and Edward Evans of Aberdare. He changed the name of the bardic meetings which he said had been formerly held in Glamorgan to "Gorsedd".' (To make a comment at this point: Williams's earlier theory might have been regarded indulgently by Welsh scholars, for in a sense it was a harmless romantic fiction which existed only in a corner of his mind; but by going farther back than 1450 and claiming that his 'bardism' went back to the Druids, Williams was now contaminating the main stream of Welsh scholarship.) In 1791 he started to promulgate his new ideas, and in 1792 he induced some of his friends to hold a Gorsedd on Primrose Hill. 'The Gorsedd took no hold in Wales for years', and 'not until the middle of the next century was it finally associated with the Eisteddfod'.[1]

In 1819, when he was over seventy, he prevailed upon members of the Dyfed Society to hold a Gorsedd, or Session of the Bards of Britain, at an Eisteddfod at Carmarthen; today, the ritual and regalia of his invention add so picturesque an embellishment to the proceedings

---

[1] Thomas Parry, *A History of Welsh Literature*, tr. I. Bell, Oxford, 1955, pp. 302–3.

of the Royal National Eisteddfod that the association between Gorsedd and Eisteddfod appears to be closer than it really is. Prior to the eighteenth century, Eisteddfodau were more like conferences of members of a guild than the modern entertainments in which the public holds the stage and fills the auditorium. To some extent, Williams's Gorsedd preserves the older meaning of the Eisteddfod, and in a romantic fashion it also preserves a memory of the place once held by the Bards in the Gallic hierarchy. But the visionary who was so concerned for the good name of the poet lost his own good name, and it has now been evident for some time that his inventions overlay and distort what he knew about the actual practices of the professional Bards. Some of the features of his Gorsedd have their roots in the literature which has been described here. The meaning he gave to the word 'Ovydd', his title for the member of the Gorsedd who is the equivalent of the Vates, is taken from Henry Rowlands: 'Ovydd', however, is the anglicized spelling of the name in Welsh of the poet Ovid.[1] As for the stone circle in which, according to Williams's prescription, a Gorsedd should on occasion be held, this tradition of the Druids goes back only to the pages of Aubrey's 'Templa Druidum'.

Williams's version of Druidism was published in English in *Poems, Lyric and Pastoral* (a title which pays a quiet compliment to Michael Drayton's *Poemes* of 1606) in 1794. Since its publication was delayed, his book was only partly in print when William Owen's *Heroic Elegies of Llwyarç Hen* appeared in 1792. (Owen adopted the additional surname of Pughe in 1806; he is here called by the name by which Williams first knew him.) Owen had seen the other's work, and he had also received 'communications and assistance'[2] from Williams while writing the preface to his *Elegies*. Williams's ideas were thus by chance published in English under another's

[1] T. Garel Jones, op. cit., p. 250.   [2] op. cit., lxii.

name. Owen, then, speaks for Williams as much as for himself, and it would seem that at this stage Williams was specially concerned with an obvious obstacle to the successful promulgation of his views. The Druid who once presided over the holocaust had cast a long shadow, and Williams was determined that this should not fall over his Druids. Owen observes that Druidism was characterized by a 'severe inflexible morality',[1] but he did more for his Bards by asserting of the Druids' three 'orders': 'each of the orders had a peculiarity of estimation, yet neither was held to be more intrinsically excellent than the others'.[2] This 'peculiarity of estimation' placed the Druid in a kind of quarantine. '*Bardd Braint*', Owen says, 'was peculiarly the ruling order, *Derwydd* the religious functionary, and the *Ovydd* was the literary, or scientific order.'[3] Elsewhere he makes it even clearer that the Bard was the superior of the Druid, and partly in order to isolate and minimize the forbidding associations attached to the name of 'the religious functionary', the hierarchy was turned upside down. Williams's own detailed account of the relationship between the orders was posthumously translated and published under the title of 'The Voice Conventional of the Bards of Britain' in *Iolo Manuscripts*, 1848: more is made here of the Druids and their white robes, but in his reorganization of the orders, the Bards are promoted to a position which is quite inconsistent with Strabo's remarks on their standing in the hierarchy.

In the context of Owen's interesting dissertation on the metres of Welsh poetry, Williams's theories might well be expected to make a good impression on English readers; they had the appearance of being grounded on good authority, and some of his readers were understandably inclined to believe him. As it has been said, the word 'Ovydd' does not mean Vates, and circumstantial evidence of this kind justifies the tart criticism of Williams

[1] ibid., p. xxxviii.   [2] ibid., p. xlii.   [3] loc. cit.

by other readers who were from the first suspicious of his claims, but who could not always say precisely what was wrong. In speaking of 'bardic mysteries', he was not concerned with poetry alone: he was also concerned with such matters as initiation and the oral transmission of Druid doctrine, and here again he gives himself away, for Owen asks 'the pious not to be alarmed at the idea of Druidism being still alive in this island': 'the *British* patriarchal religion is no more than that of *Noah*, or of *Abraham*'.[1] Williams is more careful to bring the Bards to the fore, and he expands Owen's remarks: he thus cites a tradition of the Druids which goes back only to the pen of Annius of Viterbo:

The *Patriarchal Religion* of ANCIENT BRITAIN, called by the Welsh most commonly *Barddas*, (BARDISM,) though they also term it *Derwddoniaeth*, (DRUIDISM,) is no more inimical to CHRISTIANITY than the religion of NOAH, JOB, or ABRAHAM:—it has never, as some imagine, been quite extinct in Britain; the *Welsh Bards* have through all ages, down to the present, kept it alive.[2]

Williams is here self-evidently writing for the English reader, who would naturally take it to mean that these terms and their meanings were current in Wales. It is not surprising that he failed to convince his Welsh friends in London of the truth of his assertions. He goes on immediately to say:

there is in my possession a manuscript synopsis of it by *Llewelyn Sion*, a *Bard*, written about the year 1560; its truth and accuracy are corroborated by innumerable notices, and allusions in Bardic manuscripts of every age up to TALIESIN in the *sixth century*, whose poems exhibit a complete system of DRUIDISM, by these (undoubtedly authentic) writings it will appear that the *Ancient British* CHRISTIANITY was strongly tinctured with DRUIDISM.

[1] op. cit., p. xxxviii.   [2] *Poems*, vol. ii, p. 194.

This 'manuscript synopsis', Taliesin's 'complete system' and Williams's collection of 'aphorisms' of the Druids evidently mean much the same thing. In the form in which Williams offers his aphorisms, they do not so much expound Druidism as divulge it, and he placed so high a value on them that elsewhere he remarks of his 'outlines of *Bardism, Druidism*' that the '*Sermon on the Mount* is a set of Aphorisms very much like those of the *Bards of Britain*'.[1] Nothing quite like this had appeared before. While Stukeley's Druidism turns out to be in effect a form of Christianity so early as to anticipate the foundation of the Church, Williams's version more ingeniously suggests a corpus of archaic belief, and it is more compactly organized.

> Thou, skill'd in deep Druidic lore,
> TALIESIN, through the world renown'd,
> Thy verse embalms the sacred store
> Of bardic mysteries profound—[2]

in this apostrophe Williams alludes to an historical poet whose name became a legend, and who as a legendary figure had ascribed to him a quite different kind of poetry from that written by the original poet.

The historical Taliesin was a sixth-century figure, and poetry ascribed to him has been preserved in the 'Book of Taliesin', a manuscript written *c.* 1275. . . . Twelve of the historical poems in this mixed collection probably date from the sixth century, and most of them, if not all twelve, are now considered to be the genuine work of Taliesin. . . . Taliesin grew into a legendary figure and became the central character of a saga dating possibly from the ninth century but based on an earlier Welsh folk tale. The mythological poems in the 'Book of Taliesin' form the verse elements in this saga; the folk tale, recorded in later manuscripts with additional verse elements inserted, provides the prose setting.[3]

[1] ibid., vol. ii, p. 225.
[2] ibid., vol. ii, p. 7.
[3] *Correspondence of Percy and Evans*, p. 37: editor's note.

The *Book of Taliesin* contains religious and mythological poetry, and prophetic and historical poems of various dates; the texts which so perplexed Evan Evans may have yielded more of their meaning to Williams, but precisely what he made of them cannot possibly be gone into here. Nevertheless, the posthumous publication in *The Cambrian Quarterly* for 1833 of his translation into English of 'The Mabinogi of Taliesin' gives a general though incomplete picture of what he knew about the legend of Taliesin, and there is no reason to think that he discriminated between the historical and the legendary Taliesin.[1] The accompanying Welsh text of 'The Mabinogi of Taliesin' is the source of Lady Charlotte Guest's translation of the story of Taliesin in her *Mabinogion*, 1838–49.[2] This does not materially differ from Williams's translation, and to quote from her more familiar version of the legendary Taliesin's poetry, the poet declares in the course of the story of his death as Gwion and his rebirth as Taliesin:

> My original country is in the region of the summer stars. . . .
> I was with my Lord in the highest sphere,
> On the fall of Lucifer into the depths of Hell:
> I have borne a banner before Alexander. . . .
> I have been loquacious prior to being gifted with speech. . . .
> I am able to instruct the whole universe.
> I shall be until the day of doom upon the face of the earth;
> And it is not known whether my body is flesh or fish.[3]

A romantic splendour falls on the page as Williams translates; nevertheless, the text which he read was striking enough to inspire the cautious Evan Evans to remark that Taliesin 'seems to have been well versed in the doctrine of the Druids' on metempsychosis, 'which accounts for the extravagant flights of fancy frequent in his poems'.[4]

[1] op. cit., vol. v, pp. 200 ff., 366 ff.

[2] D. R. Phillips, *Lady Charlotte Guest and the Mabinogion*, Carmarthen, 1921, p. 30.

[3] op. cit. (Everyman), pp. 273–4.   [4] *Specimens*, p. 53.

It also happens that 'derwyddon' are mentioned in the *Book of Taliesin*, and in, for instance, the poem 'Armes Prydein', which was written in about A.D. 930, these Druids are spoken of as vaticinators. They are, however, not precisely the same Druids whom Caesar described, but men who have inherited their name, and who, in the contexts in which they appear in the earliest Welsh poetry which mentions them, are seen as prophets, magicians, and Bards. It should be added that what is here said about them does not suggest anything which throws further light on the doctrines of the Druids of classical antiquity. Since Williams believed that these texts dated 'up to' the sixth century,[1] he obviously thought that their references were to the original Druids; but though they are both mentioned in the same manuscript, these derwyddon and Taliesin's 'extravagant flights of fancy' can only be related to each other by a misunderstanding of the text or by a free association of ideas.

The *Book of Taliesin* contains very remarkable poetry. To quote from Sir Ifor Williams's translations of verses from the poem 'Angar Kyfyndawt' which he gives in a lecture on early Welsh poetry,[2] Taliesin declaims a number of lines starting with 'I know' as though he is omniscient. 'I know', he says:

> I know why there is an echo in the hollow,
> Why silver gleams . . .

This list of the wonders that have yielded their secrets perhaps suggests that the simplest of things are the most mysterious; then Taliesin suddenly changes his theme and says:

> I have been a blue salmon,
> I have been a dog, a stag, a roebuck on the mountains,
> A stock, a spade, an axe in the hand.

---

[1] He speaks of 'Bardic manuscripts of every age up to TALIESIN': *Poems*, ii, p. 194.   [2] Though not from the accompanying interpretation.

The poet whose awareness has pervaded the universe, who has been present in all things and at all events, who has acquired his knowledge by being what he knows, has also risen above the confederacy of life and death:

> I have been dead, I have been alive,
> I am Taliesin.[1]

To see in this a poem about metempsychosis seems to be inconsistent with Taliesin's existence as 'an axe in the hand'. Sir John Morris-Jones, however, argues that the poem shows an affinity with the teachings of the Druids;[2] returning to the opinion of a critic who was a contemporary of Williams's, Peacock understood it in the same way:

That Taliesin was thoroughly initiated in these mysteries [of the Druids] is evident from several of his poems. . . . One of them, a shade less obscure than its companions, unquestionably adumbrates the Druidical doctrine of transmigration. According to this poem, Taliesin had been with the cherubim at the fall of man, and with Alexander at the fall of Babylon; in the ark with Noah, and in the milky way with Tetragrammaton . . . showing that, although the names and histories of the new religion were adopted, its doctrines still had to be learned.[3]

But though Williams responded with fervour to its striking poetry, and though he found his metempsychosis and passing allusions to derwyddon in the *Book of Taliesin*, he did not read it in such a way as passively to absorb an explicit 'system' of Druidism from it. Such a 'system' is simply not there. That he thought they were 'Patriarchal Druids' shows how much he had been influenced in his wide reading in eighteenth-century English literature, and in his remarks on a religious poem which he attributes to Taliesin he shows a tendency to strain his interpretation of his Welsh sources:

---

[1] *Lectures on Early Welsh Poetry*, Dublin, 1944, pp. 58–59.
[2] J. Morris-Jones, 'Taliesin', *Y Cymmrodor*, vol. xxviii, 1918, p. 248.
[3] *The Misfortunes of Elphin;* ed. R. Garnett, 1891, p. 67.

I have in one passage mentioned a *qualified sense* in which the *Christian Bards and Druids* believed in the *Metempsychosis*: this was, that the depraved soul of man passes in a state beyond the grave into progressive modes of existence corresponding with the nature of Earthly worms and brutes, into whom in the literal sense, the Aboriginal or Patriarchal Druids believed it passed. TALIE-SIN places this probationary, divestigating, or purifying, *Metempsychosis* in the *Hell* of *Christianity*, whence the soul gradually rises again to *Felicity*, the way for it having been opened by *Jesus Christ*; for, this is his obvious meaning when he says,

(and here Williams quotes the Welsh verse, translating it)

i.e. multitudes were, ignorant of their state, in Hell, in the miser-able progression of deliverance, during the world's five ages, until released by *Christ* from the captivities of the immense deep, of the abyss of *Abred*; all those has GOD taken into his protection.[1]

But the poet 'obviously' says that the world was benighted until the coming of Christ, the 'five ages' being a reference to St. Jerome's division of pre-Christian history into five periods. If this is typical of his interpretation of the poetry he ascribed to Taliesin, Williams saw in it a Druidism which had never existed.

Returning to the question of the authenticity of his 'deep Druidic lore': a summary is given below of the 'synopsis' which he says was recorded in 1560 of 'the outlines of *Bardism, Druidism,* or the Ancient British *Philosophy*', of the collection of 'aphorisms' which purport to reveal the doctrine of the Druids on the relationship of man to the universe:

1. 'All animated beings originate in the *lowest point of existence*': they rise in its scale until they arrive at the highest state of happiness that finite being may experience.

2. All states below the human state are evil, but there is no 'culpability' in this domain: here Fate reigns.

3. All beings rise from the condition of animals to the

[1] op. cit., vol. i, pp. xxi–xxii.

human state, and then they attain to 'some degree of negative goodness'.

4. Every being fills its allotted place in creation.

5. In the human state, the balance of good and evil produces liberty: the will is now free to exercise itself.

6. Here, a being has the power of 'coacting with the Deity'.

7. All states above the human are good; having attained to one of these, a being cannot relapse.

8. An evil man falls, after death, into 'an animal state of existence [which] corresponds with the turpitude of his soul'. Eternal misery, however, is incompatible with the attributes of God.

9. Finite beings cannot comprehend infinity, therefore God 'manifests himself to *finite* comprehensions as a *finite being*, as in the Person of JESUS CHRIST, &c.'

10. The ultimate states of happiness permit 'delightful *renovations* in endless succession', for a finite being cannot 'endure the *taedium* of ETERNITY'.

11. Memory exists in the lower states.

12. In the higher states man remembers his past.

13. Knowledge can be gained only by experience.

14. Knowledge of the higher states is communicated by celestial beings: 'BARDISM always owes its origin to *Divine communications*'.

15. Beasts of prey are the instruments of Divine benevolence: they expedite the passage of souls.

16. It is meritorious to die for Truth, Justice and Virtue.

17. A criminal should voluntarily give himself up for execution.

18. The sacrifice of animals hastens their progress to the human state.

19. No inferior being should destroy another except to save its own life.

20. Every act conducts to ultimate good: the victim of injustice is compensated for his sufferings.

21. Fortitude is the greatest of virtues.

22. Pride is 'the utmost degree of human depravity'.

23. 'The soul is an inconceivably minute particle of the most refined matter'.

24. From a perfect knowledge of the causes of evil, liberty ensues.

25. Humanity's is the *State of Probation*.

26. Creation is still in its infancy.

27. When recognized as such, evil is hated; 'but being in itself possible, it will, with all other possibilities, eternally exist in its abstract principles'.

28. All states of existence, when purged of evil, will remain 'as beautiful varieties in the Creation'.

29. They may then be occupied by 'celestials', when they will all be equally honourable.

30. The 'infallible rule of Duty' is 'not to do or desire anything, but what can eternally be done . . . in the *celestial states*'. The good of one being must not arise from the misery of another.[1]

This, then, is the doctrine which had at last become, as Caesar puts it, 'common property', a doctrine in which man is shown standing above a state where, as Williams says in one of his poems, the unfortunate soul is doomed

> to creep
> A groveling worm, or, in the deep,
> To dread the billow's angry swell,
> Or wing the skies, or through the desart yell,[2]

and beneath 'the *taedium* of ETERNITY'. It cannot be said that it is impossible to take this system seriously: some of his readers believed Williams. They evidently did not realize that they also accepted it as a body of beliefs that the Druids held in common with Noah. Williams's abilities do not show to advantage here; in an alleged transcript of a sixteenth-century manuscript which

[1] op. cit., vol. ii, pp. 195 ff.   [2] ibid., vol. ii, p. 204.

is translated by his son under the title of 'The Roll of Tradition and Chronology', he attempts quite another kind of exposition of 'bardic mysteries'.[1] In effect, it opens with a vivid and magnificent commentary on the first verse of the Gospel according to St. John, and it serves to remind one that Williams had many sides to his character: if he is remembered as a scholar with exasperation, his frauds may be remembered with indulgence.

Williams used to visit the British Museum frequently, and a friendly bookseller allowed him to rummage through recently published books,[2] and he may well have incorporated in his aphorisms some ideas that his wide reading in contemporary literature had suggested to him. The parallels that are pointed out here may be fortuitous, but three of them are taken from eighteenth-century poetry on the Druids, a field that does not give coincidence much room. In 1780 John Smith stated that none could die in the hell of the Druids, where the damned dwelt among savage beasts, the lowest of them being almost immersed in snakes.[3] This recalls what Williams says of 'Earthly worms and brutes' in his comments quoted above on a verse which he attributed to Taliesin, a remark which slightly amplifies what he says in his eighth aphorism. A little later, John Ogilvie said of the Druids:

> The rageful soul, in yelling wolves they found;
> The proud, in reptiles grov'ling on the ground:
> Pale envy croaking in th'obscener toad

while others, of better character,

> Frisk'd in the lamb, or mid' the sacred grove
> Uninjur'd, wanton'd in the sportful dove:
> Till the freed thought a happier seat possess'd,
> And man's fair form receiv'd the welcome guest.[4]

---

[1] *Iolo Manuscripts*, Llandovery, 1848, pp. 424 ff.
[2] See E. Waring, *Recollections of Edward Williams*, 1850, pp. 10, 25.
[3] *Galic Antiquities*, Edinburgh, 1780, pp. 21 ff.
[4] *The Fane of the Druids*, 1787, p. 33.

It is quite likely that Williams knew these lines: in his own verse, it is noticeable that his unfortunates, like Ogilvie's, grovel and yell.

The suggestion that sacrifice assisted promotion to higher states was put forward in a drama published only four years earlier than Williams's poems. The Druids, in Frank Sayers's *Starno*, insist on sacrificing the young Kelric: there is no last-moment reprieve, and the play ends as

> (The priest completes the sacrifice.)

> CHORUS 'Tis not in mortal mould confin'd
> That deathless souls shall share
> Unmingled bliss—
> Vainly the storms of fate shall dash
> Th'immortal spark of vital fire,
> That quenchless cleaves aerial space,
> And glides, in mystic round,
> Through ever-changeful forms.[1]

Aphorism 9 may have been suggested by Erasmus Darwin, who thought that 'the world may be still in its infancy, and continue to improve FOR EVER AND EVER'.[2] Aphorism 10, with its 'delightful *renovations*' that alleviate the tedium of eternity, is little more than a paraphrase of James Thomson's lines from *Winter*:

> We, shifting for relief, would play the shapes
> Of frolic fancy; and incessant form
> Unnumbered pictures, fleeting o'er the brain,
> Yet rapid still renew'd.[3]

And again, Thomson's remarks on his spiritual ascent from the lower planes of existence

> From seeming evil still educing good,
> And better thence again, and better still,
> In infinite progression[4]

---

[1] *Poetical Works*, 1830, pp. 108–9.
[2] *Zoonomia*, 1794, I, section XXXIX, ix, 4.
[3] op. cit., ll. 610 ff.   [4] 'A Hymn', ll. 114 ff.

fit Williams's context very well: in his lower states, evil
exists but 'culpability' does not, and this has some
affinity with Thomson's 'seeming evil'. There is, in fact,
something very familiar about Williams's cosmology.
Both he and Thomson have the same conception of a
hierarchic universe whose superior states are occupied by
the same endless process of metempsychosis. Both are
involved in one odd contradiction, for in their view the
nearer the soul gets to the Divine unity the more it gets
attached to multiplicity. If Williams claimed that this was
the philosophy of the Druids, might it not have originated
with the Druid who lay in Richmond Churchyard?

There was a public for novelties that did not try its
sense of decorum, and by some of his contemporaries his
ideas were favourably received. 'The Bardic system',
writes the historian Sharon Turner

as at present known, expresses an ardent benevolence, a sublime
theology, mixed with the peculiar notion of transmigration, which is,
however, put into its most plausible shape, and a valuable morality.[1]

Williams's version of Druidism is summarized in Robert
Southey's *Book of the Church*,[2] and Mrs Hemans has
recorded her impressions of the holding of a Gorsedd.[3]
Far more striking was the reaction of hostile critics.

'I must confess', says Edward Davies in the preface to
his *Mythology and Rites of the British Druids*, 1809,

that I have not been the first in representing the *druidical*, as
having some connection with the *patriarchal religion*; but I know
of no work already before the Public, which has unravelled the
very slender threads by which the connection was maintained.[4]

To this casual dismissal of everything that Williams had
said on the subject, Davies adds some remarks which

[1] *History of the Anglo-Saxons*, 1799, p. 195.
[2] op. cit., 1824, Bk. I, pp. 4 ff.
[3] Quoted in T. Bulfinch, *The Age of Fable*, New York, 1935, p. 433.
[4] op. cit., p. vii.

reflect on the other's character, but Davies's own exposition of Druidism offers no acceptable alternative to
Williams's inventions. It reads as though some mutation
of the imagination had reached out to and flowered in a
world that cannot possibly exist, and so removed is it
from reality that it enters into no opposition with it. It
was presented as a scholarly study, but just as the men of
the Renaissance had discovered themselves in the Druids,
and just as the Druids of the eighteenth century were
sometimes surrounded by an Augustan ritual of rationalization, so the Romantics inadvertently possess a Druid of
their own. Yet the author was still the same man who had
painstakingly traced the origin of language back to Eden,
who had so sympathetically shared Adam's first efforts to
speak. In the meantime, however, he had come under the
influence of the Reverend G. S. Faber's *Dissertation on
the Mysteries of the Cabiri*, 1803. Faber's work is based on
the euhemerist theories that had led to Jacob Bryant's
discovery of the meaning of the symbolism of the histories
and legends of antiquity, and to recondite learning Faber
adds a readily employed terminology of esoterism in order
to show that many of the gods of Greece and Rome could
ultimately be identified with Noah. It was his thesis that
when the veneration of the Patriarch was coupled with
sun-worship, this produced what he calls the helio-arkite
religion. He goes on to say that the crescent moon,
according to the Chaldean astronomers, was 'no unapt
symbol of the Ark', and since Varro says that the crescent
moon was called Jana, Faber infers that Janus was originally Noah.[1] The frontispiece of the third volume of his
Origin of Pagan Idolatry[2] illustrates some features of this
thesis: it shows engravings of various religious symbols
and other objects from all parts of the world, and these,
he argues, demonstrate the homogeneity of ancient beliefs which were at first centred on Noah. The trident of

[1] op. cit., pp. 16–17.   [2] Published in 1816.

Shiva is here taken to be a symbol of the crescent moon, or the Ark; megalithic remains at New Grange and near Maidstone are also shown as symbols of the Ark, symbols of rebirth after confinement to initiatic chambers.

Davies was convinced that Druidism had been surreptitiously practised in Britain until the sixth century. Early Welsh poetry, was, he thought, contemporary with Druidism in its last stages. It was very difficult to understand. The texts were defective, but the poems also seemed to have been made obscure by design, and this led him to believe that they were a repository of the secrets of the Druids: their guarded language was a necessary expedient in a country which had long been converted to Christianity. After reading Jacob Bryant[1] and Faber on classical mythology, Davies was certain that he could decipher this cryptic literature.

He took Druidism to be a debased form of Patriarchal religion; this, having been contaminated by worship of the sun and moon, had then turned into the Helio-arkite and Lunar-arkite superstitions. Its central theme was the story of Noah, and Davies thus found in the greater part of the poetry he examined covert allusions to some aspect or other of the story of the Deluge. He translated copiously into English, sometimes placing whole passages before the reader, sometimes interspersing a running commentary; in the specimen given below it can be seen what he made of some lines on a cow, which in the original run— as they are translated by a modern scholar: 'At mid-day it will be lowing, at midnight it will be boiling; it will be boiled on land, it will be eaten in ships.'[2]

The chief of the Diluvians, and therefore *Hu* the *Mighty*, is styled *Cadwaladr*, the *supreme disposer of battle*, and described as a druid. He is attended by a *spotted cow*, which procures blessings. *On a serene day she bellowed*, I suppose as a warning presage of

[1] *A New System, or an Analysis of Ancient Mythology*, 1774–6.
[2] Quoted in J. Morris-Jones, 'Taliesin', p. 19.

IV. Symbolical representations in ancient architecture of the landing of the Ark on Ararat: *see pp.* 211–12.

the deluge; and afterwards *she was boiled, or sacrificed, on May Eve*, the season in which British mythology commemorated the egress from the ark. The *spot where she was sacrificed*, afforded rest to the deified patriarch, who is here styled *Yssadawr*, the *consumer* or *sacrificer*.[1]

But merely to say that he thought this poetry commemorated Noah would misrepresent Davies: his interpretation of the story of the Deluge is itself far from being simple. In his commentary on the legend of Taliesin, different lines of thought, each of them with surprises for the classicist, the historian, the Welsh scholar, the theologian, the student of esoterism, not to mention his fellow exponents of Druidism, are closely interwoven, and his argument then leads to remarks that have no obvious relationship to either truth or falsehood.

In *Hanes Taliesin*, the tale of Taliesin, Cyrridwen (whom Davies calls Ceridwen) is the mother of the ugliest man in the world, and in order to provide her son with some compensation for this defect, she brews in her cauldron a potion which will produce for him the essence of inspiration. One Gwion Bach, a boy, is given the task of tending the cauldron. It suddenly throws out three drops of the elixir: these fall on the boy's finger, which he promptly puts to his mouth and sucks. By swallowing the precious liquid, he acquires the powers that Cyrridwen had tried to obtain for her son. She bears down on the boy to kill him, and in an ecstasy of panic he flees from her, constantly changing his shape. She swiftly follows him through this desperate sequence. The hare is hounded, the fish is chased by an otter. Finally he changes himself into a grain of wheat, but a hen appears and swallows him. Cyrridwen lays her egg and waits until her prey is hatched. He is now at her mercy, but she is struck by the child's beauty, and instead of killing him there and then, she puts him into a leather bag and throws him into the sea.

[1] op. cit., pp. 221 ff.

He is later discovered and exclaimed over, and called Taliesin, the radiant browed, a prodigy who replies when asked if one so small can speak: 'I can say more than you can ask.'[1]

In seeking the underlying meanings of a story of death and rebirth told with grim wit and irony, Davies's approach is defensible. But in trying to elucidate it, he did not see it as a cipher which might contain its own key. He saw it in the light of a theory in which a rationalizing euhemerism was combined with the cultivation of the occult. The legend, far from being illuminated by this treatment, was eclipsed by it. Nevertheless, Davies was solicitous of his readers, careful to explain each step in his reasoning, and his delicately conducted arguments lose much by being summarized. But to do Davies this injustice: he says that in the legend of Taliesin 'we may discover constant allusions to the history of Ceres and her mystical rites'. To the unfamiliar perspectives of classical mythology with which he illustrates his arguments he adds a kind of Biblical exegesis which is not today often met with, and he then explains that the Ark was the symbol of initiatic death. When he comes to describe how Gwion tried to escape from the furious Ceridwen by turning himself into a hare, Davies comments: 'The goddess then transforms herself into a bitch. However degrading the symbol, these animals seem to have a particular connexion with the mysteries of Ceres and Isis.' Ceridwen is thus identified as the Ceres or Isis of the Druids, and the fleeing boy as a candidate for initiation into her mysteries —or, as Davies puts it, an 'aspirant'. When Gwion changes himself into a grain of wheat and Ceridwen turns herself into a hen and pecks at him, Davies arrives at the heart of his interpretation: 'the singular representation of Ceridwen as swallowing the aspirant', he urges, 'must imply something more than the mere introduction into the sanc-

[1] Based on Sir Ifor Williams's synopsis, *Early Welsh Poetry*, p. 60.

tuary . . . and we have here the history of his enclosure
into some *ship*, *cell*, or *cave*, which more immediately
symbolized the person of the mystical goddess. Here he
studied the fanatical rites, and imbibed the sacred doctrines of Ceridwen'.

But Ceres, he goes on to say, might also be 'considered
as the genius of the ark', and uniting the various strands of
his exposition, he declares that

the very process here described, evidently relates to a connected
series of mystical rites, allusive to one history; and the character
and connexions of Ceridwen, the great agent, compared with the
import of the mysteries of Ceres . . . abundantly prove, that the
reference must be made to the history of the deluge.

In revealing to him the hidden meaning of Druid
symbolism by way of Ceridwen and the mysteries of
Greece and Rome, and in leading him back to the Ark
whose truly profound mystery is rightly only adumbrated,
Davies is mindful of the reader, but when he describes
the landing of the Ark, Davies temporarily leaves his
audience to its own thoughts and goes into a trance in
which random images from Celtic and other literatures
converge and are seen in a single vision.

The *landing* of those who escaped from this drowned country,
upon the mountains of *Snowdon*, is like the landing of Deucalion
upon Mount Parnassus. . . . The district of *Snowdon*, from the
remotest period of British mythology, was famous for its Arkite
memorials. Here was the city of *Emrys*, or the *ambrosial* city—
this was also called the city of *Pharaon*, or *higher powers*; that is,
the *Baalim*, or Arkite patriarchs. Here the dragons were concealed
in the time of *Beli* (the solar deity) and in the time of *Prydain*,
the son of *Aedd the great*, a mystical person of the same family.
As dragons were harnessed in the car of the British *Ked*, as well
as in that of Ceres, the concealing of these animals, in a city of the
higher powers, must imply an establishment of her mysteries.

The land of Gwyddno is said to have been inundated in the
time of *Emrys*, the sovereign. This is the person from whom the

temple of Stonehenge, as well as the *sacred city* in Snowdon, derived its name. If the Britons of the fifth century had a monarch who bore this title, we can only say, like his successors *Uthyr* and *Arthur*, he was complimented with a name out of the vocabulary of the Druids; and that the age of *Emrys* was *any age*, which acknowledged the *Helio-arkite* superstition.[1]

In intention, *The Mythology and Rites of the British Druids* offers an exhaustive analysis of a body of poetry which preserves the secrets of the Druids. In so far as Davies's arguments are founded on wrongly dated texts, an approximate equivalent of the task he set himself would be an attempt to prove that the first fifty poems in *The Golden Treasury*, for instance, originally formed part of the Arthurian cycle. With this analogy in mind, it can be appreciated that his mistranslations are only a minor feature of so intricate an assembly of error and fallacy that its author's orchestration, as it were, is itself remarkable. He assumed that Druidism had flourished in sixth-century Britain, that it was a debased form of Patriarchal religion incorporating sun and moon worship, that it was centred on the story of the Deluge, that early Welsh poetry was contemporary with Druidism, that this in turn could be explained by reference to the mysteries of Ceres and Isis among others, and to Welsh mythology, and that what lay behind this elaborate symbolism had an even more profound significance which could be explained only in terms of initiatic rites. Davies's sincerity is evident, but in a work of such complexity it is not surprising to find a touch of the tendentious here and there. This is not to suggest that he was guilty of the kind of deliberate deception that Williams practised: Davies was not only convinced that he had discovered the secrets of the Druids, but he was careful to exhibit his evidence. Indeed, he firmly faced difficulties that a less scrupulous exegetist might have avoided. As it can be seen from his own

[1] op. cit., pp. 230 ff.

comments, he was apprehensive of the effect that some passages in the original text might have on his readers; nevertheless, he translated the implacable words that confronted him. References to pigs and dogs were therefore assimilated into a work which is not without a certain dignity, and he thus inspired, in their monumental book on early British costumes, the remarks of Meyrick and Smith on 'the mystical sow of the Druids', and it was on his authority that they said 'the Druids were called Dogs of the Deep of a white hue, with red shining ears'.[1] But, as it will be seen, it is in his diction that Davies comes under suspicion of preferring artifice to candour.

His interpretation of Welsh poetry was challenged by a Dean of Merton College, Oxford, who as editor of a text of the eighth-century historian Nennius was at home in the period to which the Druidism of Williams and Davies belonged. In attacking their contention that it preserved the teaching of the Patriarchs, the Reverend Algernon Herbert was relatively indulgent to Davies, who had called it 'the *Helio-arkite* superstition'. Williams, on the other hand, had affirmed the respectability of Bardism: he had actively propagated his ideas, and he had held Bardic ceremonies in 'the eye of the light' on a Welsh mountain-top and on the summit of Primrose Hill. Davies's theories were greeted by Herbert with supercilious amusement, even if he surreptitiously borrowed some of the other's phrases, but Williams was denounced as the agent of a subversive movement that had again come into the open after lying low for centuries.

Herbert did not like Druidism: 'by the strange union of knavish urbanity and philosophical trumpery with wild atrociousness, it seems to have made a compound worse than either of the discordant elements by itself, a monster

[1] *The Costume of the Original Inhabitants of the British Isles*, 1821, p. 26, plate x.

hideous and ridiculous'.[1] He argues persuasively that it
was of late creation, making its appearance suddenly, and
swiftly imposing itself on the Celts, for 'the Druidical
organisation and attainments exceeded any thing that the
savageness of the Celtae is likely to have struck out by the
mere energy of their sylvan meditations'.[2] Overthrown
by Rome, it did not disappear entirely; then, originating
along the eastern borders of the Empire, something new
spread to and infected Britain, a heresy founded on 'the
mysteries of the Persian Magi'. The heretics were 'Mithriacs', and the alleged renaissance of Druidism in post-
Roman Britain was not Druidism at all, but Mithraism.
The Mithriacs, or Neo-Druids, parodied Christianity:
they pretended to be Christians, but they worshipped the
sun and revived the doctrines of the knavish Pythagoras.[3]
The Druids of old were more boisterous and open than
the subtle and more dangerous Neo-Druids, and Herbert
sharply discriminates between them.

Contemptuous of Owen's efforts to raise the status of
the Bard in order to make him a more imposing figure
than the Druid himself, Herbert comments that 'bardism
was only the rude office of a songster'.[4] Stung by certain
phrases in Williams's version of ancient Celtic ritual—
especially where the audience is dramatically asked if
they meet in peace, Herbert remarks: 'Bardism was
formerly a war-whoop, but now it babbles of peace and
philanthropy.'[5] But he was alarmed at Williams's mention
of 'bardic mysteries profound', and he points out that the
Neo-Druids were secretive because they had 'barbarous
usages to conceal from the eye of civilisation and impious
follies from that of the Holy Church'. What specially
roused Herbert's resentment was Williams's 'organisation': this, he thought, had revived an old and sinister
conspiracy, and in its contemporary form it was the

---

[1] *The Neodruidic Heresy in Britannia*, 1838, p. 13.
[2] ibid., p. 14.   [3] ibid., pp. 29 ff.   [4] ibid., p. 36.   [5] ibid., p. 79.

'mongrel produce of Druidism, Mithraic heresy, and modern Free-Masonry'.[1] In his opinion, everything that had been recorded of Britain after the Romans—and here he took particular heed of the story of King Arthur—was a garbled version of what had really happened, and in the same poetry that had yielded to Davies 'the history of the deluge', Herbert found ample proof of camouflaged heresies that had contributed to the chaos into which the country was then plunged. To sum up the situation in Arthurian Britain as Herbert describes it:

It has been the object of this Essay to shew that the separation of the British province of the empire was not merely the case of an effete civilization giving way to irrumpent barbarism, such as its other provinces exhibit. But, that it was attended by an abandonment of established Christianity, and the rise of a strange and awful apostatic heresy; of which the historical vestiges are rare, but the internal evidences numerous and strong.

Symptoms of that change have tinged British history and literature from the separation downwards, to an indefinitely modern point of time. But it had its paroxyms; its times of greater ascendancy and power than others; times of greater publicity and more unreserved avowal, as others were of a more dissembling temper, and saw reason to prefer closer disguises of such initiation as may be termed masonic.

The long and great paroxym of this mania was the period extending, from the revolt against the Gwynethian King-Insular, Gwytheyrn of the Untoward Mouth, down to the conflict (called) of the Field-of-Iniquity or Cam-lan. Its period of extreme exacerbation was from the establishment of that power (known by the name of Arthur) which fell in the Cam-lan, unto its downfall in that revolution. After which event, the aforesaid power or principle was removed out of sight by the two chief bards of Britain, and kept alive, from thenceforwards indefinitely, in the secrecy of a charmed and magical asylum.

This long paroxym includes that remarkable period in which a most obscure and inglorious real history gives place to a romance

1 ibid., p. 36.

of heroic wonders. . . . Emmrys Wledig . . . Uthyr Pendragon, and Arthur, by whom that space is filled, were not real persons; but terms . . . while a number of real men, of inferior glory . . . were those that actually performed the brawlings and ruination of that dismal time.[1]

Little need be said here of Herbert's arguments, for where they are founded on erroneously dated poetry they are open to the same criticism that invalidates Davies's premises. Vigilant and suspicious, Herbert was a critic who placed more trust in his own insight and presentiments than on evidence as he investigated a past which had been denounced by Gildas, a present in which the same apostatic heresy had reappeared. But to show how quickly his fears could be wakened: he thought that its alleged predilection for the Gospel according to St. John demonstrated the waywardness of the Celtic Church, for in his opinion any indication of partiality was itself sufficient proof of a leaning to the heretical; and he accused St. Patrick, St. Columba, and St. Columban of mimicking Christ and the Apostles by taking with them on their missions twelve associates or disciples.[2]

The theories of Edward Williams, Edward Davies, and Algernon Herbert added quite adventitious complications to the study of early Welsh poetry, and they made the subject of Druidism even more mystifying. (Yet susceptible readers still continued to believe in its longevity, and it was perhaps a cross-current of the ideas of Williams and Thomas Maurice that moved the Archdruid Myfyr Morganwg to offer prayers to Kali at Pontypridd in 1878.)[3] Though they had so greatly differed in their interpretation of the same material, they held in common the assumption that it was written in the sixth century, and their subsequent disagreement only made their agreement on

[1] *Britannia After the Romans*, vol. ii, 1841, pp. 1–2.
[2] ibid., pp. 145, 155.
[3] Wirt Sikes, *British Goblins*, 1880, p. 277.

this point the more impressive. The very basis of everything they had to say about Druidism was then effectively
challenged by D. W. Nash in *Taliesin*, 1858.

Nash was particularly interested in dating the early
Welsh poems he inspected, and he demonstrated how
easy it was to remove anomalies in their interpretation
simply by transferring poems to later centuries than those
in which earlier students had placed them, and in some
cases, later centuries than those in which the poets had
written them. An entertainingly sardonic critic, he takes
a look at, for example, G. D. Barber's *Ancient Oral
Records of the Cimbri*, 1855, in which the sixth-century
poem *The Gododdin*, which celebrates the heroes who fell
at the battle of Catraeth, is described as a treatise on the
game of chess. Nash quotes from Barber's translation
and comments:

> Cast at it quickly. Give it up! Turn it over.
> Consider! Risk! Hurry on! Stand still! Go back!
> A pleasant game of games.

We must say, we prefer giving it up.[1]

As a translator, however, Nash does not live up to the
expectations aroused by his malice. His command of
Welsh was peremptory rather than wide, and the
'apparent good sense of his translation'[2] puts into plausible English meanings that are not always in the original
texts. Accuracy should not be looked for in the specimen
of his work given below, but his interpretation and render-
ing of the poem from the *Book of Taliesin* which he
translates as 'The Panegyric on Lludd the Great' hints at
the growing astringency of the temper of Welsh scholarship. In the Druids themselves Nash was little interested,
and he devoted a chapter to 'The Druidical Philosophy'
only because Williams, Davies, and some others had
enmeshed Welsh poetry in a cat's cradle of Druidism and

---

[1] *Taliesin*, 1858, p. 67.
[2] J. Morris-Jones, op. cit., pp. 18–19.

Neodruidism. He was delighted to give the string a final tug, and what he thought of their work may be gathered by implication from a comparison of the style of his translation of 'The Panegyric' with that of the annotated version offered by Davies.

As Davies translates it, it runs:

A song of dark import was composed by the distinguished *Ogdoad*, who assembled on the day of the moon and went in open procession: on the day of Mars, they allotted wrath to their adversaries: on the day of Mercury, they enjoyed their full pomp: on the day of Jove, they were delivered from the detested usurpers: on the day of Venus, the day of the great influx, they swam in the blood of men: on the day of Saturn – – – – – – on the day of the sun, there truly assemble five ships, and five hundred of those who make supplication, 'O Brithi Brithoi, &c. – – – – – – O son of the compacted wood, the shock overtakes me: we all attend on *Adonai*, on the area of *Pumpai*.'

In his notes, Davies explains that 'this *Ogdoad* consists of the Diluvian patriarch and his family', and that 'the accumulating deluge . . . is figuratively styled the *blood of men*'. 'The 'five hundred' are 'the wicked inhabitants of the old world'. He adds that 'their prayer is in a foreign language, probably that of the mysteries introduced by *Coll*, the Cornish hierophant'.[1] Nash for his part states that the poem is a satire on monks, that the mysterious words which Davies suggests are in the language of the Cornish hierophant are really a mockery of the monks at their prayers. The Druids and the Patriarchs vanish, and a second look at Davies's diction will disclose further traces of a compulsion that acted not only on his thoughts but on his choice of words like the pull of the tides.

In Nash's translation it runs:

> They make harsh songs;
> They note eight numbers.

[1] op. cit., pp. 564 ff.

On Monday they will be
Prying about.
On Tuesday they separate
Angry with their adversaries.
On Wednesday they drink,
Enjoying themselves ostentatiously.
On Thursday they are in the choir;
Their poverty is disagreeable.
Friday is a day of abundance,
The men are swimming in pleasures.
On Saturday . . . .
On Sunday certainly,
Five legions and five hundred of them,
They pray, they make exclamations,
'O brithi brithoi
Nuoes nuedi
Brithi brithanai
Sychedi edi euroi.'
Like wood-cuckoos
In noise they will be,
Every one of the idiots
Banging on the ground.[1]

[1] *Taliesin*, 1858, p. 257.

XI

ALL THINGS BEGIN AND END IN ALBION'S
ANCIENT DRUID ROCKY SHORE

IN the literature which has been described here, William
Blake was quite at home, and it was to its picture of
the Druid as the heir of the Patriarchs that Blake owed
much of the inspiration for the most singular of his ideas.
If, after he had absorbed himself in studies of the Druids,
the main stream of his thought went on as before, it now
flowed through a transformed landscape. Compared with
the literature from which it is derived, what Blake then
had to say is like the version of the original that shows on
the reverse of a woven pattern: in Blake's view, Druidism
did not evolve somewhere along the road from Ararat,
for it was already ancient when it entered the Ark; it
was carried to, and not from the oaks of Mamre, and his
Patriarchs are the heirs of the Druids.

But these are only incidental features of his new
cosmogony; more striking developments show themselves in his mixture of Biblical and British names and
place-names in the later Prophetic Books, and under the
stimulus of this new and exciting idea he wrote the
notable lines which have been taken from their context
and given the title 'Jerusalem'. In their original setting
they are part of the preface to *Milton*, which opens with
an exhortation in prose to young men and artists to free
themselves from the influence of 'the stolen and perverted'
classics which are 'set up by artifice against the true
Sublime of the Bible'; then, as though addressing himself
to a higher level of response in his readers, Blake exclaims:

And did those feet in ancient time
Walk upon England's mountains green?
And was the holy Lamb of God
On England's pleasant pastures seen?

And did the Countenance Divine
Shine forth upon these clouded hills?
And was Jerusalem builded here
Among these dark Satanic Mills?

Taken out of their context in *Milton*, the opening lines of 'Jerusalem' are puzzling. What they refer to has no known place in sacred history, and looked at in this light, it would seem that Blake does not mean these lines to be taken literally. Yet in their proper context—which includes *Jerusalem* (whose title should not be confused with that of the poem quoted above), the revised *Vala* or *The Four Zoas*, and *A Vision of the Last Judgement*, all of which were written or revised after he had reinterpreted Genesis—the rhetorical questions have a simplicity of meaning that matches the poem's direct emotional appeal, and their feeling springs not only from their great theme but also from Blake's sense of awe at his discovery of this island's unique importance in sacred history. Blake was convinced that Britain, and not Palestine, was the original Holy Land.

Milton forms a part of the Prophetic Books. To summarize their plot in a sentence: Albion's efforts to regain his lost primordial state are frustrated by the malevolent Urizen, who is partly a projection of his own nature; but when the 'Shepherd of Albion' finally intervenes, His words transfigure Albion and restore him.[1] By alluding to conditions as they were before the Fall, Blake extends his cycle to include by implication the vanished primordial age, leaving, for example,

[1] The standard work on the Prophetic Books is Northrop Frye's *Fearful Symmetry*, Princeton, 1947.

the nature of the earliest form of Druidism to be inferred.

Blake aimed at the statement of universal truths, and the episodes of the Prophetic Books typify states or conditions that are met with during the course of the cycle. The dramatis personae all have an archetypal character, and Blake invents, with significant exceptions, the names of both persons and places as though to give the outstanding features of his cosmology meanings which are precise within the framework of his own symbolism, but elusive if attempts are made to interpret them in any other terminology. The tone of his writing varies, and when he says that his work is visionary, he does not imply that it is divorced from mundane reality: in *Jerusalem* he intersperses his poetry with admonitory addresses that have all the bluntness of plain speaking.

Blake's theme is the predicament of Fallen Man, whose archetype, in this cosmogony, is not Adam but 'Albion, our Ancestor',[1] the eponymous first inhabitant of this island; Adam himself has a subordinate part, and he is called among other things a Druid.[2] Between Albion and the gods who people the Prophetic Books there is the closest possible relationship, for Albion was originally the mirror of the Divine, of the 'Four Mighty Ones' who rule in 'Great Eternity' in a unity which is simultaneously multiple and single;[3] after the Fall, they appear on Earth as separate gods. They can exist as such only in the conditions which bring about and perpetuate the disaster of the Fall, and Albion, instead of reflecting the Divine harmony, now sees his own plight reflected in that of the divided gods: their encounters then illustrate the permutations of human error.

Albion's enemy is Urizen, who in Great Eternity is the

---

[1] *A Vision of the Last Judgement*, pp. 80–81; K.643.
[2] *A Descriptive Catalogue*, v; K. 608–9.
[3] *The Four Zoas*, I; K. 252, 264.

principle of justice and order: hence, for Blake, 'mental strife' is a spiritual activity. In Albion's universe he is the symbol, so to speak, of the human reason when it arrogates to itself powers to which it is not entitled. He now usurps the functions of Los—who is so named, presumably, because he is the reverse of Sol, the spiritual sun. The tyrant Urizen takes it upon himself to interpret, and thereby pervert, the truths which can be grasped only by the intuition. He thus places a barrier between Albion and his return to the lost primordial state in which he lived with his wife Brittannica and their daughter Jerusalem. Literal-minded to a degree, Urizen quite fails to understand what is meant by the sacrifice which casts off 'Selfhood': instead, he sacrifices the physical body.

Jesus, as the manifestation of the Divine perfection which is unaffected by what happens below, 'Opens Eternity in Time & Space'.[1] As the Shepherd of Albion, He is present from the first, and His is the most ancient Gospel.[2] The cycle ends when He intervenes and reveals to Albion the nature of the true sacrifice which casts off Selfhood. Urizen returns to his original condition; his Druids vanish; Albion calls on Jerusalem to return from exile. The Prophetic Books close as the presence of Jerusalem removes from the world the duality of the sacred and profane.[3]

The Druids are frequently mentioned in *Milton* and *Jerusalem*. Without moving from the background, they are, like figures in a striking tapestry, intrusive. The desolate surface of Britain after the Fall is covered with 'Druid stones'; its horizons are lit by their holocausts, and they build Stonehenge from the rocks of Eden.[4] Their oppressive presence suggests the deterioration of the very

---

[1] ibid., 1; K. 264. Jer. 75; K. 535.
[2] *Jer*. 38; K. 479. *Jer*. 27; K. 463.
[3] *Jer*. 96–99; K. 563 ff.   [4] *Jer*. 66; K. 519.

ancient rather than the freshness of the primordial. Never-
theless, theirs was the earliest wisdom before they turned,
under Urizen's influence, 'mental and allegorical sig-
nification into corporeal command',[1] and the original
Druidism was providentially preserved by the Druid
Abraham, who, unlike Urizen's Druids, did not go astray.
Even classical learning stemmed from it, for 'Your Greek
Philosophy . . . is a remnant of Druidism'.[2]

The Druids are the priests of Urizen; as such, they
share some of his peculiar characteristics, and they also
have some general resemblances to the Druids that Blake
had read about. Both Urizen and the Druids—to speak
loosely—were priests, lawgivers, and philosophers. Urizen
mistakes the dimensions of space for absolute reality; the
Druids were once thought of as mathematicians, and in
the Prophetic Books, height, length, and breadth are
called 'Druidical'.[3] As sacrificers of men, they also made
appropriate priests for Urizen. One of his more subtle
faults was that he thought that a circle made a suitable
symbol of infinity. Since stone circles were in Blake's day
widely thought of as Druid temples, it seemed to him that
they very aptly demonstrated the fallacious nature of
Urizen's metaphysics, and it is among them that 'the
Mills of Satan' are found.[4]

So far, then, the Druids have been briefly described in
their relation to a major character and the essential plot
of the Prophetic Books; if they are in the background,
and give it its colour, they have every right to be there,
for it is Britain, the land in which Druidism originated,
the land in which Blake's version of sacred history started.
They also have another background, and Blake's borrowings from the literature on the Druids shows how widely
he had read in it, and how ingeniously he applied his

[1] *Descriptive Catalogue*, v; K. 609.
[2] *Jer.* 27; K. 463. *Jer.* 52; K. 497.
[3] *Milton*, I, 4; K. 379.
[4] *Europe* (1794); K. 216. *Milton*, I, 12; K. 386.

borrowings. A case in point is his mention of the 'Holy
Fiend, the Wicker Man of Scandinavia'.[1]

The Wicker Man is the colossus of osiers, described by
Caesar and Strabo, in which the Druids burned animals
and men. In Blake's symbolism, the vegetable is the image
of the purely physical nature of man: he says of his own
'vegetable' eye that he looks through it, not with it.[2]
Blake points out that the colossus of osiers comes from a
'Vegetating Root', and the burning of the Wicker Man
thus demonstrates the ineptitude of the Druids' sacrifice,
for by destroying the human body they achieve nothing.

There seems to be no special connexion between the
Wicker Man as such and Scandinavia, but a number of
authors thought that Druidism had been practised there.
Olof Rudbeck,[3] and Peringskiold's edition of Snorri's
Heims Kringla helped to foster this notion;[4] in 1758 a
thesis was presented at the University of Ulm on affinities
between the Gallic Druids and the Gothic Drotti.[5] Henry
Rowlands, Percy's translation of Mallet's *Northern
Antiquities*[6]—the most probable source of Blake's ideas—
Bishop Nicholson, and Thomas Warton also helped to
give the idea some currency.[7] It was a part of Blake's own
thesis that Druidism had spread over the world. Again,
Blake claims that the Jews had received from the Druids
'a tradition, that Man anciently contain'd in his limbs
all things in Heaven and Earth',[8] and this is in all probability a reference to the Cabbalist teaching on the nature
of Adam Qadmon, who before the Fall was the human

[1] *Jer.* 47; K. 492.
[2] *Vision of the Last Judgement;* K. 652.
[3] O. Rudbeck, *Atlantica*, Uppsala, 1675, p. 817.
[4] Snorri Sturluson, op. cit., Stockholm, 1697, vol. i, pp. 6–11.
[5] *Diss. gradualis de Gallorum Druidis cum Gothorum Drottis collatis; resp. N. Smedberg*, Lund, 1758.
[6] Mallet thought that the poetry of the Druids was preserved in the Eddas: *Northern Antiquities*, II, pp. xv, xvi.
[7] *Irish Historical Library*, Dublin, 1724, p. xxi; *History of English Poetry*, vol. i, 1774, sig. d v.
[8] *Jer.* 27; K. 463.

vehicle of the Divine attributes. The Druids, by filling
their colossus with animals and men, thought they were
following their original teaching on the nature of man; in
reality, they were parodying it. In this single image of the
Wicker Man, Blake relates his Druids to the Druids as
they had been described in the classics, castigates them
for misunderstanding what sacrifice implied, alludes to
the spread of Druidism over the world, and condemns
them for perverting an ancient esoteric doctrine which the
Jews had received from them.

The precise sources of Blake's Druid symbolism cannot
always be identified. The Druids' 'Knife of Revenge &
the Poison Cup of Jealousy'[1] are taken, in all probability,
from the frontispiece to Elias Schedius's *De Dis Germanis*,
which shows a dignified Druid standing in the foreground
of a scene of carnage holding a Saracen dagger and a
chalice. The 'Stone of Trial', which ultimately comes
from Gibson's edition of Camden, is alluded to in several
books. Quite possibly he had read Aylett Sammes on the
Druids, for Blake calls the sun a 'scythed chariot', and
Sammes was the first to claim that the ancient Britons
fixed scythes to their chariot wheels; but this idea is also
in *Caractacus*.[2]

Blake had accepted much of what the learned had to
say of the Druids. He borrowed technical archaeological
terms from Stukeley. Some eighteenth-century magazine
articles on alleged similarities between the human sacrifices of the Peruvians and those of the Druids anticipate
Blake's statement that Druidism reached South America.
A number of authors had suggested that the Cabbala and
Druidism had much in common. Henry Rowlands asserts
that Jewish religion was only a copy of 'the sacred Patriarchal Rubrick'. John Cleland, following Pezron, was
certain that Greek mythology was 'demonstrably' the in-

[1] *Jer.* 63; K. 514.
[2] *Jer.* 56; K. 504. Sammes, *Britannia*, p. 121.

vention of the Druids. Blake championed in his own way the theory that originally all mankind had the same religion. As for the subject of the Druids and the Patriarchs, Blake copied Edward Williams by calling his own Druids 'the Patriarch Druids'.[1]

Yet Blake had not always thought of the Druids as the priests of Urizen. It is only in the last two Prophetic Books that a sudden proliferation of references to the Druids appears, and at the same time, the evidence of his belief that Britain was the original Holy Land. This evidence is not confined to the completed Prophetic Books: the unfinished *Vala*, later called *The Four Zoas*, shows Blake at work altering passages to make them consistent with his new ideas. The date on its title-page is 1797, and before he started to revise it, he held no unusual views on Biblical topography and chronology, while his single reference to the Druids (in *The Ghost of Abel*) before this date is unremarkable. A picture which he drew for his illustrated *History of England* shows, from its position in the list of contents, that for him they were still stock figures of ancient history.[2]

He knew by 1794 of Stukeley's theories on Druid temples, and he accepted the other's archaeological conclusions; with Stukeley's Druids he would have nothing to do, for his own Druids were the ancestors of the deists whom Stukeley had fought. In the following year, Blake shows that he had still not changed his views on sacred history: in *The Song of Los* he says:

> Adam stood in the garden of Eden
> And Noah on the mountains of Ararat;
> They saw Urizen give his Law to the Nations.[3]

Judea is still Urizen's 'ancient place'.[4] Even as late as the first revision of *Vala*, when he describes how 'Those in

[1] *Jer.* 98; K. 567.
[2] *Poetical Works*, ed. J. Sampson, Oxford, 1913, p. xxxv.
[3] *Song of Los* (1795), 'Africa'; K. 247.   [4] ibid., 'Asia'; K. 249.

Great Eternity met in the Council of God', he shows
them doing so over the Biblical Holy Land, 'as One Man,
hovering over Gilead and Hermon'.

But between 1797 and 1804, when he began to write
and etch *Milton* and *Jerusalem*, Blake dramatically changed
his mind. He then came to the conclusion that Britain was
the original Holy Land. 'Mount Gilead', the second
version of the 'Gilead and Hermon' quoted above, is
deleted in the manuscript, and in the final draft the sacred
site over which the Council meets is the top of 'Snowdon
Sublime'.[1] In the Prophetic Books written during and
after 1804, Jerusalem is Albion's daughter, and to her
belongs a golden pillared structure rising near Paddington;[2] she is banished from Britain and exiled to the
Middle East when this island is given over to Urizen's
Druids.[3] The sons of Israel first live in Britain.[4] Zion's
'most ancient promontory' is near Paddington.[5] The island
becomes the immediate setting of Blake's story, and Palestine becomes the scene of subsequent developments. A
comment of Blake's which he made in 1810 makes it
perfectly clear what he thought was the general sequence
of events, for he then said that Albion's history 'Preceded
that of the Hebrews'.[6] The essentials of his cosmogony
are unchanged, but after 1797 Blake dwells heavily on the
unique importance of Britain in sacred history. It would
be going quite against the evidence of his text to minimize
the literal meaning of the line 'All things Begin & End
in Albion's Ancient Druid Rocky Shore', a line which he
places in three different contexts.[7]

---

[1] op. cit., 1; K. 264. See also *Prophetic Writings*, ed. D. J. Sloss and
J. P. R. Wallis, Oxford, 1926, p. 156, and *William Blake's Vala*, ed.
E. M. Margoliouth, Oxford, 1956, p. 175. The emendation is made only
once: the original versions are still shown in K. 257, 331.
[2] *Jer.* 27; K. 463.
[3] *Jer.* 48, 49; K. 494. *Jer.* 78; K. 538–40.
[4] *Jer.* 16; K. 450.   [5] *Jer.* 12; K. 445.
[6] *Vision of Last Judgement;* K. 643.
[7] Milton, 1, 6; K. 381. *Jer.* 27; K. 463. *Jer.* 32; K. 473.

Blake's belief is given explicit expression in his address 'TO THE JEWS' in the twenty-seventh section of *Jerusalem*:

JERUSALEM the Emanation of the Giant Albion! Can it be? Is it Truth that the Learned have explored? Was Britain the Primitive Seat of the Patriarchal Religion? If it is true, my title-page is also True, that Jerusalem was & is the Emanation of the Giant Albion. It is true and cannot be controverted. Ye are united, O ye Inhabitants of Earth, in One Religion, the Religion of Jesus, the most Ancient, the Eternal & the Everlasting Gospel. The Wicked will turn it to Wickedness, the Righteous to Righteousness. Amen! Huzza! Selah!

'All things Begin & End in Albion's Ancient Druid Rocky Shore.'

Your Ancestors derived their origin from Abraham, Heber, Shem and Noah, who were Druids, as the Druid Temples (which are the Patriarchal Pillars and Oak Groves) over the whole Earth witness to this day.

You have a tradition, that Man anciently contain'd in his mighty limbs all things in Heaven and Earth: this you received from the Druids.

'But now the Starry Heavens are fled from the mighty limbs of Albion.'

Albion was the Parent of the Druids, & in his Chaotic State of Sleep, Satan & Adam and the whole World was created by the Elohim.

Jerusalem, whether she is thought of as the daughter of Albion and Brittannica, as a spiritual presence, or as a pillared structure to which she has given her name, is here originally associated with Britain. By asking 'Is it a Truth that the Learned have explored?' Blake leaves the visionary realm of Los and Urizen for a world where he thinks he can appeal to printed authorities. 'Was Britain the Primitive Seat of the Patriarchal Religion?' With this question, he identifies his authorities. Round and during Blake's lifetime, at least four books were devoted to the subject of the Druids and Patriarchs. Cooke's *Enquiry into the Patriarchal and Druidical Religion* appeared in 1754, the anonymous *Complete History of the Druids . . . with an Inquiry into their Religion and its Coincidence with the Patriarchal* in 1810, and *The Identity of the Religions called Druidical and Hebrew* in 1829; D. James's *Patriarchal Religion of Britain* was published in 1836. Blake may well have assumed that his reference would be sufficiently understood. By claiming that all history had started in and would end in Britain, he reverses the opinion of the antiquaries on the origins of British megaliths: the Biblical standing stones, he says, were copies of British models, and the 'Oak Groves' at Mamre and elsewhere commemorate the earliest veneration of the oak in the island where Druidism had started. By saying that Albion was the parent of the Druids, that Adam was a Druid, that the Jews received a tradition from the Druids, he makes himself quite clear: Albion's 'Chaotic State of Sleep' belongs to the more subtle realms of his cosmogony, but once there was a physical world, history started in this island.

Possibly Rudbeck, who had argued that his native Sweden was man's original home, may have suggested this idea to Blake; nevertheless, how Blake finally came to hold his own novel views is an enigma. As a working hypothesis, it might seem that he was in the first place particularly impressed by the resemblances he could detect between Urizen and the Druids. Urizen typified everything that Blake hated: dogma, repression, stupidity, jealousy, oppression, selfishness, cruelty. The coincidence between his formal attributes as lawgiver, priest, and so on, and those of the Druids must have struck Blake with some force: he had isolated and analysed the monster that stood between man and his return to the Golden Age, and he thought that what could be said of Urizen applied with equal force to the Druids. The impact on him of the

striking things that had been said of the Druids then gave
his thoughts a new direction. They had once been held
in great esteem as the earliest of philosophers, and a
number of learned authors, approaching the subject from
different starting-points, had found many links between
the Druids and the Patriarchs. Blake was convinced that
there was substantial truth in what they had to say. For
reasons of his own, he took their theories a stage farther,
but in doing so, he simultaneously accepted and rejected
all that they had said. They had contended that the
Patriarchal teaching had been brought to Britain by the
Druids; Blake, on the other hand, asserted that it had first
been promulgated in Britain, in the original Holy Land.

It was after he came to this conclusion that he liberally
scattered British place-names about the Prophetic Books.
The fields between Islington and Marybone are where the
pillars of Jerusalem originally stood, and it was on the
earth of primordial Britain that

> Her Little-ones ran on the fields,
> The Lamb of God among them seen,
> And fair Jerusalem his Bride,
> Among the little meadows green.[1]

Returning to 'And did those feet in ancient time': to
give the poem its most literal interpretation, it means 'I
shall struggle to restore our own lost British Jerusalem'.
This bald synopsis, of course, brings out very strongly
the limitations of an exclusively literal interpretation. But
if its opening verses are read where Blake placed them,
there is a close relationship between

> And did those feet in ancient time
> Walk upon England's mountains green

and 'All things Begin & End in Albion's Ancient Druid
Rocky Shore'.

[1] *Jer.* 27; K. 464.

By capturing the popular imagination, 'Jerusalem' has in turn been captured, and since the poem no longer belongs to its context, one is now presumably free to read what one likes into the opening lines. In the Prophetic Books, however, Blake's version of Genesis is so provocative that it hardly lends itself to a willing suspension of disbelief. Nevertheless, it does not affect their central meaning, and if it is disconcerting to see the extent to which Blake was self-deluded, this is partly because his sincerity is so patent.

But sincerity is a virtue which is hospitable to illusion, and those who have written in all good faith about the Druids have evidently rarely arrived at anything like truth. Yet some of them have had brief contacts with realities of one kind or another. The German scholar whose notions about the Druids were tinged with a romantic patriotism and who as an etymologist 'deriues all from *Dutch*',[1] as Selden puts it, most nearly approached the etymologies which are derived from Indo-European roots. Stonehenge is not a Patriarchal hieroglyph, but it was the contemporary of some events which are described in Genesis, and the bluestones were brought from Prescelly to their new home long before the Exodus. Blake found Zion in Paddington, but to the south, no farther away than Wiltshire, there was a temple far older than the Temple. The venerated name of Noah has been bandied about in many a page on classical mythology, but the name of Iapetus, the father by Clymene the Oceanid of Prometheus and the grandfather of Deucalion, 'yields no plausible Greek etymology',[2] and in this enigmatic name the worlds of classical scholarship and of eighteenth-century disquisitions on mythology have a bridge, even if it would be unsafe to set foot on it.

[1] *Poly-Olbion*, p. 151.
[2] *Oxford Classical Dictionary*, Oxford, 1949, see 'Iapetus'.

CONCLUSION

I T is surprising that the progress of literature on the
Druids, particularly in the eighteenth century, met
with no opposition to speak of. Possibly the token
observance of tacitly understood conventions in writing
about them disarmed criticism: if inconsequential in-
ferences were drawn from irrelevant premises, at least the
proper gestures had been made. In John Wood's *Choir
Gaure*, 1747, for instance, Abaris—who is also called the
Archdruid Bladud—rapidly converts both hemispheres to
Druidism, uses 'Okeyhole' as an initiatic cave and estab-
lishes a seat of learning at Drewstanton. This seeming
fantasy was based on the title of Magus which was given
by Leland to the legendary King Bladud of John Hardyng's *Chronicle*[1] and on Thomas Carte's assertion that
the Druids of Britain were Hyperboreans—for the garments of the Hyperborean Abaris who visited Pythagoras
suggested to Carte that Abaris wore 'the very habit of the
Highlanders'.[2] Unconvinced by the arguments of those
students of comparative religion who thought that
Druidism had an Eastern origin, Wood insists that it had
started in Britain, and that the mysterious arrow of Abaris
was the symbol of the rapid diffusion of Druidism
throughout the world. Wood's allusion to Okeyhole, or
Wookey Hole, is a reminder that these were not the only
caves which local antiquaries thought had been inhabited

---

[1] Leland, *Commentarii*, p. 8; *Chronicle of Iohn Hardyng*, ed. H. Ellis,
1812, p. 52.
[2] T. Carte, *History*, p. 69; Herodotus, 4, 36.

by the Druids,[1] and he had clearly not learned from
Gibson's edition of *Britannia* that Stanton Drew was not
named after the Druids.[2] Wood's account of the Druids is
not pure invention.

Nevertheless, what he said was so far-fetched as to
imperil what must have sometimes been an insecure
relationship between author and reader, and even Stukeley attacked Wood's 'whimsys of his own crakt imagina-
tions'.[3] But this kind of comment is rarely met with;
though Hearne called Stukeley 'a hypothetical fancifull
man',[4] the cheerful and indefatigable Chyndonax made
more converts than enemies. Richard Cumberland's
satirical portrait of 'Dr. Druid the Antiquarian' does not
hit off anything in particular. As for more general
reviews: 'On no subject has fancy roamed', says the
Reverend Edward Ledwick, 'with more licentious indulgence than on that of the Druids and their institutions';[5]
and the historian John Pinkerton is equally sharp:
'*Druidic* is beginning to be a term for the most nonsensical
nonentity of antiquism'.[6] They were writing in the 1780s,
years after the appearance of the more daring conjectures
on Druidism, but their strictures lead only to typical
conclusions: the former says that the Druids were cannibals, and the latter that they were Phoenicians.

'Have we not found their festivals in India, their circular
temples in Judea, their rites at Delphi and Soracte? In
short, have we not found them everywhere?'[7] The critics
were overwhelmed; nothing checked the propagation of
manifestly novel ideas on the Druids, and in the first
half of the nineteenth century Algernon Herbert protests

[1] See T. D. Kendrick, *The Druids*, 1928, p. 1.
[2] Bochart, *Geographia Sacra*, II, p. 755; corrected in the 1695 edition
of *Britannia*, col. 81.
[3] *Family Memoirs*, ed. Lukis (Surtees Society, lxxx), vol. iii, 1887, p. 276.
[4] Piggott, *William Stukeley*, p. 2.
[5] *Archaeologia*, vol. vii, 1784, p. 304.
[6] *An Enquiry into the History of Scotland*, 1789, vol. i, p. 406.
[7] G. Higgins, *The Celtic Druids*, 1827, p. 281.

that he finds them 'entering the nursery . . . and becoming as it were the elements of catechetical instruction'.[1]
By this time the fame of the Druids had indeed spread
far beyond the relatively restricted circle that Milton had
in mind. Public houses were being named after the Druids.
Vauxhall Gardens once had its shaded Druid's Walk.[2] A
sloop in the Royal Navy, a London street, and a new tulip
were given their name,[3] and in the mid-nineteenth century
a well-known sporting writer styled himself The Druid.[4]
They were firmly established in the background of British
history; the topographer and the local antiquary had discovered their remains all over rural Britain, but for the
rest of the nineteenth century, outside the study of folklore they no longer inspired particularly bold conjectures.
Gnomic sayings and country customs were then scrutin-
ized for evidence of a Druid origin; as Browning puts it:

> Oh and, for their part, boys from door to door
>   Sing unintelligible words to tunes
> As obsolete: 'scraps of Druidic lore',
>   Sigh scholars, as each pale man importunes
> Vainly the mumbling to speak plain once more.[5]

But the student of folklore seemed to track down his
Druids by a free association of ideas, and because the
Welsh for 'wren' is 'dryw' (in which the vowel sounds of
'Druid' are reversed) he found traces of Druidism in
wren hunts; the Druids he detected in the ballad of True
Thomas (Druid Thomas) and in kissing beneath the
mistletoe are also random examples of his discoveries.

With the severing of the long association of the Druids
and the Patriarchs, something that had greatly complicated

[1] *The Neodruidic Heresy*, f. 2.
[2] F. Burney, *Evelina*, ed. F. Mackinnon, Oxford, 1930, p. 559.
[3] *Gentleman's Magazine*, XLVII, 1777, p. 504; *Dictionnaire Universel*, Paris, 1720, 'Druide'.
[4] H. H. Dixon, author of *Silk and Scarlet*, 1859 &c.
[5] Robert Browning, *La Saisiaz; The two poets of Croisic*, 1878, p. 96.

the earlier literature on the Druids then disappeared. Yet the theme had an essential simplicity which made it a convenient frame of reference: Mason, who would have nothing to do with the road from Ararat, is more clearly seen as a man who kept far closer to the classics than anyone else who wrote at length on the Druids; Toland, by comparison with those who wrote of Noah, may in spite of his many failings be appreciated as a man who prized the neglected Irish texts. The theme was based on a number of fallacies, but it had the merit of keeping in an intelligible relationship to each other the allusions, in the works which have been mentioned here, to the caves of Elephanta, the galoshes of the Druids, the Ark which carried the future Bacchus, the sons of the May, Christmas decorations, the gray-musing son of a rock, the oracular horses of Cyrus, the foundation of Cambridge, and Olwedd of the luminous teeth.

SELECT BIBLIOGRAPHY

Unless otherwise indicated, the place of publication is London.

AELIANUS, *A Regystre of Hystories*, tr. A. Fleming, 1576.
Annual Register, The, 1761.
ANNIUS VITERBIENSIS, J., *Commentaria super opera diversorum auctorum de antiquitatibus loquentium*, Rome, 1498.
ANON., *A Description of Stonehenge*, Salisbury, 1776.
A Complete History of the Druids . . . with an Inquiry into their Religion and its Coincidence with the Patriarchal, Lichfield, 1810.
The Identity of the Religions called Druidical and Hebrew, 1829.
ARNOLD, MATTHEW, *The Study of Celtic Literature*, (Everyman edn.) 1916.
ASHMOLE, ELIAS, *Theatrum Chemicum Britannicum*, 1652.
ATKINSON, R. J. C., *Stonehenge*, 1960.
AUBREY, JOHN, *Monumenta Britannica*, Bodleian MS. Gen, Top. c 24.
Boldleian MS. Aubrey 12, 13.
ST. AUGUSTINE OF HIPPO, *Works*, tr. M. Dods, 1871.
Monseigneur saint Augustin dela cité de Dieu, tr. Raoul de Presles, Abbeville, 1486.

BACON, NATHANIEL, *An Historical and Political Discourse of the Laws & Government of England*, ('collected from some manuscript notes of John Selden'), 1689.
BAILLY, J. S., *Lettres sur l'Origine des Sciences*, Paris and London, 1777.
BALE, JOHN, *The Actes of Englysh Votaries*, 1546.
Scriptorum Illustrium Maioris Britanniae Catalogus, Basle, 1557.
BANIER, ANTOINE, *The Mythology and Fables of the ancient Peoples explain'd from History*, 1739–40.

BARCLAY, ALEXANDER, *The Shyp of folys of the worlde*, 1509.

BAUDEAU, NICHOLAS, *Mémoire à consulter pour les anciens druides Gaulois*, n.p., 1777.

BLAKE, WILLIAM, *The Poetical Works*, ed. J. Sampson, Oxford, 1913.

The Prophetic Writings, ed. D. J. Sloss and J. P. R. Wallis, Oxford, 1926.

Blake's Poetry and Prose, ed. G. Keynes, 1946.

William Blake's Vala, ed. E. M. Margoliouth, Oxford, 1956.

BOCHART, SAMUEL, *Geographia Sacra*, Caen, 1646.

BOECE, HECTOR, *Scotorum historiae a prima gentis origine*, Paris 1526.

Heir beginnis the hystory and croniklis of Scotland, Edinburgh, 1536.

The Buik of the Croniclis of Scotland, a metrical version by William Stewart, [1535], ed. W. B. Turnbull, 1858.

The Works of John Bellenden, Edinburgh, 1822.

The Mar Lodge Translation, ed. G. Watson, Edinburgh, 1946.

BORLASE, WILLIAM, *Observations on the Antiquities Historical and Monumental, of the County of Cornwall*, Oxford, 1754; ibid., 1769.

BOSWELL, JAMES, *Boswell's Life of Johnson*, ed. G. B. Hill, Oxford, 1934–50.

Journal of a Tour to the Hebrides, ed. F. A. Pottle and C. H. Bennett, 1936.

BRANT, SEBASTIAN, *Das Narren schyeff*, Basle, 1494.

BREBEUF, GEORGES DE, *La Pharsale de Lucain*, Paris, 1670.

BROUGHTON, RICHARD, *The Ecclesiatical Historie of Great Britain*, Douai, 1633.

BROWN, THOMAS, 'A short Dissertation of the Mona of Caesar', in William Sacheverell, *An Account of the Isle of Man*, 1702.

BRYANT, JACOB, *A New System, or an Analysis of Ancient Mythology*, 1774–6.

BULAEUS, CAESAR, *Historia Universitatis Parisiensis*, Paris, 1665.

BUNTING, HENRY, *Itinerarium et Chronicon Ecclesiasticum Totius Sacrae Scripturae*, Magdeburg, 1597.

CAESAR, *Caij Julij Caesaris: Inuictissimi imperatoris commentaria*, (ed. Lucas Panaetius), Venice, 1511.

CAIUS, JOHN, *De Antiquitate Cantabrigiensis Academiae*, 1568; ibid., 1574.

Cambrian Quarterly, The, 1833.

CARTE, THOMAS, *A General History of England*, 1748.

CAREW, THOMAS, *Poems*, ed. R. Dunlop, Oxford, 1949.

CELTES, CONRAD, *Conradis Celtes, Protucij quatuor libri amorum secundum quatuor latera Germaniae*, Nuremberg, 1502.

CHASSENEUX, BARTHÉLEMY DE, *Catalogus Gloriae Mundi*, Lyons, 1546.

CHOTZEN, T. M., 'Some sidelights on Cambro-Dutch relations', *Transactions of Cymmrodorion*, 1938.

CLELAND, JOHN, *Specimens of an Etymological Vocabulary*, 1768. *The Way to Things by Words*, 1776.

CLEMENT OF ALEXANDRIA, *Works*, tr. W. Wilson, Edinburgh, 1876.

CLÜVERIUS, PHILIPPUS, *Germaniae antiquae libri tres*, Leyden, 1616.

COLGAN, JOHN, *Acta Sanctorum Veteris et Maioris Scotiae*, Louvain, 1645.

COLLIER, JEREMY, *An Ecclesiatical History of Great Britain*, 1708–14.

COLLINS, WILLIAM, *Odes*, 1747. *Ode Occasion'd by the Death of Mr. Thomson*, 1749; ibid., in *The Poetical Calendar*, ed. W. Woty, 1763.

COLLINGWOOD, R. G., and J. N. L. MYRES, *Roman Britain*, Oxford, 1937.

Contributions to a Dictionary of the Irish Language, 'dodénta—dúus', Dublin, 1960; ibid., 'F—fochraic', 1950.

COOKE, WILLIAM, *An Enquiry into the Druidical and Patriarchal Religion*, 1754.

COTGRAVE, RANDLE, *A Dictionarie of the French and English Tongues*, 1611.

CRADOCK, JOHN, *Literary Memoirs*, vol. iii, 1828.

CROMWELL, THOMAS, *The Druid*, 1832.

CUMBERLAND, RICHARD, *The Fashionable Lover*, 1772.

ST. CYRIL OF ALEXANDRIA, *Opera*, Basle, 1546. *Pro Christiana Religione contra Julianum libri decem*, Leipzig, 1696.

DARWIN, ERASMUS, *Zoonomia*, 1794–6.

DAVIES, EDWARD, *Celtic Researches*, 1804.
The Mythology and Rites of the British Druids, 1809.
DAVIES, JOHN, *Antiquae Linguae Britannicae*, 1621.
DAVIES, MYLES, *Athenae Britannicae*, 1716–[19?]
DELAPORTE, Y., 'Les Druides et les traditions Chartrains', *La Voix de Notre-Dame de Chartres*, n.p., Sept., 1936.
DES MOULINS, JACOB, *Antiqua Restaurata*, 1794.
DIAPER, WILLIAM, *Dryades*, 1713.
DICKINSON, EDMUND, *Delphi Phoenicizantes*, Oxford, 1655.
DIONYSIUS OF HALICARNASSUS, *Roman Antiquities*, tr. E. Cary, 1937.
DRAYTON, MICHAEL, *Englands Heroicall Epistles*, 1598.
Poemes Lyrick, and Pastorall, 1606.
Poly-Olbion, 1612; ibid., ed. J. W. Hebel, Oxford, 1933, (vol. iv of *The works of Michael Drayton*).
D'URFÉ, HONORÉ, *Astrea*, tr. J[ohn] D[avies], 1657–8.

EVANS, EVAN, *Some Specimens of the Poetry of the Antient Welsh Bards*, 1764.
The Correspondence of Thomas Percy and Evan Evans, ed. Aneirin Lewis, Louisiana, 1957.

FABER, GEORGE STANLEY, *A Dissertation on the Mysteries of the Cabiri*, Oxford, 1803.
The Origin of Pagan Idolatry, 1816.
FISHER, P. F., 'Blake and the Druids,' *Journal of English and Germanic Philology*, Illinois, 1959.
FLOWER, ROBIN, *The Irish Tradition*, Oxford, 1947.
FOOT, JAMES, *Penseroso*, 1771.
FRANCKLIN, WILLIAM, *Researches on the Tenets of the Jeynes and Boodhists*, 1827.
FRYE, NORTHROP, *Fearful Symmetry*, Princeton, 1947.
FULLER, THOMAS, *The Church-History of Britain*, 1655.
The Appeal of Injured Innocence, 1659.

GALE, THEOPHILUS, *The Court of the Gentiles*, Part I, Oxford, 1669; Part II, Oxford, 1671; Part III, 1677; Part IV, Book iii, 1678.
GALTRUCHIUS, PETRUS, *The Poetical Histories*, tr. M. d'Assigny, 1671.

Geiriadur Prifysgol Cymru, Cardiff, vol. xv, 1960.
GEOFFREY OF MONMOUTH, *Historia Regum Britanniae*, ed. A. Griscom, 1929.
GIBBON, EDWARD, *The Decline and Fall of the Roman Empire*, ed. J. B. Bury, 1913.
GODWIN, FRANCIS, *A Catalogue of the Bishops of England*, 1601; ibid., 1615.
GORDON, ALEXANDER, *Itinerarium Septentrionale*, 1726.
GOROPIUS BECANUS, J., *Opera*, Antwerp, 1580.
GRAY, THOMAS, *Correspondence of Thomas Gray*, ed. P. Toynbee and L. Whibley, Oxford, 1935.
Grove's History of Music, ed. H. C. Colles, 1927.
GENEBAULT, JEAN, *Le réveil de l'antique Tombeau de Chyndonax*, Paris, 1623.
GUEST, LADY CHARLOTTE, *The Mabinogion*, (Everyman edn.)
GUICCARDINI, LUDOVICUS, *Description de tout les Pays-Bas*, Antwerp, 1586.

HARDYNG, JOHN, *The Chronicle of John Hardyng*, ed. H. Ellis, 1812.
HAVET, L., *Le Querolus*, Paris, 1880.
HEARNE, THOMAS, *A Collection of Curious Discourses*, 1720.
HELVICUS, CHRISTOPHER, *Theatrum Historicum*, Marburg, 1629.
HENRY, ROBERT, *The History of Great Britain*, 1771.
HERBERT, ALGERNON, *An Essay on the Neodruidic Heresy in Britannia*, 1838.
  Britannia after the Romans, vol. ii, 1841.
HEYLYN, PETER, *Certamen Epistolare*, 1659.
HIDGDEN, RANULF, *Polychronicon*, tr. John de Trevisa, 1482.
HIGGINS, GEOFFREY, *The Celtic Druids*, 1827.
HIPPOLYTUS, *The Refutation of All Heresies*, tr. J. H. Macmahon, Edinburgh, 1868.
HOLINSHED, RAPHAEL, *The First Volume of the Chronicles of England*, 1577.
HOLMES, ROBERT, *Alfred*, Oxford, 1778.
HOWELLS, JAMES, *Dodona's Grove*, 1645.
HOWES, EDMOND, 'An Historical Preface': John Stow, *Annales*, 1631.

IRENICUS, FRANCISCUS, *Germaniae Exegeseos*, Hagenau, 1518.

JAMES, D., *The Patriarchal Religion of Great Britain*, 1836.
ST. JEROME, *Sancti Eusebii Hieronymi . . . Opera Tomus Sextus*, Verona, 1736.
  Liber Hebraicarum Quaestionum in Genesim, in *S. Eusebii Hieronymi . . . Omnia Opera*, (Migne, *Patrologia Latina*, vol. 23), Paris, 1845.
Jewish Encyclopaedia, The Universal, vol. v, New York, 1941.
JONES, INIGO, *The Most Remarkable Antiquity of Great Britain, vulgarly called Stone-Heng, Restored*, (ed. John Webb), 1655.
JONES, ROWLAND, *The Origin of Language and Nations*, 1764.
  Hieroglyfic, 1768.
  The Philosophy of Words, 1769.
  The Circles of Gomer, 1771.
  The IO-Triads, 1773.
JONES, THOMAS, *Of the Heart and its Right Soveraign*, 1678.
JONES, T. GAREL, *The Life and Works of Henry Rowlands*, National Library of Wales MS. Theses 1936/14.
JONES, SIR WILLIAM, *Discourses delivered before the Royal Asiatic Society*, 1824.
JOSEPHUS, *Jewish Antiquities*, (Bohn edn.), 1889; *The Works of Flavius Josephus*, tr. Sir Roger L'Estrange, 1702.

KEATING, GEOFFREY, *The General History of Ireland*, tr. Dermod O'Connor, Dublin, 1723.
  The History of Ireland, vol. i, ed. D. Comyn, 1902; vol. ii, ed. P. S. Dinneen, 1908.
KENDRICK, SIR THOMAS, *The Druids*, 1928.
KENNEDY, MATTHEW, *A Chronological Dissertation of the Royal Family of the Stuarts*, Paris, 1705.
KEYSLER, J. G., *Antiquitates Selectae Septentrionales et Celticae*, Hanover, 1720.
KING, EDWARD, *Munimenta Antiqua*, 1799–1805.
KYFFIN, MAURICE, *Deffyniad Ffydd Eglwys Loegr a Gyfieithwyd i 'r Gymraeg*, [1595], ed. W. P. Williams, Bangor, 1908.

LACROIX, PAUL, *Ballets et Mascarades de Cour*, Paris, 1868–70.
LACTANTIUS, LUCIUS COELIUS FIRMIANUS, *Opera*, ed. X. Betuleius Augustanus, Basle, 1563.
  The Works of Lactantius, tr. W. Fletcher, Edinburgh, 1871.

LAMBARD, WILLIAM, *An Alphabetical Description of the Chief Places in England and Wales*, [1570], 1730.

LE FÈVRE, JEAN, *Les fleurs et antiquitez des Gaules*, [1532]: *Recuiel des poésies francoises de xve et xvie siècles*, ed. A. de Montaiglon, Paris, tom. 8, 1858.

LELAND, JOHN, *Commentarii de Scriptoribus Britannicis*, Oxford, 1709.

J. Lelandi antiquarii de rebus Britannicis Collectanea, ed. Thomas Hearne, Oxford, 1715.

The Itinerary of John Leland, ed. L. T. Smith, 1907.

LESCALOPERIUS, PETRUS, 'Theologia Veterum Gallorum': Cicero, *De Natura Deorum*, Paris, 1660.

LEWIS, JOHN, *The History of Great Britain*, [ed. Hugh Thomas], 1729.

LHUYD, EDWARD, *Archaelogia Britannica*, Oxford, 1707.

'A Collection of Highland Rites & Customs', Bodleian MS. Carte 269.

LIPSCOMB, WILLIAM, *Poems*, Oxford, 1784.

LLWYD, HUMPHREY, *Commentarioli Brytannicae Descriptionis Fragmentum*, Cologne, 1572.

'De Mona Druidum Insula': A. Ortelius, *Theatrum Orbis Terrarum*, Antwerp, 1574.

LLWYD, RICHARD, *Beaumaris Bay*, 1800.

LOCHER, JACOB, *Stultifera navis*, Basle, 1497.

LOT, FERDINAND, 'Nennius et l'Historia Brittonum', *Bibliothèque de l'École des Hautes Études*, vol. 263, Paris, 1934.

LUCAS, CHARLES, *A Descriptive Account . . . of the old Serpentine Temple of the Druids at Avebury*, Marlborough, 1801.

LYNCHE, RICHARD, *An Historicall Treatise of the Travels of Noah into Europe*, 1601.

MACPHERSON, JAMES, *An Introduction to the History of Great Britain*, Dublin, 1771; ibid., Edinburgh, 1763.

MALLET, PAUL HENRI, *Northern Antiquities*, tr. Thomas Percy, 1770.

MARTIN, JEAN, *La Réligion des Gaulois*, Paris, 1727.

MARTIN, MARTIN, *A Description of the Western Isles of Scotland*,

MASON, WILLIAM, *Poems*, 1764; *Works*, 1811.

MASSON, DAVID, *The Life of John Milton*, 1875.

MAURICE, THOMAS, *Netherby*, Oxford, 1776.

    Indian Antiquities, 1793–1800.

MEXIA, PEDRO, Ἀρχαιο Πλουτος *containing Ten Following Bookes to the former Treasurie*, 1619.

MEYRICK, S. R. and C. H. SMITH, *The Costume of the Original Inhabitants of the British Isles*, 1821.

MICKLE, WILLIAM JULIUS, *Poems*, 1794.

MILTON, JOHN, *The Doctrine and Discipline of Divorce*, 1643; ibid., 1644.

    Areopagitica, 1644.

    The History of Great Britain, 1670.

    Facsimile of the Manuscripts of Milton's Minor Poems, ed. W. A. Wright, Cambridge, 1899.

    The Latin Poems of John Milton, tr. W. MacKellar, New Haven, 1930.

    The Works of John Milton, ed. F. A. Patterson, New York, 1930–40.

Monthly Review, The, 1798.

MORE, JOHN, *A Table from the Beginning of the World to this Day*, 1593.

MORRIS, LEWIS, 'Celtic Remains', *Archaeologia Cambrensis*, [1877], n.p., n.d.

MORRIS-JONES, SIR JOHN, 'Taliesin', *Y Cymmrodor*, vol. xxviii, 1918.

MYLNE, JAMES, *Poems*, Edinburgh, 1790.

NASH, D. W., *Taliesin*, 1858.

NASHE, THOMAS, *The Terrors of the Night*, 1594.

NICHOLSON, WILLIAM, *The English Historical Library*, 1696.

    The Irish Historical Library, Dublin, 1724.

O'DONOVAN, J., 'An ancient Poem attributed to St. Columkille', *Miscellany of the Irish Archaeological Society*, Dublin, vol. i, 1846.

OGILVIE, JOHN, *The Fane of the Druids*, 1787.

ORTELIUS, ABRAHAM, *Theatrum Orbis Terrarum*, Antwerp, 1574 ibid., also with the title *The Theatre of the Whole World*, tr. W. B., 1606.

OWEN, WILLIAM, (later William Owen Pugh[e]) *The Heroic Elegies of Llwyarç Hen*, 1792.

PARKER, MATTHEW, *De Antiquitate Britannicae Ecclesiae*, 1572; ibid., Hanover, 1605.

PARRY, THOMAS, *A History of Welsh Literature*, tr. I. Bell, Oxford, 1955.

PARSONS, JAMES, *The Remains of Japhet*, 1768.

PEACOCK, THOMAS LOVE, *The Misfortunes of Elphin*, ed. R. Garnett, 1891.

PEARCE, WILLIAM, *The Haunts of Shakespeare*, 1778.

PELLOUTIER, SIMON, *Historie des Celtes*, La Haye, 1740; ibid., Paris, 1770.

PEZRON, P-Y., *The Antiquities of Nations*, tr. David Jones, 1706.

PHILLIPS, D. R., *Lady Charlotte Guest and the Mabinogion*, Carmarthen, 1921.

PIGGOTT, STUART, *British Prehistory*, 1949.

William Stukeley, 1950.

PINKERTON, JOHN, *An Enquiry into the History of Scotland*, 1789.

PLUMMER, CHARLES, *Vitae Sanctorum Hiberniae*, Oxford, 1910.

PONTANUS, ISAAC, *Itinerarium Galliae Narboniensis*, Leyden, 1606.

Originum Francicarum, Harderwijk, 1616.

POPE, ALEXANDER, *Brutus*, British Museum MS. Egerton 1950.

The Temple of Fame, 1715.

POSTEL, GUILLAUME, *L'Histoire mémorable des expéditions depuys le déluge faictes par les Gauloys*, Paris, 1552.

POTTER, G. R., 'James Thomson and the Evolution of Spirits', *Englische Studien*, vol. 61, Leipzig, 1926.

PRICE, SIR JOHN, *Historiae Britannicae Defensio*, 1573.

PUGH[E], William Owen: see William Owen.

PURCELL, HENRY, *The Music in the Tragedy of Bonduca*, 1842.

Querolus, ed. Peter Daniel, Paris, 1564.

RALEIGH, SIR WALTER, *The History of the World*, 1614.

RAMUS, PETRUS, *Liber de Moribus Veterum Gallorum*, Paris, 1559.

RAY, JOHN, *The Wisdom of God manifested in the Works of Creation*, 1704.

REYNOLDS, HENRY, 'Mythomystes', (1633): *Critical Essays of the Seventeenth Century*, ed. J. E. Spingarn, Oxford, 1908.

RHYS, JOHN DAVID, *Cambrobritannicae Cymraecaeve Linguae Institutiones*, 1592.

RICHARDS, WILLIAM, *Wallography*, 1682.

RINAKER, CLARISSA, *Thomas Warton*, Urbana, 1916.

ROUILLARD OR ROULLIARD, SÉBASTIEN, *Parthénie*, Paris, 1609.

ROWLANDS, HENRY, *Mona Antiqua Restaurata*, Dublin, 1723; ibid., 1766.
   Bodleian MS. Carte 10553.
   British Museum MS. Adds. 14883.

RUFFHEAD, OWEN, *The Life of Alexander Pope*, 1769.

SAMMES, AYLETT, *Britannia Antiqua Illustrata*, 1676.

SAYERS, FRANK, *Poetical Works*, 1830.

SCHEDIUS, ELIAS, *De dis Germanis*, Amsterdam, 1648.
   De Diis Germanis, Halle, 1728.

SCOTT, SIR WALTER, 'Provincial Antiquities', *Miscellaneous Works*, Edinburgh, 1870.

SELDEN, JOHN, 'Illustrations': Michael Drayton, *Poly-Olbion*, 1612.
   Analecton Anglo-Britannicon, Frankfort, 1615.
   The Reverse or Back-Face of the English Janus, tr. 'R. Westcot', 1683.
   Opera Omnia, 1720.

SENECA, *De Morte Claudij Caesaris*, Basle, 1521.

SIBBALD, SIR ROBERT, *The History . . . of Fife*, Edinburgh, 1710.

SKENE, W. F., *Four Ancient Books of Wales*, Edinburgh, 1868.

SLATYER, WILLIAM, *Palae-Albion*, 1621.

SMITH, JOHN, *Choir Gaur*, Salisbury, 1771.

SMITH, THOMAS, *Syntagma de Druidum Moribus*, Oxford, 1664.

SOUTHEY, ROBERT, *The Book of the Church*, 1824.

SPEED, JOHN, *The History of Great Britaine*, 1611.

SPENCE, JOSEPH, *Anecdotes . . . Collected from the Conversations of Mr. Pope*, ed. S. W. Singer, 1820.

SPOTSWOOD (or Spottiswoode), JOHN, *The History of the Church of Scotland*, 1655.

STILLINGFLEET, EDWARD, *Originae Britannicae*, 1685.

STOW, JOHN, *A Survay of London*, 1603.
   Annales, 1631.

STREET, HENRY, *Leaves from Eusebius*, 1842.

STUKELEY, WILLIAM, *Palaeographia Sacra*, 1736.
Stonehenge A Temple Restor'd to the British Druids, 1740.
Abury, a Temple of the British Druids, 1743.
Palaeographia Sacra, 1763.
Cardiff Public Libraries MS. 4.253.
Bodleian Library MS. Eng. misc. e 135.
A Catalogue of the genuine Library of William Stukeley, 1766.
The Family Memoirs of the Rev. William Stukeley, M.D., ed.
W. C. Lukis, (Surtees Soc.), 1882–7.

TAILLEPIED, NOËL, *Histoire de l'estat et république des druides*, Paris, 1585.
TAIT, JOHN AND WILLIAM WOTY, [published anonymously], *The Druid's Monument, A Tribute to the Memory of Dr. Oliver Goldsmith*, 1774.
TEMPLE, SIR WILLIAM, *The Works of Sir William Temple*, 1720.
THOMSON, JAMES, *Liberty*, 1736.
The Seasons, 1746.
The Castle of Indolence, 1748.
TINDAL, MATTHEW, *Christianity as Old as the Creation*, 1730.
TOLAND, JOHN, *Miscellaneous Works*, 1747.
A New Edition of Toland's History of the Druids, ed. R. Huddleston, 1814.
TOMPKINS, J. M. S., 'In yonder grave a Druid lies', *Review of English Studies*, vol. xxii, Oxford, 1946.
TURNER, SHARON, *The History of the Anglo-Saxons*, vol. i, 1799.

VAN SCRIECK, A., *Monitorum secundorum libri quinque*, Ypres, 1614.
VERGIL, POLYDORE, *Anglicae Historiae libri XXVI*, Basle, 1534.
Polydore Vergil's English History, ed. H. Ellis, 1846.

WALLACE, JAMES, *A Description of the Isles of Orkney*, ed. J. Small, Edinburgh, 1883.
WALTERS, JOHN, *Poems*, n.p., 1780.
WARING, ELIJAH, *Recollections of Edward Williams*, 1850.
WARNER, RICHARD, *A Second Walk through Wales*, 1800.
WARNER, WILLIAM, *The First and Second Parts of Albion's England*, 1589.

WARTON, THOMAS, *The History of English Poetry*, vol. i, 1774.
Poetical Works, ed. R. Mant, Oxford, 1802.

WATSON, HENRY, *The Grete Shyppe of Fooles of this Worlde*, 1517.

WEBB, JOHN, *An Historical Essay Endeavouring a Probability* that the language of the Empire of China was the Primitive Language, 1669.

WEBB, WILLIAM, *An Analysis of the History of Ireland*, Dublin, 1791.

WEST, GILBERT, *The songs, choruses and serious dialogue of the Masque called the Institution of the Garter*, 1771.

WHEARE, DEGORY, *The Method and Order of Reading Histories*, tr. E. Bohun, 1698.

WHITAKER, JOHN, *The History of Manchester*, 1771.

WHITEHEAD, WILLIAM, *Verses to the People of England*, 1758.

WHITING, G. W., *Milton's Literary Milieu*, Chapel Hill, 1939.

WILFORD, FRANCIS, 'Essay on the Sacred Isles in the West', *Asiatic Researches*, Calcutta, vol. viii, 1805, vol. xi, 1810.

WILLIAMS, EDWARD, [Iolo Morganwg], *Poems, Lyric and Pastoral*, 1794.
'The Mabinogi of Taliesin', *The Cambrian Quarterly*, vol. v, 1833.
Iolo Manuscripts, Llandovery, 1848.

WOOD, ANTHONY, *Historia et Antiquitates Universitatis Oxoniensis*, Oxford, 1674.
Athenae Oxonienses, Oxford, 1692.

WOOD, JOHN, *Choir Gaure*, Oxford, 1747.

WOODHULL, MICHAEL, *Poems*, 1772.

WORDSWORTH, WILLIAM, *Poetical Works*, ed. E. de Selincourt, Oxford, 1940–9.
The Prelude, ed. E. de Selincourt, Oxford, 1950.
Ecclesiastical Sonnets, ed. A. F. Potts, Yale, 1922.

YOUNG, EDWARD, *The Complete Works*, ed. J. Doran, 1854.

INDEX

Camden, William, 1, 39–45, 53, 62, 104–5.
Cam-lan, 219.
Cannibalism, Druids accused of, 21, 25, 160, 239.
Capitol, fire of the, 24, 153.
Caractacus, 138.
Caractacus, 43, 142, 147–51, 158, 171–2, 230.
Carmarthen, 197.
Carnedd, 76, 79.
Carnutes, 18, 99.
Carte, Thomas, 68, 109, 174, 237.
Caste, Druids and, 4, 16–17, 25, 199.
Castle of Indolence, The, 175–7.
Catholic Church, Catholicism, 29, 32, 34, 38, 65, 78, 120, 157, 218.
Catraeth, 221.
Causidiques, 45.
Caves, 11, 18, 20, 31, 96, 173, 215, 237.
Celsus, 92.
Celte, 37.
Celtes, Conrad, 44, 51, 72, 101.
Celtic Church, 4, 62, 218–20.
Celtic gods, 40, 93.
Celtic languages, 69–71, 75–77, 80, 113, 116, 132, 180, 182–6, 191.
Celtic mysteries, 57.
Celtic religion, 3, 41, 89, 93, 95, 119.
Celtic Researches, 189–92.
Celts, 2, 6, 7, 41, 69, 80, 85, 86, 90, 109, 132, 218.
Ceres, 214–15.
Ceridwen, 213–15.
Cerrig y Drudion, 41–42, 105.
Chaldea, Chaldeans, 36, 83–84, 89–90, 180, 191, 211.
Cham, 38, 127.
'Chapels', 107.
Charles II, King, 102.
Charleton, Walter, 102–3.
Chartres, 31–32.
Chasseneux, B. de, 45.
Chaucer, Geoffrey, 31, 169–70.
Cheshire, 54.
Chester, 52–53.
Chief Druid, 17, 101, 110–11, 118.
China, 11, 84, 124, 180–1.
Choir Gaur, 135–6.

Choir Gaure, 10–11, 237–8.
Chorea Gigantum, 102–3.
Christ, 5, 157, 205, 220, 225–7, 235.
Christianity, 9, 38–39, 59–65, 117, 124, 126, 157–8, 163, 187, 200, 205, 218–19.
Christmas, 170, 187, 240.
Chronicles of England, The, 36–39.
Chronologies, 65–66, 101, 190, 205, 231–2.
Church of England, 117–19, 120–31.
Chyndonax, 101, 118, 238.
Cicero, 10, 22, 89.
Cimbri, 68, 69, 123, 130, 179, 221.
Cimmeri, 68, 69.
Circles, stone, 30–31, 52 n., 104–5, 107, 111–13, 123–8, 163, 167, 171, 175, 198, 228, 238.
'Circus alatus', 127–8.
'Classerniss', *see* Callernish.
Claudian, 55.
Claudius, 21, 22–23, 43–44, 61.
Cleland, John, 70, 158, 186–9, 230.
Clement of Alexandria, 25, 57, 89–91, 100.
Cneph, 128.
Cobham, Elinor, 46.
Coins, 42, 44.
Colgan, John, 62.
Coll, 222.
Collier, Jeremy, 91–92.
Collins, William, 27, 172–8.
Colossus, 20, 148, 158, 187, 229–30. *See also* Holocausts, Wicker figure.
(St.) Columba, 5, 220.
(St.) Columban, 220.
Comerus, 37.
Comparative philology, 76–77, 179–92.
Confucius, 11.
Consortia, 3, 18.
Conversion of Britain, 39, 59–65.
Cooke, William, 180, 234.
Cormac, King, 115.
Cornwall, 99, 131–3.
Corybants, 28.
Cowper, William, 142, 152–3.
Cradock, John, 98.
Cromlechs, 43, 76, 79, 116, 134, 171.

Groves, 7, 9, 20, 23, 24, 49, 131–2, 160, 161, 164, 178, 208, 233.
Guiccardini, Ludovicus, 55.
Guest, Lady Charlotte, 202.
Gunpowder, 12, 163.
Gwîn a bragawd, 13.
Gwion, 202, 213–14.
Gwyddno, 215.
Gwytheyrn, 219.
Gymnosophists, 89.

Hakpen, 127.
Hardyng, John, 237.
Hearne, Thomas, 114, 141, 238.
Heber, 233.
Hebrew, 70, 76, 87, 128, 132, 180, 184–6, 189–92.
Hebrews, 99, 232.
Hecaerge, 55.
Hecataeus of Abderos, 55, 190.
Helio-Arkite superstition, 211–17.
Helvicus, Christopher, 83.
Hemans, Felicia, 210.
Hengist, 140.
Henoch, 93.
Henry, Robert, 100.
Herbert, Algernon, 217–20, 238.
Hercules, 76, 123.
Hercules Ogmius, 71, 116.
Hermes Trismegistus, 120.
Hermetic philosophy, 122.
Hermio, 9.
Hermon, 232.
Herodotus, 143–4.
Hesus, 128.
Heylyn, Peter, 63–65.
Hieroglyphics, hieroglyphs, 122, 128–9, 163, 191, 236.
Hierophantes, 30.
Higden, Ranulf, 106.
Hindus, 88, 96–98.
Hipperbore, 55.
Hippolytus, 25, 57, 92, 144.
Historia Regum Britanniae, 38, 49, 59–60, 66, 102 n., 106.
History of Great Britain, The, (Milton), 57–58.
History of Ireland, The, 114–15.
Holinshed, Raphael, 6–7, 35–39, 93, 94, 193.
Holland, Philemon, 53, 102, 104.
Holmes, Robert, 141, 161.

Holocausts, 20, 134, 158, 161, 164, 166–7, 199, 227.
Holy Land in William Blake's *Prophetic Books, The*, 225–35.
Horace, 129–30.
Horsa, 140.
Howes, Edmond, 142.
Hu, 212.
Humber, 128.
Huys te Britten, 46.
Hylobii, 11.
Hyperboreans, 10, 50, 54–55, 58, 81, 116, 174, 190, 237.

Iamblichus, 57.
Iapetus, 236.
Iceni, 24.
Ida, 27.
Identity of ancient religions, 83 n., 93–95, 98, 100.
Idolatry, 7, 98, 134, 187.
Immortality of the soul, Druids' teaching on, 18–19, 22–23, 38, 68, 132, 138, 144–5, 156–7.
Initiate, initiation, 11, 13, 96, 164–5, 200, 212, 214.
India, Indians, 11, 84, 89, 90, 96–98, 188, 238.
Indians, North American, 95.
Iolo Morganwg, 194. *See also* Edward Williams.
Interpretatio Romana, 93.
Ireland, Irish Druids, 3–5, 62, 74, 110, 113–17.
Irenicus, Franciscus, 156.
Irish language, 113, 116, 189, 191.
Isaac, 158.
Isis, 35, 214.
Isis, River, 35, 178.
Isles of the Gentiles, 67.
Islington, 235.
Italy, 55.

Jacob, 126.
Jacob, Henry, 70–71.
Jacob's pillar, 98.
James, D., 234.
Jana, 211.
Janus Ogyges, 94.
Japan, 95.
Japhet, 6, 38, 66–67, 179, 182–3, 186, 189, 236.

Martin, Jean, 98.
Martin, Martin, 109–13, 116, 135.
Marvell, Andrew, 27, 172.
Mason, William, 43, 142, 147–51,
  158, 171–2, 240.
Mass, 187.
Maurice, Thomas, 88, 96, 140, 160.
Maynus, King, 30.
Maypole, 187.
Maximus of Tyre, 92.
Medusa, 128.
Mercury, 41, 64, 93.
Merddin, 13.
Metempsychosis, 7, 19–20, 23, 38,
  138–9, 143, 155, 175–7, 195, 202,
  204–10.
Mexia, Pedro, 23, 156.
Meyrick, S., 13–14, 217.
Mickle, William, 154.
Midas, 85.
Mills of Satan, 228.
Milton, John, 27, 52–58.
Milton, 225–35.
Miriam, 129.
Misfortunes of Elphin, The, 158–9,
  204.
Mistletoe, 24–25, 50, 133, 136, 160,
  170–1, 239.
Mithras, 96, 123, 218.
Mithriacs, 218.
Mitzoth, 77, 81, 230.
Mizraim, 127.
Molesworth, Lord, 112, 114.
Mona, 23–24, 29, 47, 52, 58, 96,
  139, 147, 161.
Mona Antiqua Restaurata, see
  Henry Rowlands.
Monotheism of Druids, 7, 50, 62–
  65, 92–93, 97.
Monthly Review, 169.
Montmartre, 31.
Monumenta Britannica, 104–9, 119,
  198.
Moon worship, 132, 211.
Moral philosophy, 19.
More, John, 65.
Morris, Lewis, 48.
Morris-Jones, Sir John, 204, 221.
Moses, 100, 120, 122.
Myfyr Morganwg, 220.
Mylne, James, 153.
Myrddin, 14.

Mysteries, 7, 10, 103, 164–5, 170,
  181, 188, 193, 194, 200–1, 204,
  214, 218, 222.
Mythology, 10, 69–70, 78, 94, 99,
  128, 186–8, 193, 211, 214, 230.
*Mythology and Rites of the British
  Druids, The*, 13, 210–17.
*Myvyrian Archaiology of Wales,
  The*, 195.

Nash, D. W., 221–3.
Nashe, Thomas, 46.
Nativity of Christ, 32, 61, 123, 125,
  157.
Natural philosophy, Druids' study
  of, 6, 12, 17, 20, 22, 78.
Nature, 162, 169–78, 191.
Nennius, 67, 217.
Neo-Druids, 218–19, 222.
Neptune, 96, 128.
New Grange megaliths, 212.
Nicholson, William, 108, 229.
Noachidae, 191.
Noah, 14, 37, 66–67, 76, 80, 94,
  100, 123, 127, 129, 155, 181,
  185, 200, 204, 207, 211–15, 222,
  231–13, 236.
Nymphs, 52, 140.

Oak, oaks, 8, 9, 11, 24, 71–72, 77,
  86–87, 99, 152, 167, 169, 170–2,
  233–4.
O'Connor, Dermod, 114–15.
Odin, 143–4, 187.
Og, 71, 116.
Ogdoad, 222.
Ogilvie, John, 208.
'Ogum' alphabet, 116.
Okeyhole, 11, 237.
Ollamh's wand, 115.
Olwedd, 13, 240.
Orators, 110.
Orientation of Stonehenge, 135–6
Origen, 39, 62–63, 92.
Origin of Druidism, 9, 15, 35, 45,
  70, 71–72, 83–85, 88, 237.
Origin of philosophy, 6, 21, 38, 83,
  90, 142, 228.
Orkneys, 112.
Orpheus, 85.
Ortelius, Abraham, 44–47, 53 n.
Osiris, 127.